DO YOU WANT YOUR DOUBTS ABOUT WORDS "DISPELLED" OR "DISSIPATED"?

Do you "amend" or "emend" a law?

Do you prefer to sleep "prone" or "supine"?

Do you want a "guarantee," "guaranty," or "warranty" on the next car you buy?

Do you know where to find the "Tropic of Cancer" and the "Tropic of Capricorn"?

Do you think that command of the language is a "requirement" or a "requisite" for getting ahead?

The right word at the right time is an invaluable tool—just as the wrong word can be a source of confusion and embarrassment. Yet our language is full of words and terms that are easily mistaken for one another, and others with subtle distinctions that can decisively influence vital shades of meaning. This easily used and authoritative guide is designed to give you perfect confidence that the words you use are the words you want.

"The difference between the almost right word and the right word is really a large matter—'tis the difference between the lightning bug and the lightning."

—MARK TWAIN

THE
NEW AMERICAN
DICTIONARY
OF
CONFUSING
WORDS

by

William C. Paxson

A SIGNET BOOK

SIGNET
Published by the Penguin Group
Penguin Books USA Inc., 375 Hudson Street,
New York, New York 10014, U.S.A.
Penguin Books Ltd, 27 Wrights Lane,
London W8 5TZ, England
Penguin Books Australia Ltd, Ringwood,
Victoria, Australia
Penguin Books Canada Ltd, 2801 John Street,
Markham, Ontario, Canada L3R 1B4
Penguin Books (N.Z.) Ltd, 182–190 Wairau Road,
Auckland 10, New Zealand

Penguin Books Ltd, Registered Offices:
Harmondsworth, Middlesex, England

First published by Signet, an imprint of New American Library,
a division of Penguin Books USA Inc.

First Printing, December, 1990
10 9 8 7 6 5 4 3 2 1

REGISTERED TRADEMARK—MARCA REGISTRADA

Printed in the United States of America

Contents

Preface and Acknowledgments

Why this book? After all, dictionaries provide all sorts of definitions, don't they?

Well, we users of English are creating some sort of mess. For centuries we have been making up new words and using old words in new ways. At present, hundreds of millions of people are hard at work each day in the English-language factory, giving fresh twists and turns to the meanings of some million or so words. Our imaginative efforts in this regard frequently become a lasting part of the language and are faithfully recorded in dictionaries.

Consequently, a good modern dictionary, for all of its value, can be something of a pain in the neck to use. It is big, and for many words it will present so many definitions that what is available is confusion instead of a solution.

Consider a classic case of confusing words—*affect* and *effect*. Dictionaries have recorded so many meanings for *affect* and *effect* that the distinction between the two is blurred, in effect (affect?) allowing us to treat them as synonyms. As any hard-nosed editor or uncompromising English teacher will tell you, *affect* and *effect* are indeed not synonyms, and you'd darn well better mind your *p*'s and *q*'s about how you use them.

You shouldn't feel bad (badly?) about being confused by dictionary definitions. Instead, you should infer (imply?) that what is needed is some sort of guide that will simplify the most confusing of words and definitions. That's one thing that this book does.

In addition, confusing words frequently travel in pairs. With some pairs, the definitions in a dictionary can be separated by hundreds of pages. A lot of page flipping is involved when it's time to sort out the differences between combinations like *anonymous* and *pseudonymous*, or *augment* and *supplement*.

Therefore, it'd be nice to have a time-saving little guide that reduces the flipping of pages by placing definitions of confusing words on the same page. That's a second thing that this book does.

By way of acknowledgments, thanks go to my wife, Diana, for admirable performance in her usual role as first reader; to Ted Johnson, for an excellent job of editing the manuscript; to Hugh Rawson at New American Library, for the support that he has provided in a number of ways; to all the other fine people at NAL for the excellent help that they have given me on this and other books of mine; and to Michael Larsen and Elizabeth Pomada, for bringing author and publisher together.

I also thank the friendly and helpful staff of The Library, California State University, Sacramento. The enduring high quality of services provided by that library is testimony to taxpayer money well spent.

Introduction:
On Using the Book

The Book at a Glance

- This book defines more than 2,000 commonly confused words and terms.
- Terms are listed alphabetically; an index at the back of the book provides additional help in locating main entries and terms in the text.
- Advice and examples help you cope with the most vexing problems of confusing words.

The people who will benefit from using the book are writers, speakers, editors, teachers, students, executives, people in various professions, young men and women on the way up, and anyone who just wants to know more about words.

To use the book, the steps to follow are these:

- Search for the word you want in the alphabetical listing.
- Pay attention to the cross-references.
- Check the index if you need more help.

But first, you should read the rest of the introduction. It provides additional information about the book.

Is the Subject Important?

A witness testifying before Congress said "suppository" when the word that he meant to use was *supposition*.
Then there was the college student who wrote in a report, "Because the campus cafeteria does not cater to

students in a hurry, the erection of a local Burger King has created fierce competition." A better word would have been "construction," for sexual inferences can be drawn from "erection." Place "erection" near "Burger King" and you wonder if Shakespeare's words apply: "Ay, every inch a king."

Is the subject important? You bet it is. Words make us laugh, whether intentionally or unintentionally. Words make us cry. Words tell of our love and of our hate. Words lead to war and bring about peace.

No way exists to estimate the raw power of the right word.

And no way exists to guess at the total confusion that can be caused by the wrong word.

What Kinds of Words Are Defined?

Entries define words from American English. Words are chosen from popular use (*capital, capitol*), or are technical terms that occur in popular use or that can be confused with a similarly written or similarly pronounced word in popular use (*bit, byte*).

Most entries are about words that pose problems in meaning (*allusion, delusion, illusion*). The book also shows how to use words that are frequently confused whether or not the confusion has anything to do with meaning (*who, whom*).

The definitions are comparative definitions only. That is, an entry gives the definitions that are most often confused, but may omit other definitions. For additional definitions, a desk or reference dictionary will have to be consulted.

Who's Doing the Defining?

I derived the definitions from modern desk and reference dictionaries; a list of the sources used appears at the end of the book. That list gives complete facts of publication for general and specialized reference works. In the text an occasional reference work is mentioned by its short title.

For any definition, I started with these principal American dictionaries: *American Heritage Dictionary of the English Language* (1976); *Random House Dictionary of the English Language* (1987); *Webster's New World Dictionary of American English* (1988); *Webster's Ninth New Collegiate Dictionary* (1983)—cited in the text as *Webster's Ninth*; and *Webster's Third New International Dictionary of the English Language Unabridged* (1976)—cited in the text as *Webster III*.

I also used the *Oxford English Dictionary* (1989), which traces the history of a word and provides thorough definitions along with illustrative quotations.

For questions on fine points of word usage, I relied mainly on Roy Copperud's *American Usage and Style: The Consensus* (1980). Copperud's book is valuable because it is exactly what he calls it—a consensus, in this case a consensus of usage as reported by major dictionaries and usage critics. Because *American Usage and Style* was last published in 1980, I also used the 1985 edition of *The Harper Dictionary of Contemporary Usage*, by Mary and William Morris.

When specialized definitions had to be provided, I used dictionaries written for the various professions. These dictionaries are listed in the bibliography.

Is the Book Prescriptive or Descriptive?

If you haven't heard of the descriptive-prescriptive argument, you haven't missed much, for it's one of those pastimes that exists mainly to give scholars something to fret about. Nevertheless, it's an argument that has to be considered by anyone who writes or reads a book such as this.

The prescriptive side of the argument says that a book such as this should make rules on how to use language. Without rules, the prescriptivists say, the language will disintegrate, chaos will follow, and civilization will surely fall apart.

The descriptive side says that a book such as this

should *not* make rules but instead just report how people use language. According to the descriptivists, the people who speak and write a language are the people who make the rules on how to use it.

In the true and safe spirit of compromise, it's necessary to point out that both sides are right.

We do need some kind of written rules, some kind of operator's manual on how to use the machinery of the language. However, grammar teachers and writers of books such as this—if we are doing our job right—don't arbitrarily and capriciously make the rules. Instead, we merely report the rules.

The rules themselves are made by the people who use the language. In the case of American English, the number of rule makers is equal to the population of the United States. In essence, our language is run by a committee—one heck of a huge committee.

As all of that applies to this book, where research shows a usage that can be prescribed, the book is prescriptive. Otherwise, where research differs on usage, the book is descriptive. The whole idea is to provide a book that will reflect the changing nature of language while helping to prevent confusion.

Do I Need to Know Any Special Terms?

The word *preferred* appears frequently in this book, but it does not indicate any special preference of mine. Instead, *preferred* means that a particular usage is favored by a majority of American writers and speakers, as reported by dictionaries.

In addition, words such as *connote* and *imply* (which are defined in the dictionary) appear in many entries to indicate that the meaning of the word is a slippery thing. Consequently, you may think that the book has acquired a somewhat wishy-washy tone. That impression is unavoidable. When you combine the complex richness of our language with the frailties of the human mind and our creative approaches to using words, it's a large miracle that any certainty of meaning exists at all.

The Dictionary

An *A* to *Z*
of Confusing Words
with Definitions, Examples, and Advice

A

a, an. Should you write or say "*a* history book" or "*an* history book"? That's an example of the confusion that accompanies these two words.

But why? A writer of gothic novels wouldn't succeed with sentences like "She was frightened by *an* hiss in the dark." Similarly, a sportscaster would be laughed off the air for saying "He got *an* hit each time he came to bat."

Whether to use *a* or *an* before a word can be resolved by relying on pronunciation. That is, think of the sound of the words, not what they look like.

- Before a consonant sound, use *a*: "*a* surface-to-air missile."
- Before a vowel sound, use *an*: "*an* air-to-air missile."

Accordingly, if a word begins with a pronounced *h*, as in a consonant sound, use *a* in front: "*a* habitual failure"; "*a* hacksaw"; "*a* historian"; "*a* human being"; "*a* hum in the machinery."

Otherwise, if a word begins with a silent *h* and a vowel sound, use *an* in front: "*an* heir" (pronounced "*an* air") or "*an* hour" (pronounced "*an* our").

Pronunciation also determines that *a* is used before a word with a long *u* sound. The reason is that a long *u* sounds like the consonant *y* in *you*. Correct examples are "*a* euphemism"; "*a* useful device"; "*a* unanimous decision."

In addition, when you use *a* or *an* before a series of words, the sound of *a* or *an* is applied to the first word in the series. Both of the following are correct: "*an* obscure, devious policy"; "*a* devious, obscure policy."

These same principles apply when you use *a* or *an*

before an abbreviation. Again, write them as you would say them. "*A* registered nurse" becomes "*an* RN," not "*a* RN." The pronunciation is as though the *R* began with a vowel, "*an* are en."

abbreviation, acronym, initialism. Some people say *acronym* when they mean something other than an *acronym*, and few people use the term *initialism* even though it's part of this category. Basically, an *abbreviation* is any shortened form. However, for the sake of reference, *abbreviations* are sorted into the three types described here.

An *acronym* is made up of the initial letters of all the words or sometimes just the principal words of an expression. An *acronym* is read or spoken as a word rather than letter by letter. The word *laser* (*l*ight *a*mplification by *s*timulated *e*mission of *r*adiation) is an *acronym*, as is the U.S. Postal Service's *ZIP* (*Z*one *I*mprovement *P*lan).

An *initialism* is also composed of the initial letters of an expression but is pronounced letter by letter rather than as a word. Examples of *initialisms* are *rpm* (*r*evolutions *p*er *m*inute) and *GNP* (*g*ross *n*ational *p*roduct).

Any shortened form that doesn't fall into the above categories can be called an *abbreviation*. Examples that occur under this definition are *Dr.* (Doctor) and *Calif.* (California).

Some degree of confusion is attached to the writing of plurals of *abbreviations*, *acronyms*, and *initialisms*. These plurals can be divided into two types—*final-word plurals* and *internal-word plurals*.

When the final word of a shortened form is a plural, a small *s* is added to the end. An apostrophe is sometimes used before the *s*. Thus one *CPO* (chief petty officer) may be written as several *CPOs* or *CPO's*.

When an internal word is a plural, a small *s* is occasionally added to the end of the shortened form. An apostrophe is sometimes used before the *s*. Thus "runs batted in" may be written as *RBI* or *RBIs* or even *RBI's*. Strictly speaking, it doesn't make sense to say or write *RBIs*, for that literally stands for "runs batted ins"; "runs" makes sense, but what about "ins"? However, ballplayers use "*RBIs*," and many writers do the same so that their writing will sound natural.

Whether to use an apostrophe with the plural of an abbreviation defies logic. In current use are expressions such as *snag* (*s*ensitive *n*ew *a*ge *g*uy, pluralized without an apostrophe as *snags*) and *rpm's* (*r*evolutions *p*er *m*inute, pluralized with an apostrophe).

Usually the apostrophe isn't necessary, and its presence may contribute to confusion. That is, the apostrophe may allow the shortened form to be interpreted as a contraction, a possessive, or a plural.

ability, aptitude, talent. *Ability* and *talent* are usually thought of as demonstrated or obvious, while *aptitude* pertains to what is generally predictable.

Ability means a power or skill to do something; *ability* can be natural or taught. *Talent* means a marked natural *ability*; *talent* is frequently used when referring to artistic skills. *Aptitude* means a person's inclination or suitability to perform a certain task, or to learn something.

SEE ALSO **apt, liable, likely.**

-able, -ible. *Lovable? Collapsible?* Both suffixes mean capable of. Dictionaries show the spellings for words already in use. If you're coining a word, dictionaries show a preference for *-able* over *-ible*.

abnormal, subnormal. *Abnormal* literally means any departure from the normal, whether above normal or below normal. A strict interpretation of that definition means that Einstein would have been classified as *abnormal*. *Subnormal* means less than or below normal.

above, greater than, more than, over. In the following sentence, fill in the blank with a word or words from the choices provided: "The price of each gadget is _____ $50." Choices: (a) *above*; (b) *greater than*; (c) *more than*; (d) *over*.

Before you proceed, you can rest assured that the meaning of that sentence is the same regardless of your choice. Otherwise, the dictates of careful usage are as follows:

a. *above.* A poor choice. Refers to something that is higher in terms of space, rank, priority, or place: "the stars *above*"; "ethics *above* greed"; "ten miles *above* Oahu."

b. *greater than*. Another poor choice. Should be used to refer to the largeness of size, bulk, degree, or extent: "no city *greater than* Paris"; "a whale *greater than* Moby Dick"; "a ruler *greater than* Caesar."

c. *more than*. An excellent choice. Refers to number or quantity. For certain, $50 is a number and a quantity.

d. *over*. Also acceptable, but less formal than *more than*. *Over* should not be used when the thought leads downward: "The price is down $50 *over* (substitute *from*) last year."

SEE ALSO **fewer, less.**

abrasion, contusion, laceration.   The medical profession's *abrasions*, *contusions*, and *lacerations* are known to the rest of us as *scrapes*, *bruises*, and *tears* or *cuts*.

abridged, unabridged.   An *abridged* book is one that has been shortened from a previous edition of the same book. An *unabridged* book is one that has *not* been shortened from a previous edition of the same book. These words frequently come into play when people refer to dictionaries.

A common misconception is that an *unabridged* dictionary defines all the words in the English language. That can't be so, because no one knows how many words are in the language. *Webster's Third New International Dictionary* defines 450,000 words, but that number could easily be only one-half of the total.

Moreover, it would be pointless and expensive to keep producing dictionaries that contain all the words found in previous editions *plus* all the new words formed. Words come and go, and out-of-date words would just take up space that could be put to better uses. An exception is the *Oxford English Dictionary* (*OED*). The *OED* is a historical record of English usage and an attempt to grow with the language and therefore includes many obsolete words. The *OED*, however, is a massive reference work in a class by itself.

The word *unabridged* also has nothing to do with size. That is, a small desk or pocket dictionary can be an *unabridged* version of a previous one.

Therefore, the term *unabridged* can be a misnomer, and an *unabridged* dictionary is anything so labeled.

SEE ALSO **dictionary, encyclopedia, glossary, lexicon, thesaurus.**

abstruse, obtuse. *Abstruse* describes an argument or a statement that is hard to understand; the meaning may be deep, the words may be difficult, or both. *Obtuse* describes a person with insufficient mental ability to understand something. Thus a scholar's *abstruse* argument can be wasted even on an intelligent audience, and a simple argument can be wasted on an *obtuse* listener. In addition, *obtuse* is a broad word; its use implies that the *obtuse* person could be that way because of willful action or because of inborn inability.

Obtuse is not necessarily restricted to geometry (an *obtuse* angle), for the word is descended from a Latin word meaning blunt or dull.

SEE ALSO **acute angle, oblique angle, obtuse angle, right angle.**

abuse, misuse. The choice between these terms depends on whether damage is done.

In general, *abuse* carries with it some sense of harm: "Child *abuse* leaves long-lasting emotional scars." "*Abusive* language frightened the young girl."

Misuse refers to incorrect use that may not lead to harm: "*Misuse* of language is common, but we communicate quite well anyway."

You can also make this distinction: When you *abuse* a chisel, you damage the chisel; when you *misuse* a chisel, you stand a chance of damaging yourself.

Acadia, Arcadia. The spread of Cajun cooking has introduced many Americans to the word *Acadia*, which is easily confused with *Arcadia*.

Acadia is an early name for the part of Canada now known as New Brunswick and Nova Scotia. In the mid-eighteenth century, British soldiers deported *Acadians* who refused to take an oath of allegiance to the British king. Many of these people fled to what is now southern Louisiana—Cajun country.

As for *Arcadia*, it is an administrative area of Greece, an area whose history has been recorded since ancient times.

accelerate, exhilarate. It is true that a rapidly *accelerating* car can give the driver a feeling of *exhilaration*. That's about as close as these two words should be connected. Otherwise, the gadget on the floor is not an *exhilarator*, as it is sometimes carelessly mispronounced, but an *accelerator* pedal, speed control, or whatever term the manufacturer gives it. The word *exhilarating* refers to a cheerful, stimulating feeling.

accept, except. Two words with such vastly different meanings can be confused only because of a nonchalant attitude toward the sound of language.

Accept refers to what is willingly taken in, adopted, or admitted: "Students are *accepted* into college." "A Christian will *accept* certain beliefs."

Except can frequently stand in place of *but* or a similar term: "The dogs all barked *except (but)* one." "The couple liked the house *except (but)* for the pool."

If you happen to have a hard time remembering the distinction, keep in mind that the prefix *ex* very often indicates *out* or *outside*: *ex*hale, *ex*communicate, *ex*ile. *Accept* means to take in.

SEE ALSO **except, exempt.**

access, excess. *Access* refers to permission or ability to approach, enter, or make use of: "In the fall, he regularly grants hunters *access* to his land." "She has *access* to state secrets." "A narrow hall provides *access* to the inner chambers of the palace." "A password allows *access* to the central database."

Although traditionalists are resisting the change, current usage has established *access* as a verb: "By using a password, you may *access* the central database."

Access is sometimes used to refer to an outburst: "An *access* of jealousy"; "an *access* of anger"; "an *access* of patriotism." This use is rare, and it should not be confused with *excess*.

Excess refers to whatever goes beyond what is normal, usual, or lawful: "*excess* profits"; "an *excess* of wheat"; "an *excess* of enthusiasm"; "*excess* charges levied on property owners."

Excess can also mean intemperance or overindulgence: "His sexual *excesses* earned him an unsavory reputation." "The *excesses* of the period's style are an affront to good taste in art."

accident, incident. An *incident* is an event or an occurrence. An *incident* may be good or bad, expected or unexpected. If an *incident* is unexpected and occurs because of chance, it is safe to say that the *incident* is an *accident*.

Not all *accidents* are bad. We tend to say that someone's car was "damaged in an *accident*," which can be true even though *collision* is a more accurate word. Other *accidents* can be considerably different, as for lovers whose *accidental* meeting leads to a long and happy marriage.

SEE ALSO **incidence, incidents.**

accordion, concertina. Either of these musical instruments can also be called a squeeze-box. Both are small enough to hold in the hands, although the *accordion* is larger and more bulky than the *concertina*. Both operate by squeezing a bellows to force air through reeds. The air causes the reeds to vibrate, and the vibration produces music; the sound is something like that of a harmonica.

What we call an *accordion* is also known as a *piano accordion* because one of its keyboards resembles that of a piano. The *concertina* does not have a piano-type keyboard; on a *concertina* the notes are selected by pressing buttons.

ache, pain. A *pain* is something that hurts, in varying degrees of severity, for varying lengths of time. An *ache* is a constant, dull, prolonged *pain*.

act, action. *Act* refers to the thing done. *Action* is the doing of it or a collection of *acts*. "The *action* of the play took place in three *acts*." "Caught in the *act* of running away, the escaped prisoner said that the *action* of the chase was exciting."

activate, actuate. Organizations, people, and chemistry *activate*: "The governor *activated* the national guard." "Water *activates* the reaction."

Mechanical devices *actuate*: "Hydraulic push rods *actuate* the wing flaps."

acute, chronic. *Acute* refers to anything that is sharp in nature: "an *acute* observation"; "an *acute* crisis." *Chronic* refers to anything that lasts a long time: "*chronic* absenteeism."

In medical terminology, *acute* describes a disease or disorder of rapid onset, short duration, and pronounced symptoms; *chronic* describes one of long duration or one that recurs periodically. With *chronic leukemia*, life expectancy is longer than with *acute leukemia*.

Not all *acute* ailments are devastating. *Acute* rhinitis, as severe as it sounds, can be nothing more than a runny nose caused by an allergy.

SEE ALSO **disease, illness.**

acute angle, oblique angle, obtuse angle, right angle. In geometry, an *acute angle* is one of less than 90 degrees, and an *obtuse angle* is one greater than 90 degrees but less than 180 degrees. Either of these is also known as an *oblique angle*, as opposed to a *right angle*, a *right angle* being 90 degrees.

SEE ALSO **abstruse, obtuse.**

adapt, adopt. *Adapt* means to adjust. *Adopt* means to choose someone or something as one's own: "People may *adopt* a child, but the child may not be able to *adapt* to a new home."

addled, muddled. *Addled* pertains mainly to mental confusion: "*addle*-brained." *Muddled* pertains to anything that is confused or in a mess: "a *muddled* argument."

adhesive, cohesive. Things that are *adhesive* stick to other things: "An *adhesive* bandage sticks to the skin." Things that are *cohesive* stick together: "Members of the group are *cohesive*."

adjacent, adjoining, contiguous, coterminous. *Adjacent* refers to things that are close to each other but not touching: "Islands are *adjacent* to the coast."

Adjoining seems to mean *add* plus *join*—that is, touching or hooked onto. Dictionary definitions aren't that limited, however, and show synonyms ranging from *near* to *neighboring* to *next to*, along with *adjacent* and *contiguous*.

Contiguous defines things that touch: "the *contiguous* states of Florida and Georgia."

Coterminous (also spelled *conterminous*) refers to things that are contained within the same boundaries or limits: "The lower forty-eight states are known as the *coterminous* states."

administer, administrate. *Administer* has a broad meaning. A person can *administer* (manage) a business or governmental organization, *administer* (dispense) punishment or justice, *administer* (give) first aid to victims of an accident, or *administer* (say and have someone repeat) an oath of office.

Administrate is limited to managing or directing, as in an office or organization.

admission, admittance. These two words are often used interchangeably, but sometimes one is more appropriate than the other. *Admission* applies to formal acceptance as into a club or university, an acceptance that allows for rights, privileges, or membership: "He attended college mainly to achieve *admission* to his father's fraternity." *Admittance* pertains more to physical entry: "He was denied *admittance* to the boardroom."

admission, confession. *Black's Law Dictionary* provides a handy means of distinguishing between an *admission* and a *confession*: "A confession is a statement admitting or acknowledging all facts necessary for conviction of a crime. An admission, on the other hand, is an acknowledgment of a fact or facts tending to prove guilt which falls short of an acknowledgment of all essential elements of the crime."

In law and in general usage, *confession* is the more encompassing and more binding of the two terms.

adolescence, puberty. *Adolescence* is a period of transition from childhood to adulthood. The term has no precise biological meaning, but the period is roughly taken to begin with the onset of *puberty* and last until about the age of twenty. *Puberty* is the time in a person's life when sexual development intensifies.

Persons in the period of *adolescence* are known as

adolescents. No worthwhile name has been coined to pin on teenagers who are undergoing the shock and frustrations of *puberty* and are taking out their frustrations on their parents. *Puberts* perhaps? As an obnoxious label that parents can use in an attempt to get even?

SEE ALSO **child, infant.**

adopted, adoptive.   *Adopted* children. *Adoptive* parents.

adverse, averse.   *Adverse* and *averse* both express contrariness—but from different points of view. People are *averse* to things, and things are *adverse* to people: "A person may be *averse* to running for exercise, especially when faced with *adverse* terrain."

aerobic, anaerobic.   An *aerobic* process is one requiring oxygen. An *anaerobic* process is one without oxygen. *Aerobic* exercises are exercises meant to increase the efficiency with which the body takes in and uses oxygen. *Anaerobic* bacteria are ones that thrive in the absence of oxygen.

affect, effect.   These two words could be stricken from the language with no loss whatsoever. Dictionaries list so many meanings for the pair that they can be taken as synonyms. Editors, writers, and teachers confuse the meanings and the uses of them. Bureaucrats and scientists like them because the dilution of meaning allows for vague expression. Otherwise, neither *affect* nor *effect* appears frequently in the works of the best professional writers—a sure clue that something is rotten with the pair.

If you want a quick check on the commonly confused meanings of *affect* and *effect*, try this table:

Word	Meaning
effect (verb)	bring about; cause to come into being
affect (verb)	influence; change
effect (noun)	consequence; result

To get some idea of how these terms should be used, you can arrange them into a before-during-after sequence. Before something happens, you *effect* it; that is, you *bring about* its start, or you *cause it to come into being*.

During the course of an action, you *affect* it; that is, you *influence* or *change* it. After the course of an action, you can talk about its *effects*—its *consequences* or *results*.

Therefore, "The new administration will *bring about (effect)* a change in policy that will *influence (affect)* the *consequences (effects)* of government spending."

However, it is also quite possible that "The new administration will put into *effect* a change in policy." In this case, *effect* is a noun standing for whatever is produced by an action or process.

Affect as a verb also pertains to the pretenses that a person might pose. "She *affected* indifference to his amorous overtures" does not say that she was in fact indifferent but that she was pretending to be so. Similarly, "His tone was *affected*" refers to a person's willingness to show off or put on airs.

What's the best solution here? Abandon *affect* and *effect* and use more precise words.

SEE ALSO **impact.**

afflict, inflict. *Afflict* and *inflict* mean to cause some kind of suffering, or damage.

Afflict is generally used with living beings: "The itching that fleas *afflict* upon a dog seems endless." "People in the village were *afflicted* with dysentery."

Inflict is generally used with inanimate objects: "A storm such as this will *inflict* great damage upon the crops." "The hail *inflicted* great damage."

aggravate, irritate. To *aggravate* is to worsen an already bad or uncomfortable situation: "Cold weather always *aggravated* his old wounds." "Her insolence only served to *aggravate* her offenses." "The solvents *aggravated* his open sores."

To *irritate* is to vex, to exasperate, to annoy, or to drive someone to anger: "His smugness *irritates* me." "It's the little things in life that are the most *irritating*." "The solvents *irritated* his skin." "His mother's snooping *irritated* him so much that he ran away from home."

Aggravate should not be used as a synonym for *irritate* or *annoy*, for *aggravate* is the stronger of the three words.

agnostic, atheist. An *agnostic* is a person who believes that the human mind cannot know whether there is a God or gods or anything else beyond material substance. As far as an *agnostic* is concerned, there isn't enough evidence to say for certain.

An *atheist*, however, has an opinion on the subject and is not a fence-sitter. That is, an *atheist* rejects all religious beliefs and denies the existence of a God or gods.

aid, aide. An *aide* is a person who gives assistance or help: "editorial *aide*"; "the general's *aide*"; "a State Department *aide*." *Aid* is sometimes used in those senses but is better restricted to a mechanical form of assistance: "Because her leg was in a cast, she used a crutch as an *aid* in getting around."

à la carte, table d'hôte. The expression *à la carte* describes a meal in which each menu item is priced separately. *Table d'hôte* describes a complete meal as listed on the menu with one price for the entire meal.

alibi, excuse, reason. In law, an *alibi* is (1) a plea, proven or unproven, that places the accused elsewhere than at the crime or (2) the fact that the accused was elsewhere than at the crime.

In everyday usage, an *alibi* is an *excuse* as used in an attempt to avoid blame: "She used a flat tire as an *excuse* (or *alibi*) for being late to work." An *excuse* may also be a note of explanation: "If you miss school, you'll need an *excuse* from your parents."

The verb *excuse* has several meanings. One meaning is that of apology: "He *excused* his clumsiness." Another meaning is that of forgiveness: "She *excused* him for forgetting their anniversary." *Excuse* also means to grant exemption to or to release: "They *excused* classes early so that the teachers could go to a meeting." "The court *excused* him from paying the rest of his fine."

The word *reason* refers to a logical explanation or justification: "Science has established the *reasons* for earthquakes." "He explained his tardiness with *reasons* that were quite satisfactory."

Anyone who has spent at least one day in the military knows full well the difference between an *excuse* and a *reason*. If you do something wrong, the rebuke goes like this: " 'There is no such thing as an *excuse* for your behavior,' yelled the sergeant at the private. 'But there may be a *reason*.' "

alligator, crocodile. An *alligator* has a broader, blunter snout than a *crocodile*; the shape of the snout gives the *alligator's* head a triangular-shaped appearance. In addition, when a *crocodile* closes its mouth, the lower fourth tooth sticks out, a peculiarity not found in the *alligator*.

Alligators are found in the New World and in China. *Crocodiles* are found in the New World, Africa, Southeast Asia, Australia, and on islands in the South Pacific.

Alligators are said to be less vicious than *crocodiles* —but this book should not be considered as a guide to safety around large creatures with fangs.

all ready, already. *All ready* refers to complete readiness: "Everything is *all ready* for the party." *Already* expresses time: "We have *already* written a report on this subject."

all right, alright. The best bet is to use *all right* and not *alright* to describe what is satisfactory or correct: "The car is *all right*." "They were late, *all right*." *Alright* is occasionally used in that sense and may someday be on equal footing with *all right*. At present, however, *alright* is frowned upon by teachers and other critics.

all together, altogether. *All together* means collectively or in a group: "The sheep crowded *all together* by the shearing shed." *Altogether* means completely or entirely: "The plan is *altogether* workable."

The euphemism *in the altogether* is another way of saying "naked"; in this sense, *all together* is not used.

allude, refer When these two are compared, *allude* means to make an indirect reference to; *refer* means to name. "His letters *alluded* to financial difficulties, which, as a matter of pride, he wanted to conceal and would not *refer* to directly."

allusion, delusion, illusion. An *allusion* is an indirect reference to something. If a poem contains *allusions* to nature, nature is indirectly referred to or hinted at, *alluded* to, without being specifically named.

Allusion is sometimes confused with *illusion*, the latter word referring to deception or a false perception of reality: "Like all mirages, this one was an *illusion*." "The ghost was an *illusion* that frightened the child."

In this same area of confusion is *delusion*, a stronger word than *illusion*. An *illusion* is a deception that a person eventually sees as false. A *delusion* is a belief that is maintained in spite of arguments and evidence that should reasonably be sufficient to destroy it.

Care should be taken in the use of *delusion*. Columbus's crew thought that their captain's idea that the world was round was a *delusion*, but they turned out to be wrong.

all ways, always. When these two are compared, *all ways* as two words means the total amount or total extent of means or methods, and *always* as one word means ceaselessly or forever. "He promises to love her in *all ways*" speaks of a love that will express itself in every possible way; but for an unspecified term; "He promised to love her *always*" speaks of an enduring love.

alpha, omega. In the Greek alphabet, *alpha* is the name for the first letter, and *omega* is the name for the last letter: "I am the *alpha* and the *omega*, the beginning and the ending" (Revelation 1:8).

alternate, alternative. Strict usagists would prefer restricting *alternate* to describing things that occur one after the other and *alternative* to describing a choice between two things or among several things. However, the wishes of strict usagists don't hold up in practice, as the following three popular uses demonstrate.

One, when faced with bad weather at the planned landing field, pilots speak of an "*alternate* landing field." They obviously don't mean that they're going to play aeronautical hopscotch, going from one runway to the next. Here *alternative* would please the nitpickers in the crowd.

Two, there's a lot of talk, in the media and elsewhere, about *alternate* fuels to replace gasoline. In this usage, *alternate* refers to methanol, propane, or natural gas, and not the possibility that a car is a gas guzzler that has to stop at one filling station after the other.

Three, courts across the nation use "*alternate* jurors," not "*alternative* jurors."

It's hard to think of a good reason to use an extra syllable when surrounding words make the meaning clear. Sadly, about the only reason to do so is to avoid criticism. After all, there are plenty of critics around whose minds are made up and who do not wish to be confronted with facts or logic.

Of course, it still makes sense to say "My *alternatives* are . . ." when the intent is to refer to choices. But in that situation, you could substitute *choice(s)* or *option(s)*.

although, while. *While* has a meaning that refers to two events going on at the same time: "*While* the others worked, he went fishing." *While* is also used in place of *although* to stand for *though* or *in spite of the fact that*. The use of *while* for *although* allows for different interpretations of sentences such as this one: "*While* laws have forbidden age discrimination, no reasonable guidance has been given." If *although* is meant, that's the word that should be used.

alumna, alumnae, alumni, alumnus. These words were once restricted to specify graduates of schools, colleges, or universities. Usage has changed so that the words now also refer to former employees of organizations and former inmates of prisons.

Regardless of where the individual served time, the meanings are: *Alumna*, feminine singular. *Alumnae*, feminine plural. *Alumnus* (singular) and *alumni* (plural), by virtue of their Latin spellings, were once masculine, but are now used to refer to either sex.

Because many other terms are being rephrased into sex-neutral language—as examples, *stewardess* to *flight attendant* and *freshman* to *first-year student*—it is difficult to find a good reason to differentiate between men and women who graduate from a university. Even the *coed* of years past has largely become the gender-free *student* of today.

Graduate is certainly a clear enough word without being

sexist, and some people have taken to using *alum* or *alums*. If either one of these last two terms looks strange to you, remember that many words look strange when they are first coined.

amaze, surprise. *Amaze* as a verb means to experience wonder, bewilderment, or perplexity: "The starving hiker was *amazed* and dismayed that the furry marmot had so little meat on its bones."

Surprise as a verb means to be caught unprepared by something that is unusual, unexpected, or unanticipated: "The attack *surprised* the enemy completely, coming as it did on the holyday." *Surprise* can, of course, be a noun: "Because the editor long ago had learned to expect only poorly prepared manuscripts, each good piece of writing was a *surprise*."

The difference between *amaze* and *surprise* can be seen in this sentence: "The power of Japanese industry is no longer *surprising*, but its continued strength does *amaze* many observers."

SEE ALSO **astonished, astounded.**

ambrosia, nectar. In Greek and Roman mythologies, *ambrosia* was the food of the gods, and *nectar* was the drink of the gods. Today, *ambrosia* is used to refer to any delectable or pleasing flavor or fragrance, and *nectar* to refer to any delicious or refreshing drink.

amend, emend. Both *amend* and *emend* mean to correct. *Emend* is limited to the editing of written material: "The editor decided to *emend* the text to make it more readable." *Amend* conveys a broader sense and pertains to improving or correcting in general: "The legislature *amended* the law by adding three sections; no *emending* (editing) of the original language took place."

American plan, European plan. If you obtain lodging on the *American plan*, the price covers the room and meals. On the *European Plan*, the price does not cover the meals.

amiable, amicable. *Amiable* describes a person who is friendly, pleasing, and easy to like. *Amicable* describes a relationship that exists in a peaceful state, and shows goodwill and a desire of the parties to get along with each other.

among, between. Advice on *among* and *between* is divided into basic and advanced. The basic advice is to use *between* when referring to two persons or objects, and *among* when referring to three or more: "*Between* innings the players on the losing team argued *among* themselves." Certainly that advice makes sense with passages like "caught *between* a rock and a hard spot" or "Weeds grew *among* the roses."

As for the advanced advice, it comes from the *Oxford English Dictionary*, which says: "In all its senses *between* has been, from its earliest appearance, extended to more than two. . . . It is still the only word available to express the relation of a thing to many surrounding things severally and individually, *among* expressing a relation to them collectively and vaguely."

In other words, *between* rather than *among* is the better word to use when the relationship is each to each to each: "*Between* you and me and the gatepost"; "*Between* the three of them, they chopped down the tree"; "A treaty was reached *between* the four nations." In any of those examples, *among* would not convey the same relationship.

amoral, immoral. *Amoral* means without morals, indifferent to right or wrong. *Immoral* means contrary to established morals.

amuck, berserk. *Amuck* (also spelled *amok*) has to do with the committing of indiscriminate murder. *Amuck* is from a Malay word referring to men who went out in the streets and killed anyone they met. *Berserk* refers to a frenzied rage; the word is descended from a reference to Norse warriors—*berserkers*—who fought with fury and rage.

amuse, bemuse. *Amuse* means to entertain or provide with pleasure. *Bemuse* means to bewilder or confuse. "Humor books *amuse* readers." "The students' term papers were so poorly written that they *bemused* the professor."

analysis, synthesis. *Analysis* is the breaking of a whole into its parts. *Synthesis* is the opposite—the putting together of the parts to make a whole: "This book is a *synthesis* of the books listed in the bibliography." "Each of those books is an *analysis* of an individual topic."

and/or. Some 100 interpretations of *and/or* appear in *Words and Phrases*, the legal profession's multivolume guide to meanings that have been established by court judgments and verdicts. The meanings are conflicting and contradictory. In addition, various dictionaries define the virgule (/), an integral part of *and/or*, as meaning *and, or,* or whatever meaning will suit the surrounding text.

No one can say for certain what *and/or* means, whether or not the practice of law is involved. Therefore, *and/or* should be made null and void—not null *and/or* void, but null and void period.

androgen, estrogen. For people who have lost track of which hormones are associated with sexual characteristics, an *androgen* is a male hormone, and an *estrogen* is a female hormone.

   SEE ALSO **X chromosome, Y chromosome.**

anesthesiologist, anesthetist. Both administer *anesthetics*—drugs or gases that cause a complete or partial loss of sensations. An *anesthesiologist* is a medical doctor, fully licensed by the state in which he or she practices, who specializes in administering anesthetics. An *anesthetist* can be an *anesthesiologist,* a nurse, a dentist, or anyone else trained to administer anesthetics.

animal, mammal. An *animal* is any living organism other than a plant. With very few exceptions, *animals* are mobile and have to obtain food, while plants are not mobile and produce their own food. A *mammal* is an *animal* fed with milk from female mammary glands.

annual, perennial. As plants go, an *annual* is one that lives for a year or a season, not one that blooms once a year. Opposed to the *annual* is a *perennial*, a plant that has a life span of at least two years. *Perennial* also means persistent in general: "*perennial* optimism."

anonymous, pseudonymous. *Anonymous* means that no name is known or acknowledged. If no author's name is shown on the title page of a book, the author is said to be *anonymous*.

Pseudonymous refers to a fictitious name or a pen name used by an author. When a pen name is shown as the author of a book, the book is a *pseudonymous* work.

anorexia nervosa, bulimia nervosa. By itself, *anorexia* refers to a loss of appetite; by itself, *bulimia* refers to an insatiable appetite. Things are never what they seem, however, for the problem with appetite can be caused by a physiological or mental disorder. With *anorexia nervosa* or *bulimia nervosa*, the problem is a mental disorder. Moreover, both terms are misnomers to an extent, for rarely is there any true problem with appetite.

The popular view is that *anorexia nervosa* and *bulimia nervosa* are opposites. That is incorrect, for they are very similar. Both are disorders characterized by a disturbed sense of body image and a great fear of obesity. Both occur primarily in young women. Both are manifested by abnormal patterns of handling food and by self-induced weight loss.

Anorexics suppress their appetites, are preoccupied with food, and study diets and calories. Many *anorexics* indulge in binge eating and self-induced vomiting and purging; these are also characteristics of *bulimia nervosa*, and some people suffer from both disorders. *Anorexics* become emaciated and suffer nutritional deficiencies. *Anorexia nervosa* leads to a greater weight loss than does *bulimia nervosa*.

Bulimia nervosa is marked by binge eating and a feeling of loss of control over eating; the *bulimic* regularly engages in self-induced vomiting and purging, or rigorous dieting and fasting to overcome the effects of binge eating. *Bulimics* worry about becoming obese, but they seldom become as emaciated as *anorexics*.

Antarctic Circle, Arctic Circle. The *Antarctic Circle* is an imaginary line in the southern hemisphere that runs parallel to the equator and is about 66 degrees south of the equator—somewhat more than two-thirds of the way between the equator and the South Pole. The *Arctic*

Circle is the same, but in the northern hemisphere, 66 degrees north of the equator.

SEE ALSO **Tropic of Cancer, Tropic of Capricorn.**

ante-, anti-.   The prefix *ante* means before, whether in time or location: "The *antebellum* period was the time before the Civil War." "An *antechamber* is a small room that opens into a larger room."

The prefix *anti* means opposed to: "*Antiaircraft* guns shoot down airplanes."

antiperspirant, deodorant.   Perspiration is odorless until it comes into contact with bacteria on the skin. To fight the odor that arises from this contact, two classes of consumer products—*antiperspirants* and *deodorants*—have been developed.

Deodorants act in one way—by retarding the growth of the bacteria. *Antiperspirants* act in two ways—by retarding the growth of the bacteria and by restricting the movement of perspiration from the sweat glands to the skin. This last action alters a natural function of the body.

antiques, collectibles, memorabilia.   An *antique* is an object, frequently decorative, typically made more than 100 years ago. A *collectible* (also spelled *collectable*) is any object collected by people who like that sort of stuff. *Memorabilia* are objects that stir memories or are worthy of remembrance.

anxious, eager.   Connect *anxious* with anxiety—a sense of foreboding, worry, apprehension, or an uneasy feeling or state of mind. Connect *eager* with zeal, enthusiasm, or impatience. If you are driving home for Christmas, you could be *eager* to get there while being *anxious* about the road conditions.

anybody, anyone, any one, everybody, everyone, every one.   *Anyone* and *everyone* (one word) are pronouns that mean the same as the pronouns *anybody* and *everybody*: "Is *anybody* (*anyone*) home?" "There's plenty of room for *everyone* (*everybody*) in the room."

Everyone implies a collective sense that is not present

in the two words *every one*. The phrase *every one* implies each person individually: "He had something good to say about *every one* of his followers." The test is whether *everybody* can be substituted; that is, you would not say "He had something good to say about *everybody* of his followers."

The same is true of *any one*; any one emphasizes an individual: "*Any one* of you may go first." Substituting *anybody* would produce an awkward sentence: "*Anybody* of you may go first."

A lot of effort has been wasted in a dispute over whether *everyone (everybody)* or *anyone (anybody)* is singular or plural. At a glance, each seems to refer to *one* and therefore would seem to be singular. That isn't always the case, especially with *everyone* or *everybody*.

When we say *everybody*, we are generally using the word in a collective sense to mean all. Therefore, it is common to see constructions such as "*Everybody* must exercise their right to vote." *Everybody* has been used in this manner for four centuries, despite the cries of unbending usagists who insist that the word can be used as a singular word only.

The "*everyone* . . . their" construction seems to be gaining popularity, perhaps because of attempts to make the language gender-free. Certainly, it is sexist to write "*Everyone* should exercise his right to vote." Women do have the vote these days, but it's difficult to lump them in with men because English lacks a combined *his-her* pronoun.

Careful writers avoid combinations such as "*Everyone* must exercise his or her (his/her) right to vote." That kind of writing is tiring to read and falls dead on the ear.

One way out is to use the second person: "You must exercise your right to vote." Another way out is to remove the offending possessive and substitute *the*: "*Everyone* must exercise the right to vote." No need exists to specify *your* right to vote, because the only vote you have is yours, unless you live in an area of creative political chicanery.

In *Modern English Usage*, the revered H. W. Fowler surveyed the "*Everyone* . . . their" situation and concluded that it is a question that we'll have to answer for ourselves. That is essentially what happens. *Everyone* does what they want to do.

However, we're not yet ready for "Are *everybody* happy?"

apogee, perigee. The words *apogee* and *perigee* apply to the orbital paths of celestial bodies. If the earth is used as a reference, the *apogee* is the point of the orbit that is farthest from the earth, and the *perigee* is the point that is closest to the earth.

SEE ALSO: **nadir, zenith.**

apostle, disciple. *Disciple* is the broader term, referring to any person who believes in the teachings of a master and helps to spread them. *Apostle* is usually restricted to a religious or missionary sense, that is, one sent on a mission to teach the gospel. Jesus had many *disciples* but only twelve chosen *apostles*. The twelve administrative officials of the Mormon Church are also called *apostles*, yet Mormonism has many *disciples*.

appraise, apprise. *Appraise* means to evaluate, often as to the dollar value of something: "Real estate agents *appraise* property before putting it on the market." "The *appraisal* was higher than any bids." *Apprise* means to tell, to inform: "Apprise them of their rights under the law."

apt, liable, likely. *Apt* and *likely* are interchangeable when followed by *to*: "She is *apt (likely)* to succeed."

Apt has additional meanings over *likely*. *Apt* can refer to whatever is suited to a purpose: "an *apt* turn of phrase." *Apt* can also imply aptitude and intelligence: "an *apt* student of foreign affairs."

Liable refers to what is undesirable: "You are *liable* to slip if you get out on the ice." "The drunken driver was *liable* for damages."

SEE ALSO   **ability, aptitude, talent; libel, slander.**

Arab, Arabian, Arabic, Saudi, Saudi Arabian. The word *Arab* is loosely connected with any non-Jewish person from the Middle East—a huge area that includes *Saudi Arabia* and other nations. In that context, *Arab* is an imprecise word. It is also sometimes used in a derogatory sense, as is *Jew*, for that matter. People from *Saudi Arabia* are rightly called *Saudi Arabians* or *Saudis*. Things from that nation may also be called *Saudi* or *Saudi Arabian*. The language is *Arabic*.

arbitrate, mediate. To *arbitrate* a dispute is to settle it through the use of a person called an *arbitrator*. Legal procedure and legal apparatus are used, and the *arbitrator's* decision is binding. A *mediator* serves as an intermediary to help other parties reconcile their differences themselves. To *mediate* a dispute is not as strong an act and may not be as binding as to *arbitrate* it.

ardor, passion. *Ardor* refers to a warm, sometimes short-lived feeling or emotion: "His *ardor* cooled off during the course of their affair."

Passion refers to a deep, overpowering feeling or emotion. *Passion* applies to extremes such as love and sexual desire, and anger and hatred: "She had so captivated him that he idolized her and looked with *passion* into her eyes." "With maniacal *passion* he attacked the ruling powers and the prime minister."

Used lightly, *passion* implies an enthusiasm for a hobby or pastime: "a *passion* for golf"; "a *passion* for knowledge"; "a *passion* for chess."

SEE ALSO **zeal, zest.**

aristocracy, nobility, royalty. An *aristocracy* is any class considered superior or best: "an *aristocracy* of poets." *Aristocracy* can also refer to the ruling class, and at one time *aristocracy* referred to a government by the best citizens or a government by a privileged ruling class.

Nobility was once limited to mean the class consisting of nobles—people with high hereditary rank or title. The word today figuratively refers to a high station or position in society.

Royalty consists of monarchs and their families—kings, queens, princes, and princesses.

arithmetically, exponentially, geometrically. When a rate of change varies *arithmetically*, a constant is *added* to each number in the series. An *arithmetical* progression beginning with 2 and with a constant of 2 would be 2, 4, 6, 8.

When the rate of change is *geometrical*, each number in the progression is *multiplied* by a constant. A *geometrical* progression beginning with 2 and with a constant of 2 would be 2, 4, 8, 16, 32.

When the rate of change is *exponential*, the numbers increase according to the value of an *exponent*. In an *exponential* progression with an exponent of 2, the progression would begin, 2, 4, 16, 256, 65,536.

SEE ALSO **linear, logarithmic.**

around, round.   *Around* can refer to all sides: "The doghouse measures ten feet *around*." *Around* can also refer to something less than all sides: "He couldn't swim, so he walked *around* the lake." "Patton maneuvered *around* the enemy flank."

Round means circular or nearly circular in shape: "She has a *round* face." *Round* is sometimes used in place of *around* in expressions such as "Rally *round* the flag"; this usage is probably more common in Britain than in the United States.

SEE ALSO **year-around, year-round.**

arouse, rouse.   *Arouse* pertains to waking someone from sleep, or stimulating or stirring up: "*arouse* sexual desire." "His speech *aroused* debate." *Rouse* can have the same meanings except that it generally applies to a stronger reaction: "He was *roused* to anger." "The angry mob was *roused* to action."

arraign, indict.   In law, *arraign* means to bring a person to court; *indict* means to charge a person with a crime.

arrant, errant.   *Errant* means *roving* or *wandering*: "a knight-*errant*." *Errant* also refers to a deviation from a standard: "*Errant* spelling spoiled his dissertation." *Arrant* means extreme, and applies to an attribute, usually bad, that a person or thing has through and through: "This is *arrant* stupidity!"

arteriosclerosis, atherosclerosis.   In the human body's plumbing, the arteries are the large blood vessels that carry blood to the limbs and organs. When artery walls thicken and lose their elasticity, they are suffering from *arteriosclerosis*. *Arteriosclerosis* is often referred to as hardening of the arteries. The commonest form of *arteriosclerosis* is *atherosclerosis*—fatty deposits on the inner walls of the arteries.

Atherosclerosis is almost always present in the middle-aged and elderly. Severe *atherosclerosis* causes a variety of problems including heart attacks and strokes.

SEE ALSO **heart attack, heart failure.**

arthritis, rheumatism. Arthritis is a painful inflammation of a joint or joints. *Rheumatism* is a broader and imprecise term for various afflictions of the joints leading to discomfort and disability.

artisan, artist, craftsman. The word *artisan* means someone who is skilled at producing things with the hands. *Artist* means a higher order of creator, particularly in painting, drawing, sculpture, literature, or music.

Craftsman is a synonym for *artisan*, but the use of *craftsman* ignores the fact that many women are skilled at producing things with the hands; in short, *craftsman* is sexist. Nonsexist substitutes include *crafter, craftworker, craftsworker, handicrafts worker,* and *handicrafter*. If the sounds of those aren't appealing, use *artisan*.

Asian, Oriental. *Asian* describes people or things characteristic of Asia: "*Asian* artifacts"; "an *Asian* attitude." Asia is the largest continent in terms of landmass and number of people; it extends from Africa and Europe in the west to the Pacific Ocean in the east. The word *Asian* should be used in place of *Asiatic*, the latter sometimes being offensive. Exceptions exist, however, as with the recognized disease of *Asiatic* cholera.

Oriental describes people or things characteristic of the Orient, which is the eastern part of Asia. Any references to Orient or *Oriental* are largely poetic and imaginative. As an example, the Orient Express was a fanciful name for a train that went toward the Orient but in reality never left Europe. The train ran from Paris to Istanbul (that name being officially changed from Constantinople in 1930).

The unique thing about Istanbul is that it is the only major city in the world that sits on two continents—Europe and Asia. Passengers on the Orient Express got off the train in the European part of Istanbul and were ferried across the Straits of Bosporus if they wanted to go any farther. Once across the straits, and properly in Asia, they could continue their travels eastward to the Orient. Similarly, today's cruise ships to the Orient go to eastern Asia—the Far East—mainly China and Japan.

We owe this imprecision to beliefs fostered centuries ago when Europe considered itself the source of knowledge and the center of earthly existence. Then and there the term *Occident* came into being to refer to the West, the place where the sun set, and *Orient* came to mean the opposite, the East, the place where the sun rose.

Although *Occident* and *Occidental* are seldom heard today, *Orient* and *Oriental* are. They are vague terms, terms that exist largely in the language of travel agents and people of a romantic bent.

as, like. Confusion over *as* and *like* is not concerned with meaning but with a rule of grammar that is frequently applied and probably just as frequently misapplied. The rule says to use *as* (not *like*) as a conjunction when introducing a clause, a clause being a group of words that contains a verb: "This month was warm, *as* should be expected." "Do *as* I tell you to do." Otherwise, *like* is used when comparing nouns: "His car is *like* mine." "Their kitchen is *like* a pigpen."

For some reason, this little rule is hard to remember or to use correctly. As Roy Copperud shows in *American Usage and Style*, misapplication of the rule produces horrible-sounding constructions like "He ate *as* a beast" and "She trembled *as* a leaf." In both instances *as* is wrong, and *like* would be right.

Moreover, the rule is not universal, according to *Webster's Ninth New Collegiate Dictionary:* "After 450 years of use, *like* is firmly established as a conjunction. . . . While the present objection to it is perhaps more heated than rational, someone writing formal prose may want to use *as* instead."

If you are writing formal prose, your best bet is to follow the rule. If you forget the rule or if you don't like the sound of what you've written, rewrite the passage using *the way* or some other phrase.

This example is correct according to the rule, but may not sound good to some people: "He took to driving *as* a fish takes to water."

This example is *in*correct according to the rule, but may sound better than the so-called correct version: "He took to driving *like* a fish takes to water."

This example is rewritten to avoid the problem: "He took to driving *the way* a fish takes to water."

SEE ALSO **like, such as.**

asphalt, blacktop. *Blacktop* refers to a material, usually *asphalt*, that is used to pave roads or cover roofs. *Asphalt* itself is refined as a petroleum by-product, although some natural deposits exist.

assault, attack. *Assault* refers to physical or verbal attack and can imply bodily harm and intense violence: "An *assault* on the beaches was a vital part of the D-Day invasion." "His preaching is an *assault* on the teaching of evolution in the schools." "In court he was charged with *assault* for beating his wife."

Attack refers to any offensive action, whether physical or verbal: "His method is to *attack* his enemies in print." "Air Force units *attacked* the dam." "The Colorado River *attacked* the rock, carving a magnificent canyon in the plateau."

assay, essay. To *assay* is to analyze, evaluate, examine, or test: "The man who *assayed* the prospector's ore had to tell him it was nothing more than fool's gold." To *essay* is to try or attempt: "Diplomats *essayed* further negotiations."

assent, consent. *Assent* means to agree to an opinion or a proposal: "I *assent* to the proposition that all persons are created equal." *Consent* means to grant or yield to a demand or request: "I *consent* to whatever you wish."

assume, presume. These are compared here because of their use when inferring or believing a certain thing to be true. Of the two, *assume* is more closely tied to logic or reason.

When you *assume* something, you might not have proof, but study or investigation or research allows for a reasonable *assumption*: "We *assumed* that the conclusions in this report were based on competent experimental work."

When you *presume* something, you take it for granted, by guesswork, or without complete knowledge: "The injured pedestrian had *presumed* that the car would stop for him."

assure, ensure, insure. Are you unsure about when to use *assure, ensure,* and *insure*? If so, consult the dictionaries listed as references for this book, and you will be more unsure. From them you can learn that (1) the words are synonyms or (2) the words can be matched up with popularly assumed differences. The popularly assumed differences are these: *Assure* pertains to making a person sure of something; *ensure,* to making sure in general; and *insure,* to money to be paid in case of loss.

Here is one instance where a person, to be secure, can literally go shopping for definitions. However, for safety's sake, nothing is wrong with sticking to the popularly assumed differences. This is especially true of *insure,* which is the only form for compensation in case of loss.

astonished, astounded. These terms refer to a high degree of surprise. *Astonished* means momentarily overwhelmed, dazed, or speechless. *Astounded* refers to a condition of shock caused by something incredible. *Astound* is the more powerful word and means to *astonish* greatly: "A person can be *astonished* by magic tricks." "I was *astounded* when I won fifty million bucks in the lottery."
    SEE ALSO **amaze, surprise.**

astrology, astronomy. *Astrology* is a belief in the use of the positions of celestial bodies as a supposed means of predicting human affairs. *Astronomy* is the scientific study of celestial bodies.

at, near. Although crossword puzzle writers treat these words as synonyms, they aren't. When you are *at* a place or time, you are present there. When you are *near* a place or time, you are close to it. Being ready for a break *near* lunchtime is not the same as being ready *at* lunchtime, especially when you are hungry.

atoll, island. An *atoll* is an *island* shaped like a ring and nearly or completely encircling a lagoon. An *island* is a piece of land, other than a whole continent, surrounded by water.

attest, testify. *Attest* and *testify* mean to say that something is true or genuine or that it did happen. Both may involve the taking of an oath: "A notary public or other certifying officer *attests* that a document is correct." "A witness is sworn in and *testifies* in court." In careful usage, *attest* applies in situations where an oath is not part of the idea: "The size of the house *attests* to the wealth of its owner."

attic, garret, loft. An *attic* is the space between the ceiling of the top floor and the roof. This same space can also correctly be called a *loft*. A *loft* can also be the upper space in a barn (hay*loft*) or in a church (organ *loft* or choir *loft*). A *garret* is a room in the *attic* or *loft*.

attorney, lawyer. An *attorney* is someone who is appointed and authorized to act in place of another. A *lawyer*, according to *Black's Law Dictionary*, is a person who "is learned in the law" and who is licensed to defend or prosecute cases and dispense legal advice. Some *lawyers* call themselves by the term *attorney at law*, which *Black's* defines as a "person admitted to practice law in his respective state and authorized to perform both civil and criminal legal functions for clients."

Because *lawyer* has gained many negative connotations, many *lawyers* call themselves *attorneys*. After all, there are a lot of *lawyer* jokes but not many *attorney* jokes. The use of *attorney* for *lawyer* is also popular in telephone books where the yellow pages under *lawyers* will often say "see *attorneys*."

augment, supplement. *Augment* means to add more of the same thing: "Each year, Congress *augments* the budget." *Supplement* also means to add something, but usually to make up for a deficiency: "Vitamins *supplemented* his diet."

auspicious, propitious. These are two closely related words, but a distinction can be made. *Auspicious* describes a favorable omen that portends success before the start of something: "The large crowd on opening night was an *auspicious* sign." *Propitious* can mean the same but often describes continuing favorable circumstances: "Large crowds at all performances were *propitious* signs."

author, writer. Both write. Dictionaries define the word *author* as someone who originates or creates a literary work; the word *author* is descended from a Latin word for *originator*. The word *writer* is descended from Old English for *scratch, draw,* or *inscribe*. These dictionary definitions ignore the fact that many people who call themselves *writers* produce original literary works.

Author is generally a tonier word than *writer*, and *author* implies publication. *Writer* is broader: "She's a writer of advertising copy." "He's a *writer* of greeting-card verses." "As a journalist, I see myself as a *writer* and not an *author*."

authoritarian, authoritative. *Authoritarian* describes dictatorial power; *authoritative* describes an expert source. A boy fascinated with big words might complain that Dad was *authoritarian* but not *authoritative*. That is, the old man was bossy but didn't know very much.

automation, mechanization. *Mechanization* is the use of a machine to do the job; a human being must be present to run the machine. When the machine can do the job without a human at the controls, then *automation* has taken over. For instance, a factory worker operating a drill press is using *mechanization*. If the factory worker is replaced by a computer, then the drill press is *automated*.

avenge, revenge. *Avenge* means to right wrongs done to someone else: "In *The Avengers*, John Steed and Tara King sought justice for crimes committed against the British government." *Revenge* means to *avenge* wrongs done to oneself: "She sought *revenge* for the theft of her car."

SEE ALSO **feud, vendetta.**

avert, avoid, evade. *Avert* means to turn away: "She *averted* her eyes from the scene of the accident." *Avert* also means to prevent, ward off, or keep from happening by taking some action: "We can *avert* war by talking about our difficulties."

Avoid refers more to escaping or sidestepping some danger or difficulty: "The typical bachelor uses a number of ruses to *avoid* marriage."

Evade implies deceit or subterfuge: "By constantly changing his disguises, he *evaded* capture as he fled through the countries of Europe."

The classic distinction between *avoid* and *evade* is the one about income taxes. That is, it is legal to *avoid* paying taxes, but it is illegal to *evade* paying them.

avid, rabid. *Avid* means vigorously eager or enthusiastic. *Rabid* technically refers to the disease of rabies, or at least to actions that are violent, raging, or uncontrollable. Many *avid* sports fans exist, but to refer to "a *rabid* fan," as has been done, is to create the image of a raging spectator frothing at the mouth.

avocation, vocation. An *avocation* is a hobby or interest in addition to a person's *vocation*. *Vocation* broadly means the work in which a person earns a livelihood. *Vocation* also refers to a strong inclination, such as a divine calling to the religious life: "the *vocation* of the priesthood."

SEE ALSO **career, job, occupation, profession, trade; hobby, pastime; job, position.**

award, reward. An *award* is a prize or trophy based on competition or judging: "The winning essayist was *awarded* a gold medal." A *reward* is something, often money, given for the performance of a good deed: "She received a *reward* for turning in the criminal."

a while, awhile. *Awhile* as one word is an adverb referring to a short time. *A while* as two words consists of an article and a noun that can be used in place of *a time*.

Either of the following is correct: "Stay *awhile* (a short time)"; or "Stay for *a while* (a time)." The word *for* generally goes in front of *a while* but not *awhile*.

axle, axel.   An *axle* is a rod on which a wheel turns. An *axel* is a figure-skating maneuver named after the Norwegian figure skater Axel Paulsen (1855–1938).

B

back, behind, rear. In reference to the human anatomy, it is true that the *back* is the *rear* portion of the body that runs from the neck to the base of the spine. However, *back* and *rear* in this respect are not synonymous. *Rear* and *behind* stand for the *buttocks* and various other terms of varying degrees of crudeness or sophistication: *ass*, *backside*, *bum*, *buns*, *gluteus maximus*, *posterior*, *prat*, and *rump*.

Otherwise, if you are in a house and at the far end of the house as opposed to the front, then you are at the *back* or the *rear* of the house; either choice is correct. Once you step into the backyard, you are *behind* the house. Some people would refer to the backyard as *in back of* or *back of* the house, but strict stylists say that *behind* is the only correct choice.

bacteria, germ, virus. Here *germ* is the term with broadest meaning: (1) a small mass of living substance that can develop into an animal or plant; (2) any primary source from which growth and development can occur—"the *germ* of an idea"; or (3) a microorganism that can cause disease.

For a brief time in the history of our language, a *germ* was known as a *contagium*—the agent that spread sickness and death. *Germs* exist in several forms, two of the most frequently talked about being *bacteria* and *viruses*.

Bacteria (singular *bacterium*) can be harmful, poisonous, or beneficial. Beneficial *bacteria* aid in the digestion of food, are used in the making of dairy products, and produce antibiotics. Only a few *bacteria* lead to disease.

Viruses are smaller than *bacteria* and make up a large

group of infectious agents. *Viruses* are responsible for a large number of diseases, including the common cold, herpes, influenza, measles, and mumps.

bad, badly.   It is not *bad* grammar to say "I feel *bad*." Neither is it wrong to say "She looked *bad* (ill)." In both cases, *bad* is an adjective describing a condition, and the adverb *badly* would be out of place. Along these same lines, it is also acceptable to say "The water tastes *bad*"; "The locker room smelled *bad*"; and "The fish tasted *bad*." Again, *bad* is being used as an adjective.

These forms are correct because words such as *feel, taste, smell, look,* and *sound* are linking verbs. A linking verb functions chiefly as a connection between the subject and the predicate of the sentence; a linking verb does not fit the ordinary definition of a verb as a word that specifies action. In these cases, each linking verb is followed by an adjective that describes a condition—*bad* health, *bad* taste, *bad* smell. An adverb would be out of place.

However, when it's necessary to modify the meaning of a verb, then the correct form is the adverb *badly*: "The child acted *badly*"; "I did *badly* on the exam"; "His head ached *badly*"; and "She was *badly* injured."

Incidentally, some people forget these distinctions or are uncomfortable with saying "feel *bad*." For those people the options are: "I don't feel good"; "I feel like death warmed over"; "I feel depressed"; "I feel terrible"; or "I feel awful." To really be impressive, you could list your symptoms.

SEE ALSO   **good, well.**

bail, bale.   *Bail* means to dip water out of, as in "to *bail* water out of a boat." *Bail* also means to help someone out of trouble: "The bank *bailed* him out of the financial mess he was in." You can also, if you're brave enough and if the situation warrants, "*bail* out of an airplane," and you can "*bail* out of a bad deal," although that last expression is viewed by some people as being slang. *Bail* as a noun is quite familiar: "We posted his *bail* so that he could get out of jail."

As for *bale,* as a verb it means to tie in a bundle: "*bale* hay." Once the hay is *baled*, it becomes a noun, "a *bale* of hay."

baking powder, baking soda. The starting point with these two terms is *baking soda*, which is also known as bicarbonate of soda and sodium bicarbonate. *Baking soda* is a kitchen chemical that is a white, granular powder. *Baking soda* is a basic ingredient of *baking powder*, which is used as a leavening agent to raise dough.

Baking soda has a number of other uses in addition to the role it plays in cooking. It is used as an antacid to relieve heartburn or acid indigestion, it absorbs refrigerator odors, and it is used in fire extinguishers. *Baking soda*'s mild abrasiveness makes it adaptable for cleaning everything from teeth to silverware to kitchen utensils to heel marks on the floor.

balloon, blimp, dirigible, zeppelin. *Balloons, blimps,* and *dirigibles* belong to a class of aircraft known as lighter-than-air craft. Each has a bag filled with hot air or a gas such as helium; accordingly, they are buoyant, able to float in the air. A *balloon* is in a class by itself, for it is not power-driven. On the other hand, *blimps* and *dirigibles* have engines to power their flight.

Power-driven lighter-than-air craft are known as airships. These are *blimps* and *dirigibles*. The difference between a *blimp* and a *dirigible* is that one has an internal structure and the other does not. A *dirigible*'s gas bag does have an internal structure, making a *dirigible* a rigid airship. A *blimp's* gas bag doesn't have an internal structure, making a *blimp* a nonrigid airship.

The fourth word in this category, *zeppelin,* memorializes the German Count Ferdinand von Zeppelin. Zeppelin was an observer with the Union Army in the American Civil War, but his real claim to fame is that he invented the first rigid airship, in 1900. Hence, some people use the word *zeppelin* to casually refer to *blimps* or *dirigibles.*

baluster, banister. In general usage today, a *banister* is the handrail of a staircase, and the *banister* is supported by *balusters*. The *balusters* are short, vertical posts that are sometimes elaborately carved or shaped.

It wasn't always so, and diehard traditionalists among architects may insist on holding to the older definitions.

Those were: *baluster* and *banister* both meant the vertical post, and an assembly of *balusters* along with the handrail was called a *balustrade*.

band, orchestra.   A *band* is a group of musicians playing mainly wind and percussion instruments. A *band* is usually thought of as not having any stringed instruments, even though most *bands* have a bass violin or guitar or both. This definition doesn't always hold up, for some groups call themselves string *bands* or vocal *bands*.

As for an *orchestra*, it is a mixed body of string, wind, and percussion instruments.

bane, boon.   *Bane* refers to death, destruction, distress, or ruin. *Boon* refers to something that is welcome, beneficial, or pleasant. If you need some way to make the two less confusing, *boon* derives from the French *bon* or *bonne*, meaning good or kind.

bangle, bauble.   A *bangle* is a stiff decorative bracelet or anklet, or an ornamental disk hanging from such a bracelet. A *bauble* is any cheap, showy trinket.

bankruptcy, insolvency.   *Bankruptcy* was once considered involuntary, and *insolvency* was voluntary. That is, creditors would bring a *bankruptcy* action against a debtor who was unable to pay up, and a debtor would start an *insolvency* action to liquidate assets and distribute the proceeds to creditors.

Today the term *bankruptcy* and the *bankruptcy* laws cover voluntary and involuntary actions.

banquet, feast.   Both of these refer to a large, sumptuous, elaborate meal, usually with many guests, often featuring a ceremony or entertainment, and often in honor of a special event. The differences are in the formality of the event and in how elegant a term one wants to apply to it.

That is, if the outgoing president of the United States is to be honored with a farewell dinner, the invitations would specify *banquet*, not *feast*. The inevitable after-dinner speakers would appear, and the whole thing could be quite dull. A *feast*, however, carries with it the idea of fun, partying, and good times.

barbarian, barbaric, barbarism, barbarity, barbarous. The word *barbarian* and its forms deal not so much with savagery and brutality as they do with snobbery and the dislike of one people for another.

To the ancient Greeks, any non-Greek was a *barbarian*. Over the centuries, non-Romans and non-Christians became *barbarians*, as labeled by Romans and Christians. In the nineteenth century, the Western world lost its monopoly on the word when the Chinese began applying it contemptuously to foreigners. The *Oxford English Dictionary* shows the earliest recorded use of the word in 1549 when a Scotsman complained, "Every nation reputes other nations to be barbarians." As for what these words mean today, the definitions are as given below.

Barbarian: a person or a civilization regarded as primitive, inferior, unrefined, and uncivilized.

Barbaric and *barbarous*: behavior typical of a *barbarian*.

Barbarism: an act, especially the use of a word or expression that is not standard, such as "dem chicks" for "those girls."

Barbarity: cruel or brutal behavior; crude or coarse taste.

barometer, thermometer. A *barometer* measures the pressure of the air; a *thermometer* measures temperature. A *barometer* is used to forecast weather and, as an altimeter, to measure the altitude of an airplane. A rapidly falling reading on a *barometer* means that a storm is imminent; a rising reading means that good weather is coming.

basal, base, basic, basis. *Basal* is a seldom-seen adjective that pertains to the *base* of something: "the statue's *basal* area." A familiar expression is *basal* metabolism, the minimum amount of energy needed by an individual to sustain life when the individual is at rest. Although doctors can test a person's *basal* metabolic rate, such tests are not often performed today, because of the existence of better tests.

Base is a noun naming the foundation, bottom part, or essential ingredient, and is largely used to refer to material things: "the *base* of the statue"; "the *base* of the thumb." *Base* may also be used as a verb, as in "I *base* my argument on this proposition"; or as an adjective, as in "a *base* number" or "an oil-*based* paint."

Basic is an adjective that refers to something that is underlying and fundamental: "Every recruit receives *basic* military training"; "I see that we are in *basic* agreement."

Basis is a noun that often applies in the nonmaterial sense: "This proposition is the *basis* of my argument." "The company pays on a monthly *basis*."

base, bass. These are entered here only because of a pronunciation problem involving *bass*. *Bass*, with reference to music, is usually pronounced *base*. No matter how strange it looks, when you take the pronunciation into account, the correct spelling is *bass* violin, *bass* clarinet, or *bass* section. Exceptions: *bassoon* and *basso* are pronounced so that their first syllables rhyme with "*bass*et hound" or "*bass*inet."

Otherwise, the fish that got away is pronounced *bass* to rhyme with *gas* or *lass*.

basin, bowl. *Basins* and *bowls* hold liquids, and both can be used to transport liquids. The two words could be synonyms except that dictionaries show that *basin* is used in certain limited and technical senses. Among them are a protected mooring space for boats; a treatment tank for solutions; a depression in the surface of the land or in the ocean floor; a land area that holds or drains water; and a land area in which air is trapped.

bathos, pathos. *Bathos* is an unwanted effect in literature. *Bathos* can take the form of an unintentional anticlimax, a sudden going from the sublime to the ridiculous, or an unexpected transition from the sincere to the trivial. If a scene or a line or a complete movie or novel or play tries to make you cry but instead makes you laugh, the result is *bathos*.

Pathos is a quality that arouses feelings of pity, sorrow, sympathy, or tenderness in the observer. *Pathos* can exist in reality, literature, or a work of art.

beach, coast, shore. A *beach* is a level and sandy or pebbly sea*shore* or lake*shore*. The word *shore* is the general word applied to any land directly bordering a lake, ocean, river, or sea. *Coast* refers only to land along an ocean or a sea. Thus the states around Lake Michigan have *shores* and *beaches* but not *coasts*; the states along the Atlantic Ocean have *beaches*, *coasts*, and *shores*.

beast, brute. In general, a *beast* is a large, four-footed animal, and a *brute* is a human being.

However, when a human being arouses contempt and loathing because of stupidity, coarseness, vileness, or brutality—that person can be called a *beast*.

When a person is referred to as a *brute*, the meaning is that the person is crude, cruel, dull, lacking human intelligence, not having human rational powers, purely physical, rough, stupid, unfeeling, unreasoning, and unthinking.

SEE ALSO **brutal, brutish.**

beauteous, beautiful. When someone or something is keenly appealing to the senses and emotions, *beautiful* is a better choice than *beauteous*. *Beauteous* is not recommended as a synonym for *beautiful* because *beauteous* has connotations that range from the derogatory to the poetic. As Roy Copperud says, in *American Usage and Style*, "When encountering it [*beauteous*], the reader may suspect that *beautiful* has been sidestepped, and may assume that this has been done for a reason, perhaps to dilute the tribute."

because, since. The word *since* is often used in a sentence that has something to do with a time element: "*Since* 1933, when prohibition ended . . ." In addition, writers have been using *since* to mean *because* for five centuries. What is needed, then, is a workable practice for separating the two.

The ideal thing would be to restrict *because* to causal situations, for just the sight of the word plants the notion of cause rather than time in the reader's mind. Justification for such a practice can be found in sentences like this one: "*Since* your garage worked on my car, I have had to fix the brakes." That sentence could mean two things: (1) "*Since* the date your garage worked on my car . . ." or (2) "*Because* your garage worked on my car and botched it up . . ." The use of *since* leaves the reader in doubt.

bee, hornet, wasp. At the moment that you're stung by one of these insects, the exact name of the creature might not be too important. However, if you do see the villain, a *bee* (honey*bee*, bumble*bee*) has a heavier, hairier body than the closely related *wasp*. A *wasp* has a slender, smooth body. A *hornet* is a large *wasp,* and a small *wasp* with yellow markings is called a yellowjacket. None of this will make a difference, because you'll probably think of other names at the time.

believe, feel, think. Each day, a large amount of academic, business, and governmental correspondence is sent out with sentences like "We *feel* that the second phase of the study would be worthwhile to pursue." Unfortunately, use of the word *feel* allows readers to infer that the writer has stopped thinking and is getting along on emotions or a sense of touch. *Believe* isn't a much better choice, for it is hesitant and conveys a sense of wishfulness. If you have to stop short of saying "I know," then *think* is the strongest of the three words examined here.

A lot depends upon what you are writing. If you are writing fiction, your characters may speak in words that are not as finely defined as the words used in commercial correspondence or technical writing. But if you are writing official documents, the words should be accurate to stand up in court.

SEE ALSO **sentiment, sentimentality.**

bellicose, belligerent. *Bellicose* describes a warlike, pugnacious, quarrelsome attitude—a disposition to fight or start a war: "The rebel headquarters overflowed with *bellicose* senior officers."

Belligerent means being at war or carrying on a fight or engaging in combat rather than just clamoring for the same: "The *belligerent* nations waged war for seven years." *Belligerent* is also frequently used in place of *bellicose.*

below, beneath, under, underneath. These very closely related words can be used to observe the following fine distinctions.

Below: Lower than a point of reference or in direction: "the counties *below* Chicago"; "the telephone number

below the letterhead"; "five degrees *below* zero"; "*below* me in the chain of command."

Beneath: Sometimes, depending upon sound and rhythm, the same as *below* or *under*. In addition, deficient in moral or social senses: "This was *beneath* her dignity."

Under: Directly *below* or at least partially concealed: "the apartment *under* this one"; "a sweater *under* my jacket"; "the subway *under* the city."

Underneath: Same as *under*.

beneficient, benevolent. Both of these words pertain to acts of kindness, charity, or doing good. *Beneficient* refers mainly to the performance of the act. *Benevolent* refers more to the suggestion or indication of doing good, a feeling or disposition toward charity, as frequently demonstrated by the performance of a charitable act. The difference between the two words is minor, and *beneficient* is seldom used. In general, many Americans consider themselves to be *benevolent*, not *beneficient*, people.

beside, besides. *Beside* is at the side of. *Besides* is in addition to: "*Besides* letting the dog in, please place the newspaper *beside* the coffeepot."

best, better, good. *Good* is not bad or not poor, and having positive or desirable qualities. *Better* is greater in quality than *good*. *Best* refers to surpassing *better* and *good* in quality.

SEE ALSO **worse, worst.**

bi-, semi- (annually, monthly, weekly). If you want to schedule a meeting twice a week (or twice a month or twice a year), say "Meetings are held twice a . . ." or "We meet two times a . . ." Similarly, if you want to meet once every six months, just say "Our organization meets once every six months."

Don't confuse the issue by using *bi-* or *semi-* as a prefix. Readers will not be sure whether one or the other means, as an example, twice a week or once every two weeks. Dictionaries are no help in the matter, for they include these definitions: *biannual*, for twice a year; *semiannual*, also for twice a year; *biannual* for once every two years; and *biennial* for once every two years. *Bicen-*

tennial is taken to mean one anniversary every two hundred years.

SEE ALSO **demi-, hemi-, semi-.**

bias, prejudice. Both of these refer to a preference, outlook, or adverse opinion that prevents impartial judgment. The difference is that a person's *bias* is developed in view of the facts, but *prejudice* occurs without a person knowing or examining the facts.

SEE ALSO **tolerance, toleration.**

bigamy, monogamy, polygamy. These three words pertain to how many spouses a person can stand to have at one time. The socially, and most often legally, acceptable form is *monogamy*: one spouse. *Bigamy* means having two spouses. *Polygamy* means having two or more spouses.

Polygamy can exist as *polyandry* or *polygyny*. A *polyandrist* is a woman with two or more husbands; a *polygynist* is a man with two or more wives.

bill, invoice. If the seller of goods or services is doing things right, a *bill* or *invoice*—either term is acceptable—will list what was sold and what it cost. *Invoice* tends to be a bit of jargon, for, no matter how you say it, a *bill* is still a *bill*.

billiards, pool, snooker. All three games are played with a cue (stick) and hard balls on a rectangular table topped with felt-covered slate and having side cushions.

In *billiards*, one red ball and two white cue balls (one for each player) are used, and the table has no pockets. In *pool*, fifteen numbered and variously colored balls and a cue ball are used, and the table has pockets at the corners and in the middle of the long sides. In *snooker*, the ball count is fifteen unnumbered red balls, six numbered balls of varying colors, and a cue ball, and the table is similar to a *pool* table but larger.

Pool is sometimes called *pocket billiards*, and other versions of these games exist, some using fewer than fifteen balls. *Snooker* tables are rare in the United States.

bisect, dissect. To *bisect* is to divide something into two usually equal parts. To *dissect* is to cut apart piece by piece: "The medical examiner *dissected* the body of the murder victim." To *dissect* also means to examine or analyze in detail: "She *dissected* her opponent's argument."

bison, buffalo. The American *bison* is a large, shaggy-maned animal with a fleshy hump on its back, a large head, and horns. The *buffalo* is an ox found in Asia and Africa. Early explorers of the American continent wrongly referred to the *bison* by using the word *bufalo* (Spanish or Portuguese for wild ox) or *buffle* (English for beef), and those names became *buffalo*.

bit, byte. In computer jargon, *bit* is the abbreviation for binary digit and is the smallest unit of information that can be stored by a computer. In that same jargon, *byte* is a group of adjacent *bits*; the most common *byte* contains eight *bits*. A *byte* represents a single character or the amount of information that a computer can handle with a single instruction. Examples of *bytes* include a letter, space, numeral, or punctuation mark.

black, Negro. Both of these literally mean the same, for *negro* is Spanish or Portuguese for *black*. Throughout our history, both terms have been applied at one time or another to refer to persons of African descent. The term seen most frequently today is *black*. In theory, it and *white* should be lowercased because they are designations based on color. However, many writers uppercase *Black* and lowercase *white*, even though the practice is inconsistent, in order not to give offense. Designations based on race, such as *Negro*, *African-American*, or *Caucasian*, are uppercased.
    SEE ALSO **Caucasian, white.**

blatant, flagrant. *Blatant* refers to anything that is offensive or notorious or shocking, especially in an obvious manner. *Flagrant* refers to that which is evil or wrong, a willful violation of a pledge or flouting of law or morality. "The captain's *flagrant* neglect of duty caused his ship to strike the reef, a fact that he *blatantly* lied about at his trial."

blink, wink. Do you *blink* your eyes or *wink* them? *Blink* means to open and close both eyelids rapidly, either voluntarily or involuntarily: "His eyes *blinked* as he nodded off to sleep." "She *blinked* back tears when she heard the news." *Wink* means to close and open the eyelid of one eye to convey a message or signal or as a teasing gesture: "These days only a male chauvinist pig *winks* at a pretty girl."

blizzard, snowstorm.   A *blizzard* consists of intense cold, strong winds, and a great amount of blowing snow. The tendency exists to confuse a *blizzard* with a *snowstorm*, the latter term referring to any heavy snowfall, which may have high winds. Technically speaking, most *snowstorms* don't meet weather forecasters' requirements for a storm. A storm has wind speeds from 64 to 72 miles per hour, Force 11 on the Beaufort scale.

    SEE ALSO   **gale, storm.**

bloc, block.   *Bloc* refers to any political alignment or group of people, organizations, or nations united for a common action: "the farm *bloc*"; "European-*bloc* nations." *Block* has a large number of meanings, none of them synonymous with *bloc*.

blond, blonde.   When the noun form is used, a woman may be either a *blond* or a *blonde*. When the noun is used for males, *blond* is preferred: "He's a tall *blond*."

    The adjective *blond* applies to either sex and to things: "a *blond* bombshell"; "a *blond* cocker spaniel"; "a *blond* chest of drawers."

bloom, blossom.   *Bloom* refers to the flower or flowers of a plant. *Blossom* is used in that sense too, but is said especially of plants that, after *blossoming*, bear edible fruit.

blush, flush.   To *blush* is to become suddenly red in the face because of embarrassment, shame, or confusion. This same meaning can also be conveyed with *flush*. However, *flush* mainly refers to the sudden, rapid, and abundant flow of blood, water, or virtually anything.

    In novels, many characters *blush*, and some become *flushed*. Others get red in the face, probably because their authors preferred vivid language.

boast, brag. A *boast* is a statement of pride or vanity with reference to a person's deeds or the deeds of someone close to the person. *Boasting* can be exaggeration or a recitation of fact. *Bragging* is more obnoxious than *boasting* in that *bragging* is always exaggeration and tends to be artless and crude. Thus, "The annual report *boasted* about this year's profits," but "The men at the bar did nothing but *brag* about how much they could drink."

boat, ship. Generally speaking, a *boat* is a small craft as opposed to a *ship*, that term being a broad reference to any oceangoing craft. That definition doesn't always hold up, for a submarine crew calls its craft a *boat* regardless of size.

boisterous, roisterous. *Boisterous* suggests behavior that is noisy, rowdy, high-spirited, or unruly—all tending toward the unrestrained: "A *boisterous* mob marched from the shantytown and besieged city hall." "The young kindergarten teacher lost control of the children, and their play period quickly became a *boisterous* disaster."
Roisterous suggests noisy and lively carousing or merrymaking: "The wedding reception was staid and sober, not the usual *roisterous* affair of young people."

bolt, screw. Both of these are fasteners, usually made of metal, that pass through a hole. They are frequently confused because people forget which one needs a nut. Answer: the *bolt*. Nut and *bolt* both end with the letter *t*, which may help the forgetful. A very last resort is this piece of doggerel: "A *bolt* needs a nut./A *screw* doesn't."

bordello, brothel. These are not confusable. They are synonyms for a house of prostitution, and a man in search of one knows exactly what he wants by any name.

border, boundary, frontier. These three terms have distinct uses when referring to geographical areas. A *border* is an area, region, or thin strip of land that is part of a *boundary*. A *boundary* is the precise line that marks the limit of a piece of territory. Thus the *border* between the United States and Canada is a vague stretch of land, while the northern *boundary* of the United States is a surveyed line.

A *frontier* is often thought of as a remote area that is undeveloped or unsettled. A *frontier* can also be the *border* between two countries: "the *frontier* between France and West Germany."

born, borne. *Born* is a fact of birth: "a child *born* deaf"; "an Oklahoma-*born* cowboy"; "a newly *born* baby"; "a daughter *born* to the princess."

Borne refers to the act of giving birth or being carried: "She has *borne* three children." "Three children were *borne* by her." "Paratroopers are air*borne* soldiers."

brain, intellect, mind. The *brain* is a part of the central nervous system. The *brain* is a physical entity, the organ of thought and the higher nervous center. *Intellect* is the ability to learn, think, know, and reason as opposed to the ability to feel emotion. The *mind* is a state of consciousness that originates in the *brain* and that enables us to think, perceive, will, remember, or imagine.

brandish, flourish. "With a *flourish* of his cape, the villain bounded across the stage and *brandished* his sword." To *brandish* is to wave or shake menacingly, especially a weapon. To *flourish*, as compared with *brandish*, is to make bold, sweeping movements as an act of bravado. *Flourish* also means to grow well, to thrive, to be in one's prime.

brass, bronze. These metals are alloys of other metals. *Brass* is an alloy of copper and zinc, and *bronze* is an alloy of copper and tin. Sometimes other metals are included in either alloy.

bravado, bravery, bravura. *Bravado* is a blustering or swaggering show of false bravery or a pretense at courage. *Bravery* is the quality of demonstrating courage, of showing that one is indeed *brave*. *Bravura* can mean a display of daring in any endeavor, but has a limited definition that pertains to a musical performance: brilliant technique or style.

braze, solder, weld. *Welding* is the process by which two metals are heated until they melt and can be fused together. *Soldering* and *brazing* do not melt the metals that are to be joined but instead use a third metal, or alloy, which is heated until it flows to form the joint. With *brazing*, the third metal is brass or a *brazing* alloy.

breach, breech. A *breach* is any opening or breaking: "a *breach* of contract"; "a *breach* in the seawall"; "a *breach* of promise"; "a whale blowing upon *breaching* the surface of the sea."

Breech is the back end of anything, but is often used in reference to a rifle or cannon where the reference is to the rear of the barrel. A *breech* birth or *breech* delivery occurs when the *breech* (rear end) of the baby appears first.

breaker, roller. At the breach, a *breaker* is a wave that crests or breaks into foam when it crashes against the shore, and a *roller* is a long, heavy, swelling wave. A *roller* can become a *breaker*.

bridle, halter. Both fit around a horse's head, and both can be used to guide or lead a horse. A *bridle* consists of a bit, the reins, and various straps and rings. A *halter* is a simpler device usually not having a bit or reins.
    SEE ALSO **lariat, lasso.**

brim, rim. The *brim* is the top edge of something that contains a fluid: "Don't fill my cup to the *brim* again." "The reservoir is full to the *brim*." *Brim* is also used to stand for the outer edge or margin: "the *brim* of a hat."

Rim refers to the edge of a surface that is usually circular or curved: "the *rim* of a wheel." Other surfaces also have *rims*: "the *rim* of the Grand Canyon."

bring, take. *Bring* refers to motion toward the speaker or writer. *Take* refers to motion away from the speaker or writer.

brook, creek, river, stream. These terms refer to water that flows on the earth's surface. The broad term is *stream*, which refers to a body of running water moving under the influence of gravity in a narrow and clearly defined channel. A *river* is a large freshwater *stream* that flows into a lake, ocean, or other river and is fed by tributaries. *Brooks* and *creeks* are tributaries, a *creek* being the larger of the two.

brutal, brutish. A prosecuting attorney described a crime as "*brutal* and *brutish*." The attorney had closely read the dictionary, for the two are not synonyms.

Brutal emphasizes the cruelty of the act, the gross and inhuman action of one person toward another, without a showing of sympathy or compassion: "He tortured his prisoners in a thoroughly *brutal* manner."

Brutish emphasizes unchecked gross sensuality or absolute animal stupidity without human intelligence: "The unfeeling, *brutish* guards forced their captives into acts of sexual intercourse."

SEE ALSO **beast, brute.**

Buddhism, Hinduism. *Buddhism* is one of the major religions of the world. It was founded in India about 500 B.C. by Siddhartha Gautama, known as Buddha, which means Enlightened One. *Buddhists* believe in the teachings of one man, in this case Buddha. One of the principal tenets of *Buddhism* is the goal of achieving nirvana, a state of peace and happiness reached by eliminating attachment to worldly things. *Buddhism* is practiced throughout Asia and in some parts of the Western world. Westerners are perhaps most familiar with the term Zen *Buddhism*, which names a type practiced chiefly in Japan.

Hinduism is the major religion of India and is the oldest living religion in the world, having roots that date back to prehistoric times. Unlike *Buddhism* and Christianity, *Hinduism* is not based on the teachings of one man. In addition, *Hinduism* is composed of innumerable sects with a rich variety of beliefs including a reliance on a guru. Reincarnation is a Hindu tenet, as is karma, the latter a belief that a person's actions determine how his or her soul will be born in the next reincarnation. Yoga is a Hindu system of self-mastery. The caste system of *Hinduism* is part of Indian culture.

SEE ALSO **cast, caste.**

bug, insect. An *insect* is a small, six-legged animal; many *insects* have wings. The word *bug* is a popular term for all *insects*, but the true *bug* according to scientists is an *insect* of the order Hemiptera. The Hemiptera may look like other *insects* except that they lack teeth and do not chew; their mouth parts are adapted to piercing and sucking.

bugle, cornet, trumpet. The *cornet* and the *trumpet* are three-valved instruments that look a lot alike but have somewhat different tones. Both instruments have traditional and contemporary uses in classical and popular music. The *bugle* is a valveless instrument capable of sounding only a few notes and is primarily used for some military pieces such as "Taps."

bullet, cartridge, round, shell. A *bullet* is a projectile meant to be discharged through the barrel of a firearm. The tip of a *bullet* is often shaped to overcome air resistance.

The word *bullet* should not be used to refer to the entire piece of ammunition. That distinction belongs to the *cartridge*, which consists of a case usually made of metal but sometimes of plastic. The case contains a primer, a powder charge, and a *bullet*.

The word *shell* sometimes slips into this category, but the jargon of gun enthusiasts decrees that *shell* belongs elsewhere. In that jargon, *shell* is known as *shotshell*, that is, a loaded shotgun *shell*. This kind of *shell* consists of a case, a primer, a powder charge, and a load of shot; the shot is small, round masses of metal.

Shell is also loosely used to stand for any quantity of ammunition. Even the most linguistically precise of hunters might slip and say "I bought a box of *shells* for target practice." And *shell* is also used to stand for the much larger ammunition fired on warships.

As for *round*, it is a military term for *cartridge* or any single shot fired from any type of weapon. *Round* is also another term for a single loaded shot*shell*. In skeet or trap shooting, a *round* means firing twenty-five shot*shells* at thrown targets.

SEE ALSO   **pistol, revolver.**

burden, load. Both refer to anything that is carried or transported. *Burden* refers to a heavy or grievous weight, a *load* that is difficult to bear physically or emotionally: "The *burden* of responsibility rests upon the shoulders of the pilot." "On Mondays I feel as if I were bearing the *burden* of the world." *Load* refers to a full and adequate amount: "Each truck carries a *load* of logs."

burglary, robbery, theft. *Burglary* means wrongfully entering a building with the intent of committing a crime inside the building. "Wrongfully entering" simply means that the person isn't entitled to be inside. The expression *breaking and entering* is sometimes used, but *Black's Law Dictionary* points out that modern statutory definitions do not require *breaking* as part of a definition of *burglary*.

Robbery is the unlawful taking of the property of another by the use of force or intimidation. *Theft* is a popular term for larceny, which is the taking of someone else's property without that person's consent.

bush, shrub. A *shrub* is a woody plant that is smaller than a tree. A *bush* is also a *shrub*, but especially one that is low and densely branched.

bust, statue. A *statue* is the representation of the full figure of a person or animal. A *bust* is the representation of the head, shoulders, and upper torso. Either can be sculpted from stone or wood, molded in clay or a plastic substance, or cast in metal.

bustle, hustle. Do people really "*hustle* and *bustle*," as the saying goes? Perhaps. *Bustle* means to hurry along with energy, fuss, bother, commotion, or excitement: "In anticipation of the puppet show, the children *bustled* into the auditorium."

Hustle can simply mean to hurry: "You'd better *hustle* on over there if you want your check." *Hustle* can also mean to usher hurriedly, to push and shove, to speed up and hurry along in a rude and rough way: "The bouncer *hustled* the drunk out of the bar." In common usage *hustle* also means to cheat: "He made a living by *hustling* money out of unwary senior citizens."

butter, margarine. It was Shakespeare who, in *Henry IV*, called Falstaff "a gross fat man . . . as fat as butter."

It was Hermann Goering who, in a radio broadcast to the German people, said, "Guns will make us powerful; butter will only make us fat."

Such is the nature of *butter*, as health-conscious people become more and more concerned about exactly what is clogging up their arteries. Both *butter* and *margarine* contain large amounts of fat, but of different types. Saturated fats make up *butter*, and unsaturated fat goes into most *margarines*. Saturated fat tends to increase the amount of cholesterol in the bloodstream, thereby increasing fatty deposits in the arteries.

C

calamity, cataclysm, catastrophe. These three words pertain to disasters.

Calamity refers to distress or major misfortune: "The drought is a *calamity* for farmers." *Calamity* also can be a personal reaction, a judgment call: "Although she and her husband are very happy together, her father thought it was a *calamity* when she got married while still in high school."

A *cataclysm* is any sudden and violent upheaval of a physical, social, or political nature and accompanied by distress or suffering: "the *cataclysm* of nuclear war"; "the *cataclysm* of the Reformation."

The word *catastrophe* implies finality, a disastrous ending, a tragic outcome: "The annihilation of the village's population was a *catastrophe*." "In the ancient tragic plays, the death of the hero was the *catastrophe*."

callous, callus. *Callous* refers to mental or emotional insensitivity: "His negative remarks about the church indicated a *calloused* attitude toward religion." "She was very *callous* when mocking her former husband."

Callus refers to a physical characteristic—a thickening or hardening of the skin: "a *callus* on the finger"; "developed *callused* hands."

Calvary, cavalry. *Calvary* is the place near Jerusalem where Jesus Christ was crucified: the location is said to bear some fanciful resemblance to the human skull. The word *Calvary* is descended from a Latin word, *calvaria*, for skull. In Hebrew the name for the place is *Golgotha*, also meaning skull. The exact location of *Calvary* is thought to be marked by the Church of the Holy Sepulcher (Church of the Resurrection).

Cavalry once meant soldiers mounted on horseback, and referred to in the Wild West of frontier America as "forty miles a day on beans and hay." High-powered rifles and automatic weapons were especially hard on horses and made horse-mounted soldiers obsolete. Therefore, the *cavalry* of today uses tanks, armored vehicles, and helicopters.

camouflage, disguise. *Camouflage* is primarily a military act, the concealment of people, ships, or weapons of war. Paints and foliage are common tools of *camouflage*: "Leaves and branches were woven into a net as *camouflage* for the gun emplacement."

Disguise is a personal attempt to alter one's appearance or to hide the true nature of something: "The reporter wore old clothes to *disguise* himself as one of the homeless." "Her smile *disguised* her real emotions."

can, could, may, might. "He who can, does. He who cannot, teaches." When George Bernard Shaw wrote that line he was commenting on ability and not giving permission. His use of the word *can* to refer to ability complies with the dictates of traditional grammar. If he had wanted to write about permission, traditional grammar decrees the use of the word *may.*

In informal usage, *can* and *may* are used interchangeably to denote ability or permission. In formal usage, the dictates of traditional grammar should be observed. That is, for formal usage, use *can* to refer to ability, and use *may* to refer to permission. The often-heard example is "Yes, you *can* go, but no, you *may* not." In other words, "You have the ability to go, but not my permission."

In addition, *may* implies uncertainty in some uses: "The factory *may* get its safety equipment when the new budget is approved" means that nothing's definite yet.

Could implies ability but with conditions attached: "We *could* get new computers for the office if we had the money." "If you *could* come, we'd be very pleased." *Could* is also a polite way of asking a question: "*Could* you do this for me?"

In the swamp of greatest doubt is *might. Might* shows

less probability than *can, could,* or *may:* "The safety equipment we ordered *might* get here next week." "Sure. They've been telling us that for six months, but it *might* never get here."

SEE ALSO **may be, maybe; shall, should, will, would.**

canvas, canvass. *Canvas* is a noun that stands for the heavy cloth used for tents, sails, or for painting on: "He painted his landscapes on *canvas* tacked to a wooden frame." "A *canvas* tarpaulin covered the crates on the deck."

Canvass is a verb that means to solicit people for votes, orders, or opinions: "The public-opinion poll *canvassed* only a few citizens in each town." "Each party *canvasses* the shopping malls before election day."

capable, culpable. *Capable* refers to the ability or capacity to do something: "a first-place team *capable* of winning the trophy." *Culpable* means being blamable or responsible for a crime or wrongdoing: "Damage to the equipment occurred because of *culpable* negligence on the part of the operator."

capital, capitol. The *capital* is the city that is the seat of government; the *capitol* is the building in which government sits.

If you need a crutch to help you keep *capital* separated from *capitol*, just remember that the *o* in the last syllable of *capitol* is round like the domes on top of most *capitols*.

The *al* ending is also used when referring to assets: "*capital* goods"; "*capital* investment"; "political *capital*." In addition, *al* is correct with "*capital* letters" and "a *capital* fellow."

carat, caret, karat. The *caret* is an editing mark shaped like an inverted *v* to show where something is to be inserted in text.

As for the words *carat* and *karat*, they are often used when people talk about jewelry. *Carat* is a unit of weight for precious stones. One *carat* equals 200 milligrams. *Karat* specifies the proportion of pure gold in an alloy. Gold of 24 *karats* is 100 percent pure gold. Eighteen-*karat* gold is three-fourths gold and one-fourth other metals.

cardinal number, ordinal number. A *cardinal number* is used to compare quantity or frequency, as in how many or how often: "three, ten, thirteen." An *ordinal number* is used to compare rank, position, or order: "third, tenth, thirteenth."

careen, career. At one time these words were clearly distinguishable. *Careen* meant to sway and tilt; a sailboat heeling over was said to *careen*, and one might say that a drunk *careened* across the room. *Career* meant to move at high speed; a fast-moving car was said to be *careering* down the road. Those distinctions are falling aside, as *careen* is used increasingly for any kind of rapid and uncontrolled movement.

career, job, occupation, profession, trade. A *career* is a person's lifework or long-term pursuit of a means of earning a livelihood: "Vincenzi enjoyed a long and rewarding *career* as a concert pianist." "After a twenty-year military *career*, he became a schoolteacher."

A *job* is any kind of work, task, or chore that is sometimes performed for pay. "Cooking dinner for this family is a *job*!" "Her first *job* was delivering papers."

An *occupation* is a broad term for any activity that serves as the source of a person's livelihood.

Profession is variously defined as an *occupation* in which the practitioner possesses a college education, needs intellectual skills, has advanced training in a specialized field, adheres to ethical or technical standards, or performs an activity for money rather than being an unpaid amateur. Thus the word *profession* applies to various work done by many people. Among them are lawyers, politicians, writers, and athletes. Even a lawbreaker can be called a *professional* criminal provided that the crime is performed for money rather than as an unpaid amateur act.

A *trade* is an *occupation* usually thought of as requiring skilled labor or craftworking.

SEE ALSO **avocation, vocation; job, position.**

carnivore, herbivore, omnivore. The eating habits of animals allow them to be sorted into one of three categories: *carnivore, herbivore,* and *omnivore*.

A *carnivore* eats meat. Some *carnivores*, such as cats and weasels, are predators that kill their own prey. Other *carnivores*, such as hyenas and jackals, are primarily scavengers that eat animals they find dead.

A *herbivore* eats plants. Cattle and deer are *herbivores* that eat grasses, some birds are *herbivores* that eat seeds, and earthworms are *herbivores* that eat dead plant material.

An *omnivore* eats meat and plants. Bears and opossums are *omnivores*.

carpet, rug.   Both are heavy fabric coverings for floors. A *carpet* covers an entire floor; a *rug,* part of a floor.

cast, caste.   *Caste* refers to the major hereditary classes into which Hindu society is divided. *Caste*, meaning social status, is one's inheritance at birth. *Caste* is not a religious concept but is closely related to Hinduism, the major religion of India.

The four major *castes* are *Brahmans* (priests), *Kshatriyas* (princes and warriors), *Vaisyas* (landowners and merchants), and *Sudras* (farmers, laborers, and servants). A fifth *caste*, the Untouchables, has been theoretically illegal in India since 1950. However, the term *scheduled castes* now applies to the people who were once known as Untouchables.

As for *cast*, it has numerous meanings other than that of *caste*.

SEE ALSO   **Buddhism, Hinduism.**

castigate, chasten, chastise.   *Castigate* means to make a verbal reprimand, a censuring that can be spoken or written and is often done publicly: "The professor's plan was to *castigate* his students for their lazy approach to their studies." "The editorial *castigated* corrupt public officials."

Chasten means to inflict any trial or tribulation—corporal punishment, verbal denunciation, deprivation, pain, distress, or suffering—meant to make a person more humble and more moderate: "Heavier fines might *chasten* drunk drivers."

Chastise means to use verbal or corporal punishment in the hope of improving behavior: "The nurse scolded her patient, thinking that *chastising* him might get him up and walking."

catchup, catsup, ketchup. There shouldn't be any confusion over the meaning of these three, for all are names for a sauce made with a tomato base.

But which spelling should be used? Answer: *ketchup*, for it is closest in spelling to the original word, which the English language has taken from various dialects in Southeast Asia.

Catsup is allowed by modern dictionaries, as is *catchup*. However, *catchup* looks usual, perhaps because it can also refer to the act of catching up.

Caucasian, white. *White* is the popular term: *Caucasian* is restricted to technical or legal uses. Concerning capitalization, *Caucasian* should be uppercased because it is a designation based on race, and *white* should be lowercased because it is a designation based on color.

SEE ALSO **black, Negro.**

cave, cavern. Both are hollows, chambers, or galleries below the surface of the earth. A *cave* is smaller than a *cavern*.

celebrant, celebrator. For party-goers and revelers who want other words to describe what they are, *celebrant* and *celebrator* are equally allowed. *Celebrant* also means the chief person officiating at a religious ceremony: "Father O'McReilly will be the *celebrant* at this morning's Mass."

Celsius, centigrade. *Celsius* is the name for a temperature scale that is divided into 100 equal parts. The *Celsius* temperature scale is sometimes called the *centigrade* scale because *centigrade* means 100 equal parts. On the *Celsius* scale, the freezing point of water is 0 degrees, and the boiling point of water is 100 degrees.

The scale was developed in 1742 by the Swedish astronomer Anders Celsius. In 1948 an international conference on weights and measures officially assigned his name to the scale. The *Celsius* scale is used throughout the world for scientific applications and is in popular use in countries where the metric system is standard. In the United States, the popular measure of temperature is the Fahrenheit scale, on which water freezes at 32 degrees and boils at 212 degrees.

cement, concrete.   *Cement* is any chemical binding agent that makes things stick to it or to each other. Examples of *cement* are glue, paste, and portland *cement*.

Concrete is a construction material that consists of *cement*, water, and granular crushed material such as sand, gravel, stone, slag, and cinders.

censer, censor, censure.   A *censer* is an incense burner that is swung on a chain during a religious rite.

To *censor* is to examine items such as documents, movies, or television programs and to suppress or remove anything considered obscene, offensive, libelous, or dangerous. The word *censor* can refer to the person or office doing the *censoring* or to the act of *censorship* itself: "During World War II, *censors* read servicemen's mail and removed any reference to troop movements." "Television *censors* claim to be watching out for public morals while protecting the sponsors' interests."

To *censure* is to express strong disapproval: "The parents' group *censured* the network for X-rated language on a prime-time program." The word can be a noun: "The network was amused by the *censure*."

cerebellum, cerebrum.   The *cerebellum* is the part of the brain largely responsible for posture, balance, and muscle movement. The *cerebellum* is connected to the *cerebrum*, the brain matter in charge of intelligence. In humans, the *cerebellum* is a small part of the brain located at the base of the brain in back, and the *cerebrum* is the large, rounded structure that makes up most of the brain.

ceremonial, ceremonious.   *Ceremonial* refers to things associated with ceremonies: "Ladies and gentlemen, today's game will start after the *ceremonial* first pitch." "The *ceremonial* offering consisted of a bowl full of silver pieces."

Ceremonious refers to people and things associated with ceremonies and implies pomp, circumstance, or excessive formality: "The birthday party was too *ceremonious* for a seven-year-old." "She was totally out of place in suburbia, for she was a *ceremonious* old woman addicted to afternoon teas and dressing for dinner."

SEE ALSO   **rite, ritual.**

certificate, degree, diploma. A *certificate* is a piece of paper attesting to a fact. Quite often a *certificate* is used to show that a person has completed a course of study or is qualified in a profession: "Six courses of study are required to obtain a *certificate* in graphic arts." "Only 60 percent of those taking the test scored high enough to obtain *certificates* as professional engineers."

A *diploma* is any *certificate* showing that a course of study has been completed: "high school *diploma*"; "trade school *diploma*." People who receive college or university *diplomas* also have conferred upon them some form of academic title known as a *degree*: "master's *degree*"; "doctor's *degree*."

chafe, chaff. Whether you used the verbs *chafe* or *chaff* depends upon how serious the situation is. *Chafe* means to irritate by rubbing, to annoy or vex. The irritation can be literal or figurative: "The rubbing of the handcuffs *chafed* the skin on his wrists." "He *chafes* because of the boredom of his job." *Chaff* refers to light, teasing banter: "He *chaffed* his daughter about her red shoes."

As a noun, *chaff* refers to the husks of grain that remain after separation from the seed ("separate wheat from the *chaff*"), thin strips of metal used to interfere with enemy radar, or anything generally worthless.

charisma, charm. By rough count of the singles' ads, a large percentage of the unattached people in this country "possess great *charisma*." At least, they say they do— and one wonders if they can be sued for misleading advertising.

Strictly speaking, *charisma* is a rare talent. The word originally referred to a gift from God, and in one sense meant the power to heal. In recent times, *charisma* refers to a demonstrated ability to attract the devotion of great numbers of people. *Charisma* is highly subjective. Many people felt that President John F. Kennedy possessed *charisma*; others, depending upon their politics, applied other labels to him.

The word *charm* refers to the power to attract, enchant, fascinate, or please. *Charm* can refer to a person: "He is the most *charming* man I have ever met." *Charm* can refer to a thing: "That rabbit's foot is my good luck *charm*."

chart, map. The *Oxford English Dictionary*, in quoting Thomas Huxley's *Physiography* (1877), gives these uses: "We speak of the plan of an estate, the map of a country, the chart of an ocean." Not so, at least not so these days. Many navigators say *map* instead of *chart*, whether over land or sea or in the air. For the rest of us, *map* will suffice for things like road *maps* or trail *maps*.

A *map* is a useful device for finding your way on the highways. In that use, the term *chart* would be a misnomer, for a *chart* is a navigational aid that provides more detail than the average *map* does. A *chart* shows latitude and longitude, while most *maps* do not. A *chart* of the ocean shows water depths, reefs, and other information useful to maritime navigators. A *chart* used by aircraft navigators shows radio aids to navigation and mountains and hills (terminal granite) that could suddenly end the flight.

chary, wary. The word *chary* indicates a modest amount of caution. A *chary* person is one who is careful about taking chances, shy or hesitant about accepting compliments or favors, or reluctant to act or speak openly: "She was *chary* of offending others." "In any conversation with his supervisor, he was *chary* of saying why he was planning to quit." "A basic sense of insecurity caused him to be *chary* about the praise that his fans heaped on him."

All of the above examples could be said using the word *wary*, provided the subject is more cautious, more watchful, or more suspicious than *chary* indicates. Being *wary* also implies the use of cunning in escaping danger: "The escaped convict, *wary* at the barking of the approaching hounds, plunged into the frigid river to hide his trail."

cheap, inexpensive. Both of these words refer to something that is low in cost. The meaning of *inexpensive* says nothing more. *Cheap*, however, carries the idea further by implying that the quality of an item is also low, that it is not worthy of respect.

chef, cook. A *cook* is but a *cook*, but a *chef* . . . Ah! . . . *Il (elle?) est magnifique!* That may be true in the opinion of the *chef*, but the restaurant with a *chef* may serve food that is no better than the food at a restaurant with a *cook*.

Chefs and *cooks* cook, but the word *chef* is descended from a French word meaning head or chief. Literally speaking, the *chef* is the head *cook* or person in charge of the kitchen staff. As far as our stomachs are concerned, a *cook* is a *cook* by any name.

chest, dresser. A *chest* is a piece of storage furniture usually having drawers and also known as a *chest* of drawers. A *dresser* is a *chest* with a mirror attached to it.

Chicago, Hispanic, Latino. *Chicano* refers to Mexican-American people or their culture. *Hispanic* and *Latino* refer to Spanish or Latin American people and their culture.

child, infant. Basically, both of these words refer to young human beings, although many parents are bound to wonder if their *children* will ever exhibit human tendencies.

An *infant* is a baby, a *child* in the earliest period of life. The word *child* can be used to refer to an unborn baby, an *infant*, or any boy or girl in the period before puberty. A *child* also is any offspring regardless of age: "Woe be unto those folk who have adult *children* living at home." Under the law, *infant* can also be taken to mean a minor—any person under legal age, which is eighteen in most states.

SEE ALSO **adolescence, puberty.**

childish, childlike. *Childish* and *childlike* can be applied to persons of any age to refer to traits that are characteristic of a child. The words are generally applied when describing adults; after all, children are expected to be *childish* and *childlike*.

When describing adults, *childish* is a term of reproach and refers to any act that demonstrates foolishness or shows a lack of maturity: "It was a *childish* thing for a man of fifty to do, playing with a rubber ducky in the bathtub." Pertaining to an adult, *childlike* refers to a child's endearing traits such as innocence, trust, and delicateness: "My mother's eyes opened wide with *childlike* pleasure when she saw the presents under the tree."

chiropodist, podiatrist. No confusion should exist over the meaning of these terms, for they refer to one and the same—a state-licensed health-care practitioner who treats problems of the feet. The medical profession today prefers *podiatrist (podiatry)*, because its Greek origins translate into "foot" and "healing." The *Oxford English Dictionary* calls *chiropodist (chiropody)* "a factitious [unnatural] designation" because of uncertainty over the original meaning and purpose of the word.

choir, chorale, chorus. *Choir* and *chorus* are synonyms, names for groups of people who sing together, whether in church, at a concert, or for the fun of it. The word *chorale* originally applied to a type of musical composition, but in the United States has become a synonym for *choir* or *chorus*: "the Robert Wagner *Chorale*."

chord, cord. A musical *chord* is a combination of two or more notes sounded at the same time. *Cord* is a string, slender rope, or anything that resembles those: "electrical *cord*"; "spinal *cord*"; "umbilical *cord*."

circular, spiral. *Circular* pertains to anything having the form of a circle: "a *circular* saw"; "a satellite in a *circular* orbit"; "a *circular* staircase."

Spiral has two definitions of a technical nature, both having to do with circles. The definitions describe a *spiral* formed in one plane and in more than one plane.

A *spiral* in one plane consists of an ever-expanding circle; that is, starting from a center point, the radius of a *circular* line constantly increases. In the old days, when watches had mainsprings, the mainspring was a *spiral* in one plane; it lay flat inside the watch, *spiraling* (circling) out from its center.

A *spiral* in more than one plane is movement up or down in a *circular* motion. The movement may be shaped like a cone; the threads on a screw *spiral* in an ever-tightening circle until they reach the point. The movement may be cylindrical; a *spiral* notebook has a binding of wire wound into a cylinder.

Some people, to the chagrin of purists, also use *spiral* to refer to any kind of increase: "the inflationary wage-price *spiral*." Precise usage simply calls for "wage-price increase."

SEE ALSO **whirl, whorl.**

cite, quote. Do writers *cite* sources, or do they *quote* them? Both. *Citation* refers to the naming of the source; the source's words make up a *quotation*: "The footnotes *cited* numerous references, but the author *quoted* only a few of them."

civic, civil. *Civic* pertains to the city, to the community, or to citizenship as these entities relate more to the thing than the person: "The new *Civic* Center will open next week." "It's one of a person's *civic* duties to support higher taxes for better roads."

Civil pertains more to the person's relationship with the community: "Thoreau named the concept of *civil* disobedience." Masses of people in Afghanistan demonstrated yesterday in the hopes of increasing their *civil* liberties."

claque, clique. A *claque* is a group of fawning or admiring followers: "His *claque* of fair-weather friends deserted him when the going got tough."

A *clique* (pronounced "cleek" or "click") is a small, exclusive circle of people that tends to be snobbish: "A number of *cliques* developed within the student body."

classic, classical. Mark Twain gave us this definition of a *classic*: "A book which people praise and don't read." That's a good start, for a *classic* is (1) a work of the first class ("Melville's *classic* tome *Moby-Dick*"); (2) a standard of excellence ("a *classic* car such as they don't make these days"); or (3) a perfect instance, whether good or bad ("a *classic* case of bureaucratic bungling").

As for *classical*, it generally pertains to a period or a style: "the *classical* literature of ancient Greece and Rome"; "the *classical* music of Europe"; "a *classical* education."

Or "He liked *classical* music so much that each afternoon he relaxed by playing tapes of his favorite *classics*."

claw, talon.   A *claw* is a sharp toenail on the foot of an animal, or the pincers of a lobster or crab. A *talon* is the *claw* of a bird of prey.

clean, cleanse.   Both mean to get rid of dirt or something unwanted. *Clean* is largely literal: "You'd better *clean* up before supper!" "It's time to *clean* out the garage." *Cleanse* is largely religious, figurative, or emotional: "Absolution *cleanses* the faithful of their sins." "He used a smile to *cleanse* the cares of the world from his face."

cleanliness, cleanness.   Both pertain to a state of being clean, but *cleanliness* is the more popular of the two.

clench, clinch.   To *clench* is to hold, grip, or shut tightly: "*clenched* fists"; "*clenched* teeth"; "*clench* the arms of the chair." To *clinch* is to settle, as in "*clinch* an argument." In boxing, *clinch* refers to the less-than-loving embrace that fighters get into.

climacteric, climactic, climatic.   The word *climacteric* indicates a major turning point in a person's life and is associated with menopause or a so-called midlife crisis.
Climactic refers to the climax, the highest point of excitement: "The *climactic* scene is when everyone at General Hospital flees into the streets to escape the wrath of Kong."
Climatic refers to climate: "*Climatic* conditions here resemble those of the Arctic."

climate, weather.   *Climate* means the meteorological conditions that prevail in an area over the long term. *Weather* means the meteorological conditions that exist at a time and place over the short term: "Parts of California have a Mediterranean *climate*, even though the *weather* can vary greatly from day to day."

closure, clôture.   *Closure* can be used to refer to the closing of anything: "the *closure* of a real estate deal"; "early *closure* of shops and businesses on election day."
Clôture is the parliamentary procedure by which de-

bate is ended and the measure under discussion is put to a vote: "After a long day of hearings, everyone on the subcommittee was ready for *clôture*."

clue, cue.   A *clue* is a key or piece of evidence that helps solve a problem: "Detectives look for *clues* when trying to solve crimes." A *cue* is a signal for someone to do something. A *cue* is often a word or action in a play to signal the start of another speech or act: "The villain's snicker was a *cue* for the heroine to faint."

COD, FOB.   The abbreviation *COD* stands for cash on delivery or collect on delivery. When an item is shipped *COD*, payment is due at the delivery point and before the item is released to the purchaser.

The abbreviation *FOB* stands for free on board or freight on board and is used with a location such as shipping point or destination. When an item is sold "*FOB* shipping point," the recipient must pay all charges from the seller's shipping point. When an item is sold "*FOB* destination," the seller must pay all charges up to the recipient's address.

codger, curmudgeon.   A *codger* is a mildly eccentric person; the word *codger* is usually used in good humor. A *curmudgeon* is someone who is cantankerous, ill-mannered, or bad-tempered. Both words are generally used when referring to an old man with those traits.

cold-blooded, warm-blooded.   A cold-blooded animal has a body temperature that varies with the external temperature; fish and reptiles are *cold-blooded* animals. A *warm-blooded* animal has a body temperature that is constant regardless of the external temperature; most mammals and birds are *warm-blooded* animals.

Concerning human emotions, *cold-blooded* refers to someone who is ruthless or cruel, and *warm-blooded* refers to someone who is ardent, fervent, or passionate.

collaborate, cooperate.   *Collaborate* has two meanings, one of them unsavory. Basically, *collaborate* means to work together with someone in an endeavor of an intellectual, artistic, creative, or scientific nature: "Gilbert *collaborated* with Sullivan to write operettas." On the dark side, *collaborate* means to willingly assist an enemy: "Some Frenchmen were branded as traitors because they *collaborated* with the Nazis."

As for *cooperate*, it simply refers to the act of working together toward a common goal: "Soldiers and sailors *cooperated* in the attack on Guadalcanal." "Snow and cold temperatures *cooperated* to make the skiing season last longer."

collate, collect.   Although one meaning of *collate* is to critically examine and compare texts and data, the word seems to be more frequently seen when referring to the task of arranging things in order: "*collate* the pages of a book for publication"; "a sorting machine known as a *collator*."

The act of bringing together, gathering, or assembling is *collecting*, a word that says nothing about whether what has been *collected* is placed in any kind of order: "Chapters have been *collected* but need to be *collated*."

college, university.   The traditional view is that a *college* grants a bachelor's degree or is a large part of a *university*; a *university* consists of *colleges*, has research facilities, and grants bachelor's, master's, and doctor's degrees. Regardless of tradition, an occasional subordinate school calls itself a *university*, perhaps in an attempt to glorify its name (or charge higher tuition?).

collude, connive, conspire.   Any one of these three words can mean (a) to secretly plan or scheme with someone to do something or (b) to secretly work with someone in carrying out some action. Which one you use depends upon the sound and rhythm of the sentence.

comet, meteor.   *Comets* and *meteors* streak through the night sky. Which is which? *Comets* revolve about the sun, get their light from the sun, and do not crash to the earth's surface. *Meteors* do crash to the earth's surface; the light given off by a *meteor*—a shooting star or falling star—is caused by the *meteor* burning up from friction as it enters the earth's atmosphere.

Comets are flimsy things, made up of frozen gases,

frozen water, stone, and metal. *Meteors* are solid chunks of stone and metal. While a *meteor* is outside the earth's atmosphere, it is known as a *meteoroid*. If a *meteoroid* gets through the atmosphere and hits the earth, the *meteoroid* is then known as a *meteorite*, a rather sudden way to undergo a change of identity.

comic, comical. By and large, dictionaries treat these adjectives as synonyms, and "a *comic* moment" would mean the same as "a *comical* moment." Thus the user is left to decide which sounds best. In addition, *comic* is used as a noun to mean a humorous person: "a stand-up *comic.*"

The unabridged *Webster III* says that there is this difference: *Comic* means that a person thinks and reflects for a moment before laughing, but *comical* means that the laughter is spontaneous. Attempts to put that fine distinction to practical use are bound to reveal how hard it is to explain anything about humor.

command, direct, order. *Command* and *order* emphasize official authority and can be broad in scope: "The king *commands*; the people obey." "Factory supervisors quickly develop the habit of *ordering* people about." The word *direct* implies official authority, is not as strong as *command* or *order*, and is usually applied to specific procedures: "The judge *directed* the bailiff to bring in the witness."

common, mutual. *Common* relates to what a group at large does together or shares alike: "Hatfields fought for the *common* good of the clan." "All units in the subdivision face a *common* green belt."

Mutual applies to what two persons or two entities do together: "a *mutual* effort by the Hatfields and the McCoys to stop feuding." *Mutual* also applies to what members of a group do together: "invest in a *mutual* fund."

common stock, preferred stock. When, and if, a corporation pays dividends to stockholders, *preferred stock* is entitled to a preference in the distribution of dividends, and *common stock* is not entitled to any such preference. In other words, the holders of *preferred stock* are paid before the holders of *common stock*, and the holders of *common stock* receive whatever is left, if anything. In bad times, the results may be known as a common disaster.

compact, contract. A *compact* is an agreement between persons or organizations: "The Mayflower *Compact* was an agreement among the Pilgrims for the self-government of Plymouth Colony." A *contract* is also an agreement, but is more legally binding than a *compact*. Lawyers have established several requirements for a *contract*. Its essentials are subject matter, a legal consideration, competent parties, mutual agreement, and mutual obligation.

company, firm. Loosely used, *company* and *firm* appear as references to any form of business enterprise. That's loose usage, however, which is not the same as the usage of business law. In business law, a *firm* is a partnership or an unincorporated business; put another way, a *firm* is not a corporation.

compare, contrast. *Compare* means to describe like items while noting similarities and differences: "He *compared* the good and bad features of each car before he decided which one to buy."

Contrast means to limit the description to mentioning differences: "The excellence of her performance sharply *contrasted* with the poorly executed routines of her competitors."

compare to, compare with. To some people, the only acceptable usage is this: Use *compare to* when describing similarities only, and use *compare with* when describing similarities or differences. Awareness of this distinction is rare, and it's a fussy distinction anyway.

compendious, compendium. A *compendium*, or a *compendious* publication, is not large or thorough but is instead a summary, digest, or brief compilation. Noah Webster's *Compendious Dictionary of the English Language* (1806) was a relatively small volume compared to his major work, the two-volume *American Dictionary of the English Language* (1828). That work was the predecessor of today's unabridged *Webster III*.

compile, compose, concoct. *Compile* means to gather together from various sources and place into an orderly form: "Researchers *compile* data banks." "A book can be *compiled* of chapters written by different authors."

Compose means to create or produce, usually by mental or artistic effort: "Wortman said he would *compose* a tone poem for the concert hall's opening."

Concoct means to make something by mixing ingredients: "The researchers are trying to *concoct* a new drug in the laboratory." Only in jest would a person *concoct* a symphony.

SEE ALSO **compose, comprise.**

complacent, complaisant. *Complacent* means self-satisfied or contented with oneself. The contentedness can become a fault: "Numerous aviation accidents are blamed on pilot *complacency*." *Complaisant* means eager to please or oblige: "He was promoted because he was a *complaisant* individual, the ultimate yes-man."

complement, compliment. *Complement* means to complete: "Fine wine *complemented* the meal." *Compliment* means to praise or flatter. *Compliment* is frequently used in the sense of what one person says to another: "His boss *complimented* him for a job well done." However, *compliment* is also used to refer to a deed or a thing: "The town paid him the *compliment* of naming him honorary mayor."

"The woman who buys a new dress may have done so to *complement* her wardrobe. If she chooses wisely, the dress will *compliment* her figure."

complete, done, finalized, finished, through. When you have stopped work on a project, is it *complete*—or is it something else? In casual speech or writing, the choice of terms may not make any difference. However, precisionists, as supported by dictionaries, say the choice of the correct term makes all the difference in the world:

Complete(d): Having all necessary parts; full; whole; entire; not lacking anything. *Complete* is the only absolute expression in this list.

Done: Having arrived at the finish or end; not necessarily *complete.*

Finalized: Completed or *finished;* bears the stigma of being liked by bureaucrats, perhaps because it has a comfortable (to them) vagueness.

Finished: At the end; not necessarily *complete.*

Through: Through is vague and can mean *done, finished,* or *complete. Through* is the preferred means of showing passage: "*through* the first door on your right."

complex, complicated. These terms emphasize that some mechanism or problem requires considerable knowledge and study to understand. *Complex* seems to refer mainly to the number and variety of parts. *Complicated* seems to imply an intricate, elaborate relationship of the parts; something that is *complicated* may require more study than something that is *complex.*

Thus a *complex* sentence consists of at least two parts, one main clause and at least one subordinate clause. It is possible to look at the sentence, count the parts, and see their relationships. However, even a simple sentence can become *complicated* when its meaning is hard to understand. That analogy is an oversimplification, of course, but it does help illustrate the difference between the two words.

compose, comprise. *Comprise* means (1) to include or contain or (2) to make up or form. Definition 1 allows this usage: "A state *comprises* counties." Definition 2 allows this usage: "Counties *comprise* a state."

If you use *comprise* according to definition 2, you are subject to criticism, for this usage is viewed by many as being inaccurate. Therefore, the safe way out is to say, "Counties make up a state."

SEE ALSO   **compile, compose, concoct.**

comprehend, understand. *Comprehend* emphasizes the mental processes rather than the conclusions that are implied when *understand* is used. In addition, *comprehend* suggests less reflection and analysis than does *understand,* which can suggest a deep realization of all mental and physical aspects of a problem: "You may *comprehend* the individual words in a passage, but you may not *understand* the overall meaning of the sentence."

compulsion, obsession. *Compulsion* refers to a behavior that compels a person to act against one's own wishes: "Despite knowing that he was vastly overweight, his overwhelming *compulsion* was to eat hamburgers and chocolate sundaes."

Obsession means an idea or belief that constantly haunts a person's consciousness: "He was driven by the *obsession* of painting a masterpiece."

compulsive, impetuous, impulsive. *Compulsive* indicates that a person's actions are performed against his or her will or better judgment, often because of overwhelming psychological problems: "Fear of failure drove him to *compulsive* drinking."

Impetuous indicates a lack of thought or prudence in actions that are forceful, violent, extremely impatient, or hastily and rashly energetic: "The charge up San Juan Hill was an *impetuous* act." "She did not know what to expect from one night to the next, he was such an *impetuous* lover."

Impulsive indicates a sudden, spontaneous inclination of mind or temperament that prompts performance of apparently involuntary acts: "Modern retailers sometimes do quite well because of *impulsive* shopping on the part of consumers."

concave, convex. *Concave* means curved or hollowed inward, rounded like the inner surface of a sphere. The opposite is *convex,* which means curved or rounded outward: "Right side up, a bowl is *concave*; turn it over, and you see the *convex* side."

concept, conception. *Concept* and *conception* are often interchangeable as synonyms for the word *idea*: "This picture shows the artist's *conception* (*concept*) of hell."

If any difference exists it is that *concept* emphasizes the result, and *conception* emphasizes the process of formulating the idea: "The designer's *conception* of open space led to one of the most brilliant architectural *concepts* of the decade."

concert, recital. A *concert* is a musical performance by a group. A *recital* is a musical performance by a soloist or by two performers.

concertmaster, conductor. The *conductor* is the leader of the orchestra and is assisted by the *concertmaster*. The *concertmaster* is the principal first violinist. The *concertmaster* plays solo passages, had administrative duties, and sees to it that the conductor's wishes are executed.

condemn, contemn. *Condemn* means to make a severe and final judgment that is totally unfavorable, a declaration that something is evil or wrong, a sentence to one's doom or end: "Much to the gladiator's chagrin, the crowd *condemned* him to death." "Because the building was unsafe, the city *condemned* it."

Contemn means to express contempt, disdain, or scorn, often in reference to literature or art: "Snobs *contemn* the art of Persia without knowing why."

confound, confuse. The word *confound* implies a temporary mental paralysis caused by astonishment or frustration: "The student was *confounded* when the answer to the algebra problem was different every time he worked it."

Confuse implies being perplexed, bewildered, unclear, or disturbed in mind or purpose: "The student was *confused* by the poorly written passage in the textbook."

congenial, genial. *Congenial* means agreeable or having the same tastes and temperament: "a small circle of warm, *congenial* friends."

Genial means having a sociable and friendly nature: "one of the most *genial* hosts on the Washington party circuit."

congenital, hereditary. *Congenital* refers to a condition existing from birth but not *hereditary*. *Congenital* can be used literally ("a *congenital* abnormality") or figuratively ("a *congenital* liar").

Hereditary refers to characteristics that are passed on from parent to offspring. The reference can be literal ("a *hereditary* disease") or figurative ("a *hereditary* monarchy").

connote, denote. These two terms are often used when talking about the meanings of words. *Denote* refers to the definitions listed in a dictionary for a particular word. *Connote* refers to what a word suggests or implies to the listener or reader, the emotional impact of a word.

What is denoted by the word *father* is one thing, and you could check the *denotative* specifics of *father* by using a dictionary. However, *connotative* values such as authority and love are attached to the word *father*, and these values would be interpreted differently by different observers. To learn about Dad's *connotative* values, you'd have to set the dictionary aside and instead talk to his children.

consistent, persistent. *Consistent* means to conform to the same principles or course of action, to be steady, free from variation. *Persistent* means to refuse to give up or let go, to persevere, sometimes obstinately. A *consistent* advocate for educational reforms is one who always approaches such reforms in the same manner; a *persistent* advocate for the same reforms is one who returns to the fight time and time again.

constrain, restrain. *Constrain* means to force or compel: "She was *constrained* to agree." *Restrain* means to control, check, or to keep a person or thing from doing something: "A heavy chain *restrained* the dog."
SEE ALSO **obligate, oblige.**

consul, council, counsel. These similar-sounding words have the following uses:
Consul: An official appointed by a country to reside in another country for the purpose of representing the interests of the appointing country.
Council: A group of people who meet to deliberate problems and present advice.
Counsel: Advice provided by a *council* or a person; also another term for a lawyer.
Thus, "A city *council* is a governing body that *counsels* the mayor, but the city *counsel* is a lawyer."
SEE ALSO **councillor, counselor.**

consulate, embassy. Basically, a *consulate* is the office of a *consul*, and an *embassy* is the headquarters of an ambassador, the latter being a diplomatic official of the highest rank. Variations exist. The U.S. State Department operates embassies, missions, *consulates* general, *consulates,* and consular agencies (*United States Government Manual 1988/89*).

contagious, infectious.   A *contagious* disease is one that is spread from person to person by direct or indirect contact. An *infectious* disease is one that spreads without human contact being involved.

contemporary, modern.   *Contemporary* refers to what exists simultaneously with a period of time: "Just as the six-gun was *contemporary* with the Old West, the assault rifle is *contemporary* with today."

Modern refers to what is recent, or to what has existed or occurred from some point in the past to the present: "*Modern* Greek is the language used in Greece since about the sixteenth century." "The space shuttle is a *modern* means of transportation." Concerning that last example, it is also permissible to say "The space shuttle is a *contemporary* means of transportation," for the shuttle exists during the present time.

contempt, disdain.   *Contempt* is the attitude of despising or holding in disrespect: "Because of his outburst in the crowded courtroom, he was held in *contempt* of court." "She had nothing but *contempt* for the system that took away her children."

Disdain is scorn for what is beneath a person, an attitude of aloof superiority: "Despite the student's low income, he viewed with *disdain* the money his parents continued to press upon him."

SEE ALSO **despise, hate.**

contemptible, contemptuous.   Where a person stands with respect to *contemptible* and *contemptuous* depends upon whether the person is the receiver or the giver. One who is deserving of contempt is *contemptible.* One who expresses contempt is *contemptuous.*

continual, continuous.   *Continual* means recurring at intervals over a period of time; interruptions or breaks will occur. *Continuous* means going on without interruption or break. Dictionaries, and many writers and readers, treat the words as synonyms. Therefore, the most accurate method of getting ideas across in this case may be using *intermittent* or *recurring* instead of *continual*, and *uninterrupted* instead of *continuous*.

convince, persuade. Both of these words mean to change someone's beliefs by presenting argument or proof or both. The act of *convincing* suggests a reliance more on proof than on an appeal to the emotions; the act of *persuading* suggests an argument addressed to feelings as much as to reason.

copy, replica. A *copy* is an imitation or reproduction of an original: "The *photocopy* of their marriage license did not satisfy the minister, who insisted on seeing the real thing."

Replica at one time stood for a *copy* made by the person who created the original, and some purists still prefer that definition. However, modern dictionaries allow that a *replica* is a close reproduction regardless of who did the copying.

SEE ALSO **model, paradigm.**

copyright, patent. Products of a literary nature are *copyrighted*, and products of a mechanical nature are *patented*.

Copyright is the right granted by law to an author, composer, playwright, publisher, or distributor to exclusive publication, production, sale, or distribution of a literary, musical, dramatic, or artistic work. Works that can be *copyrighted* include books, periodicals, films, tapes, unpublished manuscripts, computer software, and any other product of authorship that is fixed in a tangible medium of expression.

A *patent* is a grant made by the government of some privilege, property, or authority. *Patent*-right is the right to the exclusive sale of an invention.

copyright infringement, plagiarism. *Copyright infringement* occurs when a person uses too much of someone else's copyrighted work without obtaining permission. *Plagiarism* occurs when a person uses any part of someone else's published work without acknowledging who the someone else is. The *plagiarist* presents others' works as his or her own.

Copyright is the legal right that authors have to prevent their work from being copied. Copyright law does not prohibit copying altogether. Instead, the law provides guidelines on how much can be copied without obtaining permission. When too much is copied without obtaining permission, *copyright infringement* occurs.

How much can be copied without obtaining permission is governed by the doctrine of "fair use." The quoting of one sentence from an article would not violate fair use. The use of the only chart that appeared in a three-page article might violate fair use. The quoting of an entire chapter from a book stands a good chance of violating fair use.

A lot depends on how you plan to use portions of the works of others. If your use poses no threat to the income of the author, you are probably not violating fair use. But if you plan to make money on what someone else has written or if your use would deprive the copyright owner of substantial income, then a court might find that you had violated fair use.

Fair use is based on a complicated set of court decisions that have grown over the years and are added to from time to time. For more information on fair use, *copyright infringement*, or any aspect of copyright, try these sources: the publisher who is going to handle your writing, if your work is to be published; the local library, under the catalogue heading *copyright*; and the Copyright Office, Library of Congress, Washington, D.C. 20559.

Plagiarism is the act of taking someone else's literary or artistic work and passing it off as one's own. *Plagiarism* may be an exact copy or an approximate copy. *Plagiarism* can be avoided by very simple means: If you use the words of someone else, whether a direct quotation or a paraphrase, name your source.

corespondent, correspondent.   A *corespondent* is a person charged with adultery; the word is no longer hyphenated *co-respondent*. A *correspondent* is a person who writes letters or memos. To spare embarrassment, care should be taken to spell the word with both *r*'s when someone is being written about as a *correspondent*.

corporal, corporeal. *Corporal* pertains to the body: "Spanking is a form of *corporal* punishment." *Corporeal* also pertains to the body, but as a physical, material form as opposed to a spiritual or ethereal form: "Our *corporeal* life is on earth; our spiritual life is in the hereafter." "The mind is not *corporeal*, but it may be regarded as having structure."

corps, corpse. A *corps* (pronounced "core") is a department of the armed forces: "armored *corps*"; "*Corps* of Cadets at West Point." A *corpse* (pronounced "korps") is a dead body, especially that of a human being.

corpus delicti. The *corpus delicti* is not the body of a murder victim as is frequently thought. The expression *corpus delicti* is Latin and literally means the body of the crime—the substance of a crime or the fact that a crime has been committed. It is true that the body of the crime can be a real corpse. It is also true that the *corpus delicti* can be the charred remains of a house that burned down. In essence, *corpus delicti* consists of two elements. One is the act, and the second is the criminal nature of the act.

corrode, erode. *Corrode* refers to a gradual wearing away, especially by chemical action: "Because acid *corrodes* metal, glass containers should be used."

Erode refers to a gradual wearing away by actions such as rubbing or the movement of water: "Centuries of wind-whipped sand *eroded* the cliffs." "The Colorado River *eroded* the land to form the Grand Canyon."

councillor, counselor. A *councillor* is a member of a council. A *counselor* is one who counsels or provides advice. A *counselor* may be a lawyer, a marriage *counselor*, a student *counselor*, or an investment *counselor*.

SEE ALSO **consul, council, counsel.**

country, nation. We have every right to be confused about these two. After all, we sing Samuel Francis Smith's

"My country, 'tis of thee," and we read of Abraham Lincoln's "a new nation, conceived in Liberty."

So which is right?

Country, a general term, refers to an open area of land, a physical territory, the land of a *nation*, or the *nation* itself: "Each Sunday they escaped the city to drive in the *country*." "Brazil is the *country* of my birth."

Nation refers to a politically organized community of people living in a fairly well-defined territory and having a government: "The three groups came together to forge a *nation*." "The United States is a *nation* with a written constitution."

covert, overt.   *Covert* means hidden, concealed, or disguised. *Overt* means open and apparent.

SEE ALSO   **secret, secrete.**

credible, creditable, credulous.   *Credible* means believable, reliable: "a *credible* witness by virtue of her expertise"; "a *credible* report because of the research behind it."

Creditable means commendable or worthy of esteem: "a *creditable* performance despite the lack of rehearsals"; "a *creditable* family with a long history of good works."

Credulous means willing to believe too easily, on the basis of slight proof: "Confidence men prey on *credulous* people."

crevasse, crevice.   These both mean a deep crack or split. A *crevasse* is usually a deep fissure in a glacier, ice field, or snow mass. A *crevice* is usually a split in a rock wall or cliff.

crime, offense.   These words are interchangeable whether speaking of the breaking of a law or the violating of a moral or social code. Thus it is possible to have "a *crime* against nature"; "an *offense* that stirs God's wrath"; "an *offense* against the state"; "or "a *crime* committed within the jurisdiction of the Ninth Judicial District."

crisis, emergency.   A *crisis* is a turning point, a decisive moment, or an unsettled time or state of affairs. "The cutting off of oil shipments caused still another *crisis* in the Mideast." "According to doctors, a *crisis* is a sudden change, for good or bad, in a patient's condition."

An *emergency* is a sudden, serious, and unforeseen circumstance that calls for immediate action. "The earthquake had created an *emergency*." "The pilot declared an *emergency* because of a fire in the left engine."

criticism, critique. Criticism implies finding fault, and *critique* implies evaluation and analysis. It wasn't always that way, and some traditionalists like to refer to times past when *criticism* meant nothing more than making judgments whether good or bad. The word is still used in that sense when talking about literary *criticism*, art *criticism*, and so forth. Nevertheless, *criticism* today is largely an offensive word, and *critique* a softer one.

crochet, crotchet. *Crochet* (pronounced "CROW-SHAY") is a form of needlework; *crochet* work is done with a *crochet* hook. *Crotchet* (pronounced "CROTCH-ett") is a quirk—an action or notion that is whimsical, eccentric, peculiar, and stubborn. "One of his *crotchets* was his insistence on wearing a heavy wool jacket regardless of the temperature."

crude, rude. When is a person *crude* or *rude*? Both words refer to people who are unrefined, primitive, ill-mannered, uncouth, blunt, gross, discourteous, or lacking tact or taste. *Rudeness* goes further by implying a lack of sensitivity for another person's feelings.

Thus a *crude* answer to a question could be one that is merely ungrammatical or one that is loaded with obscenities and profanity—yet does not hurt the listener's feelings. A *rude* answer could be a model of proper English —yet leave the listener in tears.

crypt, vault. A *crypt* is an underground chamber or *vault*, usually with reference to the dead, and especially a burial place beneath a church. A *vault* can be a place underground where the dead are kept, or a *vault* can be a place above or below ground where money is kept. In addition, electrical transformers and connections are placed in *vaults*.

SEE ALSO **grave, tomb.**

cum laude, magna cum laude, summa cum laude. These Latin labels are used on college diplomas and look good on résumés. The diploma describes the award of a degree as being *cum laude* (with honors), *magna cum laude* (with high honors), or *summa cum laude* (with highest honors).

curriculum, syllabus.   A *curriculum* consists of the courses of study offered by a school. A *syllabus* is the outline of a single course.

cynic, pessimist, skeptic.   Inherent in *cynicism* is a distrust of human nature coupled with a belief that people lack sincerity and goodness and are motivated by selfishness. It is much the same as humorist Finley Peter Dunne said, speaking through his Chicago-based Irish philosopher-commentator Mr. Dooley: "Thrust ivrybody—*but cut th' ca-ards.*"

A *skeptic* (British spelling *sceptic*) is a person who instinctively doubts or questions generally accepted conclusions. The father of skepticism was Pyrrho of Elis, who lived from 360 to 270 B.C. The basic doctrine that has descended from his philosophy is that real knowledge of any kind is unattainable. Pyrrho was too modest to write books, and he lived such a humble life that in his honor his fellow citizens exempted all philosophers from paying taxes. Truly an unusual person living in an unusual time.

And that, by roundabout means, brings us to the definition of a *pessimist*. A *pessimist* is not to be confused with a *cynic*, for a *cynic* distrusts human nature, but a *pessimist* distrusts everything. Neither is a *pessimist* to be confused with a *skeptic*, for a *skeptic* questions, but a *pessimist* knows—knows that the existing situation is the worst possible, or knows that the worst will happen in any given instance.

Pessimists are usually contrasted with *optimists,* the latter being people who see and expect only the best. The contrast was charmingly stated in McLandburgh Wilson's little verse "Optimist and Pessimist":

> 'Twixt the optimist and the pessimist
> The difference is droll:
> The optimist sees the doughnut
> But the pessimist sees the hole.

SEE ALSO   **sarcastic, sardonic.**

D

dais, rostrum. Both of these refer to a raised platform upon which public speakers stand so that they will be more conspicuous above the crowd. A *rostrum* could be larger, more ornate, or raised higher than a *dais*.

Dais comes from a word that exists in several languages and that means nothing more elegant than table or high table.

Rostrum, however, owes its roots to a Latin word of the same spelling that referred to a ship's prow, also known as the beak. Romans collected beaks as souvenirs from the ships of vanquished foes and used the beaks to decorate the orators' platform in the Forum in Rome. Other monuments and trophies that testified to the greatness of Rome were added to the beaks until the whole platform, about the size of a small house, became an ornamental monstrosity.

Given the flowery and effusive manner in which many public speakers are introduced, it is a safe bet that an introduction would contain references to the *rostrum* and not the *dais*.

SEE ALSO **lectern, podium.**

daze, dazzle. *Daze* means to stun or bewilder as with a heavy blow or shock: "The hard-hit ball glanced off his forehead and *dazed* him for several minutes." *Dazzle* means to amaze or overwhelm by using a brilliant or bright display: "The magnificent showing of the peacock's glorious feathers is meant to *dazzle* the unsuspecting female."

deadly, deathly. *Deadly* means capable of causing death: "*Deadly* diseases killed many early settlers." *Deathly* means having the appearance of death: "He was so malnourished that his face bore a *deathly* pallor."

deceitful, deceptive. Both of these indicate misrepresentation, the concealing of truth. The tendency seems to be that people are *deceitful* and things are *deceptive*. Thus we read of "a *deceitful* little boy" where *deceptive* wouldn't sound quite as condemning; and "The solid appearance of thin ice is *deceptive*" sounds better than calling ice *deceitful*.

decent, decorous. *Decent* means to conform to recognized standards of propriety, good taste, morality, dress, or deportment: "He is so *decent* that it seems as though the Boy Scout oath is tattooed on his brain."

Decorous is related to *decor* and *decorate*. *Decorous* implies beauty, grace, or outward conformity in matters of conduct, appearance, or taste. The word *decorous* is a loaded one, for it can imply that someone's behavior is not indicative of the true self; thus, a *decorous* person is not necessarily a *decent* one.

decided, decisive. *Decided* means unquestionable, unhesitating, definite, or free from doubt. *Decisive* means conclusive or final. *Decided* describes a quality or process that leads to a *decisive* outcome: "Superior numbers gave the allied forces a *decided* advantage that brought about a *decisive* victory."

dedicate, devote. These two verbs refer to different types of commitment to a cause or person. *Dedicate* implies a solemn and formal commitment: "A rare bureaucrat, he chose to *dedicate* his career to improving the status quo." "She *dedicated* her life to caring for the poor." *Dedicate* can also mean to set apart something in a formal rite: "A ceremony will be held to *dedicate* the lodge's new hall."

Devote implies compelling motives and a close attachment: "Why are dogs so *devoted* to their masters?"

SEE ALSO **devoted, devout.**

deduction, induction. Deductive reasoning—or *deduction*, the term that Sherlock Holmes and many others have used—is the basis for formal logic. *Deduction* occurs through the syllogism, which is an argument consisting of three parts: two premises, or propositions, and a conclusion that should logically follow from the premises. This is a syllogism in the simplest of forms:

Major premise: All mammals have backbones.
Minor premise: Humans are mammals.
   Conclusion: Humans have backbones.

You have to be careful when constructing a syllogism, for it is easy to go wrong:

Major premise: The Declaration of Independence says that all men are created equal.
Minor premise: Women are not mentioned in the Declaration of Independence.
   Conclusion: Women are not created equal.

Induction, or inductive reasoning, consists of a series of observations that lead to a general principle. Suppose that Rat A dies after drinking 507 cans of a beverage. Now suppose that Rat B dies after drinking 562 cans of the same beverage. Next suppose that Rat C dies after drinking 537 cans of the same beverage. Finally, suppose that all the other rats tested die after drinking more than 500 cans of the same beverage. If those are the results, then *induction* leads to the conclusion that 500 cans or more of the beverage in question will generally kill a rat.

Induction should be based on as many observations as possible. Even under the best of circumstances, *induction* is an incomplete process, for the number of observations can rarely if ever be total. Therefore, *inductive* conclusions are frequently hedged with terms such as *generally, usually, in most cases,* or *in every instance examined.*

To sum up, *deduction* consists of a three-step process known as the syllogism, and *induction* consists of a list of observations of no set number. *Deduction* establishes the relationships between facts, with the facts being provided by *induction.*

SEE ALSO **fallacious, fallacy.**

defective, deficient.   *Defective* means broken or not meeting a standard; *deficient* means not all there: "The motor failed because of a *defective* armature." "An audit revealed that the account was *deficient* by $5,000."

dejected, depressed.   *Dejected* refers to a feeling of sadness, frustration, or discouragement that may be of short duration. "The *dejected* look in his eyes vanished when she said that she would marry him."

Depressed refers to a lingering sadness, moodiness, or brooding; a *depressed* state could be related to a person's temperament or to external factors: "Let's not invite him to the party. He's always gloomy and *depressed*." "His sad story left her feeling *depressed*."

SEE ALSO **despairing, despondent.**

delectable, delicious, delightful.   These three words refer to anything that is enjoyable or greatly pleasing. Of the three, *delightful* offers the broadest uses and may apply to whatever gives great satisfaction to the heart, mind, or senses: "a *delightful* book"; "a *delightful* climate"; "a *delightful* meal with fine food and excellent company"; "the charming personality of a *delightful* girl"; "the *delightful* act of making love."

Delicious commonly refers to what pleases the sense of taste or smell: "a *delicious* cobbler for dessert"; "the *delicious* scent of her perfume."

Delectable is close to *delicious* but may apply more to whatever pleases a refined or discriminating person: "a *delectable* sherry"; "the *delectable* nuances of the sonata."

delegate, relegate.   The verb *delegate* means to assign or entrust to another: "The people *delegate* power to the legislature." "You can *delegate* authority but not responsibility." "Weak managers *delegate* many decisions to subordinates."

Relegate means to put into place—whether by banishment or exile, by assigning to an inferior place, or by naming to a classification: "Because of his inability to hit the curveball, Wilson was *relegated* to the minor leagues." "His peculiar religious beliefs *relegated* him to a very small circle of followers." "Father's belief was that small children should be *relegated* to the species *Darlingus horribilis*."

deliberate, intentional. When the Supreme Court said that desegregation was to proceed at "all deliberate speed," the word *deliberate* was carefully (*deliberately*?) chosen.

Deliberate describes an act that is thoroughly and carefully thought through, and not hasty or rash. The action is coolly and steadily carried out; facts, arguments, and consequences are considered: "He performed an elaborate and *deliberate* study of his colleagues' research." "He was cautious, *deliberate*, and methodical in arriving at any decision."

Intentional refers to any act done by *intent*, design, or on purpose. Use of the word *intentional* does not imply that the act was carefully thought through: "an *intentional* insult"; "an *intentional* breach of faith."

demi-, hemi-, semi-. *Hemi-* indicates one-half of something: "They sailed across the equator into the southern *hemi*sphere." "The human brain is divided into two main parts or *hemi*spheres." "*Hemi*anesthesia is a loss of sensation in either lateral half of the body."

Demi- stands for something less than complete or full. Thus we have *demi*tasse, a small cup of coffee, and *demi*god, a mythical being with not quite the power of a full god.

Semi- means one-half or some other portion of something: "In architecture, one-half of an arch is a *semi*arch." "The climate is *semi*tropical, being humid and warm throughout much of the year." "Two *semi*circles make up a complete circle." "A *semi*trailer is not one-half of a trailer but a trailer with no front wheels."

For what it's worth, which may be nothing more than trivia, there exists in music a note known as the *hemidemisemiquaver*. Its history is one of splitting notes as though they were atoms while tacking on syllables in the way that you would add rooms to a house.

In 1570, someone decided to use the word *quaver*, a musical trill or vibrato, to stand for an eighth note. Who knows why *eighth note* wasn't good enough, but it wasn't. In 1576, the word *semiquaver* came into being to describe the sixteenth note, which is one-half of an eighth note. When it was necessary to glorify the thirty-second note, which is one-half of a sixteenth note, the word *demisemiquaver* appeared in 1706. That was fine until 1853, when the word *hemidemisemiquaver* was born as another way of saying sixty-fourth note, one-half of a thirty-second note.

Anyway, it seems that musical gobbledygook stopped at that point, probably because it took longer to say the word than it did to play the note.

SEE ALSO   **bi-, semi- (annually, monthly, weekly).**

Democrat, democrat.   When capitalized, *Democrat* means a member of the political party. When lowercased, *democrat* means someone who believes in *democracy* as a philosophy of government.

SEE ALSO   **Republican, republican.**

denigrate, disparage.   *Denigrate*—literally *to blacken*—means to defame the character or reputation of someone, or to belittle maliciously: "Fellow scientists *denigrated* his efforts and subjected him to scorn and ridicule."

Disparage means to attempt to discredit or lower the esteem of someone by using indirect means such as insinuation, invidious comparison, or faint praise: "Critics *disparaged* the truth of her writing by saying that her characters belonged 'only to a story.' "

SEE ALSO   **deprecate, depreciate; insidious, invidious.**

denominator, numerator.   When fractions are written, the *denominator* is the number below or to the right of the dividing line (bar), and the *numerator* is the number above or to the left of the line. In other words, the *numerator* is the number divided by the *denominator*.

depository, repository.   These two words are not confusing; their meanings may be treated as synonymous. Both refer to storage or safekeeping: "He was a *depository* (*repository*) of ideas on efficiency." "The library is a *depository* (*repository*) of good reading." "A bank vault is a *depository* (*repository*) for money." Dictionaries show both terms used with either preposition—*for* or *of*.

depraved, deprived.   *Depraved* means bad, debased, or perverted; *deprived* means lacking something one needs or wants.

deprecate, depreciate. *Deprecate* means to mildly or regretfully disapprove of: "Giving up easily is *deprecated*." "He liked art, but he *deprecated* literature."

Depreciate means to lessen in value or price: "New cars *depreciate* rapidly." "Tax rules allow for *depreciation* on certain items each year."

SEE ALSO **denigrate, disparage.**

desegregate, integrate. These terms are interchangeable when discussing racial equality. Thus, a *desegregated* school is the same as an *integrated* one. *Desegregate* is the most narrow of these two words, pertaining solely to the establishment of racial equality. *Integrate* is a broader term that means to unify in general: "*integrate* the forces of free enterprise"; "*integrate* the efforts of the armed forces"; "*integrate* all branches of knowledge into the curriculum."

desert, dessert. A *desert* is a dry, barren region. *Dessert* is the sweet served after a meal. Deserved rewards or punishment are expressed with *deserts*: "He got his just *deserts*."

despairing, despondent. "Failure to sell his paintings had left him *despairing* of his future." Or was he *despondent*? If he had totally given up, he was *despairing*, for *despairing* emphasizes the utter absence of hope. If he still held out some hope and was at worst deeply dejected, then he was *despondent*.

SEE ALSO **dejected, depressed.**

despise, hate. *Despise* means to look down upon with contempt, scorn, or intense dislike: "The strong do not always *despise* the weak." "A self-made man, he *despised* laziness in his employees."

Hate is the antonym of *love*. *Hate* implies an emotional aversion that is sometimes coupled with hostility or malice: "For no good reason, he *hated* to meet strangers." "For very good reasons, she *hated* bigots."

SEE ALSO **contempt, disdain.**

destiny, doom, fate. These three nouns refer to a person's or thing's condition or end as decreed by a higher power. None of them necessarily means death, as is sometimes thought.

Destiny implies a predetermined state, the occurrence of events that are inevitable and necessary: "Ill health was his *destiny*." *Destiny* often is a favorable condition or outcome: "Stardom was her *destiny*."

Doom implies a judgment, decision, or condemnation to a severe penalty—disaster, ruin, death, or extinction: "The encroachment of civilization has caused the *doom* of many species." "In pronouncing the death penalty, the judge sentenced him to his *doom*." "An attack by superior forces sealed the fort's *doom*."

Fate implies the principle by which things happen as they do, as can be controlled by a supernatural or divine agency. *Fate* may refer to a condition of existence or an outcome: "His *fate* was to remain a bachelor." "The legislature decided the bill's *fate* by a single vote." *Fate* can also be controlled by a human agency: "Knowledge helps us to determine our *fate*."

detract, distract.   *Detract* means to lessen the quality of something: "A perpetual grimace *detracts* from her beauty." "The soprano's inability to hold high C *detracted* from her performance."

Distract means to divert in another direction, or in conflicting directions: "Loud noises *distract* me when I'm trying to think."

SEE ALSO   **distracted, distraught, distressed.**

deviate, digress, diverge.   The broad meaning of these three verbs can be the turning aside or veering from a straight line or a defined course.

Deviate means to move away from a prescribed principle or standard: "A navigational error caused the airliner to *deviate* 17 degrees off course." "A rare, honest politician, he never *deviated* one bit from his oath of office."

It is true that public speakers sometimes *deviate* from their topics. When that happens, however, the word that should be used is *digress*: "Let me *digress* a few moments to talk about . . ."

Diverge means to go in different directions from one point: "At the meadow, the lane *diverged* into two paths, one toward the mountains and the other toward the creek." "Any number of ideas may *diverge* from that one accepted tenet."

device, devise. *Device* is a noun that stands for a gadget, mechanism, invention, or contrivance. *Devise* is a verb meaning to form, plan, contrive, construct, or invent. Thus you could *devise* a *device*.

devoted, devout. These adjectives describe a person's loyalty and devotion. *Devoted* is the broader in meaning of the two. *Devout* implies strictly religious devotion: "He was a *devoted* servant and a *devout*, God-fearing man."
SEE ALSO **dedicate, devote.**

diagnosis, prognosis. Basically, a *diagnosis* says what's wrong with you, and a *prognosis* predicts how things are going to turn out. A *diagnosis* determines the nature of a disease, and relies on items such as an evaluation of symptoms, laboratory work, and X-rays or electrocardiograms.
SEE ALSO **symptom, syndrome.**

diastolic, systolic. Blood pressure is measured in two types—*systolic* and *diastolic*. *Systolic* pressure is the peak pressure that occurs at the moment when your heart contracts to pump out blood. *Diastolic* pressure is the pressure at the moment when your heart relaxes to allow blood to flow into the heart.

Since *systolic* pressure occurs at the moment of greatest pressure, it is always higher than *diastolic*. If the doctor tells you that your blood pressure is 120 over 70, your *systolic* pressure is 120, and your *diastolic* pressure is 70.

dictionary, encyclopedia, glossary, lexicon, thesaurus. To many people, *dictionaries* and *encyclopedias* are closely related, when in fact they aren't. Both are reference books, but they are intended to serve different purposes. Basically, a *dictionary* is about words, but an *encyclopedia* is about people, places, and things.

But aren't words about people, places, and things? Yes, they are. But (1) a *dictionary* definition is shorter than an *encyclopedia* article on the same topic, and (2) a *dictionary* definition is limited to helping readers understand how to use a word, while an *encyclopedia* article attempts to describe the entire subject named in the article's title.

Among word books, two of the most frequently consulted are the *dictionary* and the *thesaurus*.

A good modern *dictionary* is a storehouse of knowledge about words. A *dictionary* tells what part of speech a word may be used as; it shows a word's spelling, pronunciation, and meanings; and it often gives the word's derivation, along with synonyms and pointers on usage. Of the various word books, a *dictionary* is the most comprehensive.

A *thesaurus* is no more than a list of synonyms—words with similar meanings. Some *thesauruses* are simply called synonym finders. A *thesaurus* does not give definitions and is useless without a *dictionary*, unless a person has memorized all the possible shades of meanings that are attached to words.

A *glossary* is a vocabulary of specialized terms with definitions provided. A *glossary* does not give as much information about a word as a *dictionary* does.

Also in this group is a *lexicon*, which is simply a list of words with no information provided about them.

Dictionaries are very popular. Bookstores and libraries shelve *dictionaries* not only of words but also of food, clothing, chemistry, tools, firearms, and many other subjects. There is a reason for this popularity, as Sidney I. Landau points out in his excellent book *Dictionaries: The Art and Craft of Lexicography*: "*Dictionary* is a powerful word. Authors and publishers have found out that if they call a reference book a dictionary it tends to sell better than it would by any other name because the word suggests authority, scholarship, and precision." Gulp!

SEE ALSO   **abridged, unabridged.**

die, dye. *Die* means to cease physical life. *Dye* means to change the color of textiles, paper, leather, or plastic, using *dyes* of various kinds.

difference, distinction. When things are not alike, *difference* is the general term that applies broadly, and *distinction* applies to the slight dissimilarities that are determined by close inspection: "The *difference* between red and white may be easy to see, but it may be hard to spot the *distinctions* that exist between the various shades of any color."

different from, different than. Using *different than* is not wrong, but it is not the most common form. The argument is to use *different from* because of its relationship to *differ from*. That is, the American way of speech has us saying "Sue *differs from* Peggy," not "Sue *differs than* Peggy." Similarly, "Sue is *different from* Peggy," not "Sue is *different than* Peggy."

In roundabout constructions, "*different . . . than*" appears: "She loved him in *different* ways *than* ever before." That sentence can be recast to read "She loved him in ways *different from* ever before."

diffident, indifferent. A *diffident* person is one who is timid, shy, or lacking in self-confidence: "Small-town folk seem *diffident* in the big city." An *indifferent* person may be one with a neutral attitude on a subject: "As a juror, she decided to remain *indifferent* until it was time to analyze the evidence." An *indifferent* person may also be one who is aloof, unfeeling, or lacking interest in the subject: "He is *indifferent* to the suffering in the Third World."

SEE ALSO **disinterested, uninterested.**

dinner, supper. *Dinner* is the main meal of the day. The interpretation of that definition depends upon when and where the food is served.

Older generations who live in areas that are or were primarily rural will recall that *dinner* was (and may still be) served at midday. A large meal, *dinner* was meant mainly as fuel to keep farmhands going through the afternoon. A lighter meal, called *supper*, was served later in the day.

These days, in an increasingly urban society, the midday meal is frequently known as *lunch*, and the evening meal may be called either *dinner* or *supper*. The differences between *dinner* and *supper* are minor, except from the viewpoint of the cook who prepares a large *dinner* only to hear it referred to as *supper*.

diplomacy, tact.   Both of these words mean skill in dealing with others without offending them and to the satisfaction of all.

Diplomacy operates between nations: "Direct *diplomacy* means that responsible members of governments deal with each other face to face instead of through ambassadors." "Kissinger's shuttle *diplomacy* prevented or delayed several Third World disputes."

Tact applies on a personal level: "A secretary needs *tact* to get along with a boss as obnoxious as he is." "The chairwoman displayed great *tact* in dealing with the quarrelsome members of the committee."

disassemble, dissemble.   *Disassemble* means to take something apart: "*disassemble* an engine." *Dissemble* means to put on a false appearance, to misrepresent, to pretend, or to hide the true nature of something: "When embarrassed with questions about love, he learned to *dissemble* his feelings."

disburse, disperse.   *Disburse* means to pay money out: "His will established several *disbursements*." "A public fund was set up to *disburse* money to survivors."

Disperse means to scatter or spread widely: "The crop duster *dispersed* seeds over several acres." "Police tactical squads *dispersed* the protesters."

SEE ALSO   **dispel, dissipate; dissipated, dissolute.**

disc, disk, diskette.   The most frequently seen spelling is *disk* when referring to anything that is circular, flat, and thin: "a compact *disk* upon which a Vivaldi concerto was recorded"; "surgery upon a *disk* in the spine"; "a revolving plate upon which computer data and programs are stored, also known as a hard *disk*."

In computer jargon, the word *diskette* is another name for a floppy *disk*, the thin, semirigid *disk* that is permanently encased in a protective jacket.

discern, discriminate.   *Discern* means to see, perceive, or detect something that is obscure, distant, or difficult: "The nurse was able to *discern* the muffled moans of the patient in the next room." "Sentries *discerned* saboteurs advancing through the fog."

Discriminate means to recognize one thing as being different from another. "Clear thinking requires that a person *discriminate* between fact and fancy." "Prejudiced white people *discriminate* against blacks."

discomfit, discomfort. *Discomfit* is a verb meaning to embarrass, confuse, upset, or make uneasy: "The host's unexpected questions *discomfited* his guests." "Business cycles *discomfit* many investors."

Discomfort is a noun that refers to a condition of being uncomfortable: "He did not endure well the *discomfort* of a bad cold." "Various *discomforts* accompany downward swings in the stock market."

discover, invent. To *discover* is to find something: "Tom and Becky *discovered* a cave in the side of the hill." "Only after years of exploration did he *discover* the source of the White Nile."

To *invent* is to devise or create something: "Edison *invented* the light bulb and the phonograph." "She knew how to *invent* a good story when she was in trouble."

discreet, discrete. *Discreet* implies the showing of reserve and prudence in a person's speech or behavior, the opposite of being open and blunt: "To preserve the secrecy of their love affair, they always behaved *discreetly* in public." "The president wanted an aide who could be *discreet* about what went on in the White House."

Discrete means separate, detached, distinct, unrelated: "Numerous *discrete* events contributed to the downfall of the old regime." "Words in a sentence interact with each other and are not like *discrete* sticks in a bundle."

discrepancy, disparity. *Discrepancy* implies a disagreement or inconsistency: "A *discrepancy* exists between the evidence and the testimony in this case." "The company's financial reports were filled with *discrepancies*."

Disparity refers to a difference in degree—in rank, quality, grade, age, condition, or kind: "An obvious *disparity* exists between the enlisted personnel and the officers." "One of the most obvious *disparities* has always been that between the rich and the poor."

disease, illness.   A *disease* is an objective evaluation based on a person's symptoms as determined by a physician. An *illness* is a subjective evaluation made by a person based on how he or she feels.

SEE ALSO   **acute, chronic; symptom, syndrome.**

disinterested, uninterested.   One favorite distinction is this one: *Disinterested* means impartial, fair, or unbiased; *uninterested* means being indifferent, or lacking interest or concern. Unfortunately, dictionaries allow either meaning for either word, and editors, writers, and readers tend to confuse the two.

Therefore, to be understood, use a different word, one that is more accurate. Instead of *disinterested*, use *impartial*; instead of *uninterested*, use *indifferent*.

SEE ALSO   **diffident, indifferent.**

dispel, dissipate.   *Dispel* means to drive away: "Discipline helps *dispel* foolish notions from the untrained mind." "A renewed self-confidence *dispelled* her apprehensions."

Dissipate suggests complete disintegration, sometimes by wasteful means: "The sun will *dissipate* the fog by noon." "Because of its refusal to compromise, the union *dissipated* its bargaining power.

SEE ALSO   **disburse, disperse; dissipated, dissolute.**

disposal, disposition.   An in-sink garbage *disposal* grinds up garbage and gets rid of it; the device is not called a garbage *disposition*. That little analogy may help sort out the general differences between these two words.

Disposal refers to the getting rid of or the giving away of: "*disposal* of the body"; "the *disposal* of property when an estate is settled."

Disposition refers to the arrangement of things or to a person's temperament or nature: "the *disposition* of troops before the attack"; "the *disposition* of an argumentative individual."

dissipated, dissolute.   A *dissipated* person is one who has lost control of the pursuit of pleasure and whose health suffers accordingly: "Heavy drinking left him *dissipated*."

A *dissolute* person is one who is debauched, lawless, or

unrestrained in moral matters: "The *dissolute* conduct of the seamen caused their captain to restrict them to the ship."

SEE ALSO **dispel, dissipate.**

distinctive, distinguished. *Distinctive* refers to a peculiar and identifying mark or characteristic: "Water turns redwood a *distinctive* gray." "The albatross's *distinctive* markings are a white body and dark wings."

Distinguished refers to a person or thing that is celebrated, eminent, or outstanding: "A *distinguished* concert pianist"; "a *distinguished* translation of Chekhov's plays."

distracted, distraught, distressed. "Her love affair with Jules left her so (choose one: *distracted, distraught, distressed*) that she could not concentrate on her work."

Distracted: harassed by conflicting feelings; attention diverted in another direction or to a different object.

Distraught: extremely troubled; agitated, worried.

Distressed: suffering in body or mind from grief, pain, or trouble.

SEE ALSO **detract, distract.**

disturb, perturb. *Disturb* means to interfere with or break up the tranquillity of a settled state: "Overdevelopment *disturbed* the calm of the township." "He did not like people who *disturbed* the papers on his desk."

Perturb means to make uneasy: "She was *perturbed* by the lack of mail from her son." "Unexpected developments, no matter how trivial, easily *perturb* him."

dizziness, giddiness, vertigo. *Dizziness* and *giddiness* refer to a physical sensation of light-headedness, a whirling or reeling sensation along with a feeling or tendency to fall. *Dizziness* and *giddiness* also can refer to a mental impression of being foolish, bewildered, or flighty.

Vertigo is limited to mean the feeling that people or their surroundings seem to be whirling. *Vertigo* does not mean fear of heights; that problem is acrophobia.

These three terms are subjective evaluations on the part of people and are not diseases in themselves. However, they could be symptoms of a disturbance in the brain or in the part of the inner ear that helps us to establish our balance.

doctor, physician.   *Doctor* is a title conferred by a university on someone who receives a *doctoral* degree or a *doctorate*. Thus we have *doctors* of philosophy, *doctors* of law, *doctors* of education, and *doctors* of medicine.

The word *physician* means a *doctor* of medicine who is licensed by the state. Depending upon the field in which a *physician* specializes, the *doctor* can be a psychiatrist (a "head shrinker" or "shrink"), a surgeon, (a "blade"), an anesthesiologist (a "gas passer"), an endocrinologist (a "gland man"), or some other correctly identified specialty (with its attached medical slang).

dolphin, dorado, porpoise.   The *dolphin* is an aquatic, whalelike mammal whose snout forms a beak. The *dolphin* is often confused with the *porpoise,* which is also a whalelike mammal but has no beak and is smaller than the *dolphin.* In many aquarium shows, the highly intelligent and playful *dolphin* is the star performer.

To further the confusion, the name *dolphin* is also applied to a large, swift, and very colorful game fish, the *dorado.* The *dorado*'s coloring consists of luminous shades of gold, green, and purple. When a *dorado* is taken out of water or when it is dying, its coloring changes rapidly.

dominant, predominant.   Both of these words describe an uppermost, ruling, or controlling authority or reason. *Predominant* may be used to suggest that a reason was in effect at a particular time: "Low pay was the *predominant* reason for his turning down the job." *Dominant* suggests that the prevailing effects of the authority or reason are not limited to a particular instance: "The English language is *dominant* in the United States."

dominate, domineer.   *Dominate* means to rule or control by reason of superior power, authority, or strength: "The Tang dynasty *dominated* China for several centuries." "The Rockefeller and Mellon families *dominate* the financial scene." "Racketeers *dominated* the union."

Domineer means to prevail over arrogantly and arbitrarily, and in a despotic, overbearing, tyrannical manner: "The overseer screamed and yelled at the orphans and *domineered* them like the devil." *Domineer* can also mean to tower over: "Three lofty peaks *domineer* the landscape."

doubtful, dubious. *Doubtful* implies a strong uncertainty or a pronounced lack of conviction: "It is *doubtful* whether the spinster had ever had so much fun." "Stevenson campaigned in the *doubtful* states."

Dubious is less strong and implies hesitancy or suspicion: "The crowd was *dubious* about the politician's promises." "She was *dubious* about agreeing to an arranged marriage."

downstage, upstage. If you are on the stage of a theater, *downstage* is toward the front of the stage, and *upstage* is toward the rear of the stage.

downwind, upwind. When you face into the wind, you face *upwind*, in the direction from which the wind is blowing. When your back is to the wind, you are looking *downwind*, in the direction toward which the wind is blowing.

druggist, pharmacist. A *pharmacist* is any person who has a college degree in *pharmacy*, the preparation and dispensing of drugs usually associated with medical science. A *druggist* is any person who operates a drugstore, whether or not the individual has a degree in *pharmacy*.

dwarf, midget, Pygmy. A *dwarf* is a very small person, especially one who is afflicted with dwarfism, a medical condition. The condition is marked by unusual physical characteristics such as shortened lower limbs, shortened forearms, or a longer trunk relative to the length of the arms and legs.

A *midget* is a very small adult who is well-proportioned. *Midget* is not properly used in referring to someone who suffers from dwarfism.

Also in this category is *Pygmy*, another word for people of unusually small size. The word is capitalized when referring to the *Pygmy* tribes of equatorial Africa, lower-cased when loosely used to refer to anyone who is small.

E

eccentric, erratic. The word *eccentric* means off-center, or deviating widely from the usual or the norm: "An *eccentric* wheel is one with its axis not in its center." "Ben Franklin proposed a simplified alphabet because of his wife's *eccentric* spelling." The use of *eccentric* implies that a norm or standard exists. A person who believes in large, invisible rabbits is *eccentric*, because normal persons don't possess that belief.

Erratic means straying, wandering, having no fixed course, or unpredictable or capricious: "The rolling boulder traveled an *erratic* path down the mountainside." A standard may not exist: "Nomadic tribes are *erratic* in their wanderings across the desert, slowly crisscrossing the unmapped sands."

ecology, environment. *Ecology* is the science or study of the relationships of organisms and their *environments*. *Ecology* also means the totality or pattern of those relationships: "The *ecology* of the lodgepole pine requires adequate rainfall and good air quality."

Environment is another word for *surroundings*. The *environment* consists of all living and nonliving things in an area, whether natural objects such as the lodgepole pine or human-made objects such as buildings and cars. "The lodgepole pine does poorly in an urban *environment*."

economic, economical. *Economic* can refer to the science of *economics:* "the *economic* theories of Laffer." *Economic* can also refer to the production, distribution, and consumption of goods: "a national program to reduce imports and ensure *economic* survival." In addition, *economic* has to do with managing the money of a business, household, or nation: "the President's Council of *Economic* Advisers."

Economical refers to being thrifty: "The robotic assembly line, with its reliance on machines instead of people, is an *economical* means of production." "A man of few words, he writes in an *economical* style."

Or "The President is assisted by a council of *economic* advisers, but no one is sure how *economical* they are with taxpayers' money."

ectomorph, endomorph, mesomorph. An *ectomorph* is a thin person. An *endomorph* is a heavyset, overweight person. A *mesomorph* is a strong, well-proportioned person—somewhere between an *ectomorph* and an *endomorph*.

edification, education. Both of these refer to the process of improving an individual. *Edification* implies an informal process of bettering a person's character, morals, or religious faith: "Stained-glass windows depicting the crucifixion were for the *edification* of the parishioners."

Education can imply a formal course of study or training that is meant to develop competence, knowledge, or skill: "A college *education* is necessary in today's job market." An *education* need not be formal: "Dealing with the public provides a good *education* in human nature."

educationist, educator. An *educationist* is one who specializes in the theory and methods of education. The word *educationist* has acquired a derogatory connotation largely because of the bombastic jargon used by *educationists*. To the *educationist*, a desk is a "pupil station," a jungle gym is "a body awareness structure with a visualization tower," and "to studentize" is a vague expression that has something to do with getting children involved in school activities.

Consequently, many *educationists* prefer to be known as *educators*. The word *educator* is not as pompous as *educationist* and is basically a synonym for *teacher*. In practice, however, *educator* can apply to anyone in the educational hierarchy, from the theorist who rarely sets foot in a classroom to the school principal to the teacher who daily has face-to-face associations with students.

eerie, uncanny, unearthly, weird. These four words indicate different impressions of whatever is strange or mysterious.

Eerie implies uneasiness or fear because of something that it gloomy or supernatural: "It was an *eerie* experience to spend the night alone in the house that the villagers said was haunted."

Uncanny implies an uncomfortable strangeness because of something that is extremely puzzling or beyond ordinary powers of understanding: "In an *uncanny* performance, the autistic child solved for pi to the fiftieth decimal place."

Unearthly is something that is so unusual that it is not seemingly of this earth: "The broad desert, pockmarked with huge craters, was so *unearthly* that it resembled the surface of the moon."

Weird is the broadest of these terms and can apply to the supernatural or to the markedly unconventional or absurdly unusual: "He had the *weird* feeling that he was being watched as he strolled through the cemetery." "She likes him, but he seems *weird* to me!"

effective, effectual, efficacious, efficient. The first three of these are often interchangeable.

Effective implies the power to produce an effect or the actual production of the effect: "Money is an *effective* means of combating poverty." "A spanking was *effective* in controlling the unruly little boy."

Effectual means that there exists a proven ability to do the job: "Nighttime attacks were *effectual* in stopping enemy infiltration." *Effective* would work just as well.

Efficacious can mean the proven ability to do the job, but is frequently used to refer to the suggested ability: "A good meal and a few drinks can be an *efficacious* way of securing a large contract."

Of these four, *efficient* is the only one that specifies a proven ability marked by a maximum of output for a minimum of effort: "Henry Ford proved that an assembly line was an *efficient* way to build cars."

effeminate, effete. *Effeminate* means having qualities characteristic of a female but being a male: "Raised and surrounded solely by women, the lad soon became *effeminate*."

Effete means barren, exhausted, weary, or decadent: "Roman civilization collapsed from within because it had become *effete*."

e.g., i.e. These are Latin abbreviations, not English. The first one, *e.g. (exempli gratia)*, is vague and means *for example; i.e. (id est)* is specific and means *that is*. Because few people know Latin these days, writers and readers easily confuse the meanings of the two. Consequently, the best procedure is to write out in English exactly what is meant: "for example" or "that is."

egoist, egotist. An *egoist* is a person who is selfish and self-centered. So is an *egotist,* and more—an unrelenting braggart with an exaggerated and unrealistic concept of self-importance. It is quite possible to be an *egoist* and not an *egotist.* Of the two, the *egotist* is probably disliked the most.

élan, verve. *Élan* means self-assurance, enthusiasm, flair, impetuosity, or dash: "He was filled with the unquenchable confidence, courage, and *élan* of boyhood."

Verve is the vigor and energy apparent in movement, or the spirit or enthusiasm that animates an artistic performance: "She drew her characters with such *verve* that they seemed to leap right off the canvas." "The trapeze artists performed their act with unmatched daring and *verve*."

SEE ALSO **enthusiasm, zeal; vigor, vim, vitality; zeal, zest.**

elder, eldest, older, oldest. *Elder* and *eldest* are largely limited to indicate relative age or seniority among persons, not things: "The *eldest* of the family said grace." "The church's governing body of *elders* meets every Wednesday night."

Older and *oldest* are used for persons and things: "She is *older* than Jim." "It is one of the *oldest* cathedrals still standing." "She is my *older* (or *elder*) sister."

elect, elite. *Elect* refers to a chosen person or group: "Only the *elect* are allowed inside the gates of the Bohemian Club." *Elect* also refers to someone who has been *elected* but not yet installed in office: "the president-*elect*."

Elite refers to a person or group, whether chosen or not, regarded as the best, most skilled, or most powerful: "The Green Berets make up an *elite* force." "Ivy League graduates are thought of by some as being among the *elite*."

But "Many *elite* Americans are not among the *elect* allowed into the Pacific Union Club."

electric, electronic. Both of these words refer to devices that rely on the flow of *electrons*, an *electron* being a negatively charged particle of *electricity*. Therefore, *electric* circuits and *electrical* devices exist, as do *electronic* circuits and devices.

The difference seems to be one of size. *Electric* circuits carry current through wires in a house; *electronic* circuits carry current through wires in radios, stereos, and data processing equipment. *Electrical* devices include motors, relays, and switches; *electronic* devices include cathode ray tubes and transistors.

elegy, eulogy. An *elegy* is a poem written on a solemn subject, such as to lament the death of someone. A *eulogy* is a formal speech given to praise the deceased. However, poets know that an *elegy* can be a poem on any subject as long as it is written in *elegiac* couplets. And, broadly speaking, a *eulogy* is any speech of praise.

Nevertheless, an *elegy* is a poem, and a *eulogy* is a speech, and both are usually said over the dead.

elemental, elementary. In one sense, *elemental* applies to an object or great power of nature: "the frigid, *elemental* feel of the polar ice"; "the *elemental* force of a great storm." *Elemental* also applies to one of the chemical elements: "The experiment relied on elemental carbon."

Elementary is used to refer to that which is basic, fundamental, introductory, or simple: "A child's primer is an *elementary* reader." "Careful research is an *elementary* principle of good writing."

elevate, exalt. Both of these mean to raise or lift, but that which is *elevated* is not as high as that which is *exalted:* "The priest *elevates* the host at Mass." "His next promotion will *elevate* him to the rank of brigadier general." "He *exalts* God above all others." "He holds the *exalted* position of Chief Minister of the Privy Council."

emigrant, immigrant. An *emigrant* is a person who leaves (*emigrates* from) a country or a region to live in another. An *immigrant* is a person who settles in (*immigrates* to) a new country or region. The terms are used chiefly when referring to people who migrate or move. An easy crutch is the equating of *in* to the first syllable of *immigrant*.

eminent, imminent. *Eminent* refers to a person or thing that is conspicuous, noteworthy, prominent, or outstanding: "An *eminent* sociologist, he is the father of the theory of active avoidance." "A house of *eminent* beauty stood atop the hill."
Imminent refers to an act that is about to take place and is usually said of something that threatens: "His execution was *imminent*."

empathy, sympathy. *Empathy* is imagining yourself in someone else's situation in order to better understand the person and the situation. "The most important quality in a good parent is *empathy* with children and their problems."
Sympathy is a broad term. It can refer to a friendly interest in a person or thing; an agreement, attachment, or relationship between persons and things; or a strong emotional identification with another person: "Although I couldn't help her, I was in *sympathy* with her wish to further her education." "Gasoline prices have risen in *sympathy* with the oil embargo." "The boy went to his mother for *sympathy*, not his father."

emulate, imitate. *Emulate* means to strive to equal or excel: "He became chairman at the age of forty, *emulating* his father, who was appointed to the post at forty-five."
Imitate means to copy or to follow the example, model, or pattern set by another person or thing: "His art *imitated* that of Van Gogh." "He *imitated* Aaron's style of hit-

ting." A mocking sense can accompany *imitate:* "The comedian got laughs by *imitating* the president."

endemic, epidemic, pandemic. These three words refer to the distribution of something throughout an area or a population.

Endemic describes a disease with a low death rate that is always present in a locality or a population: "the *endemic* nature of measles among schoolchildren." It can also mean native or characteristic among a particular people: "America's *endemic* belief in individualism."

Epidemic describes a disease that breaks out, spreads rapidly, attacks many people in the area, causes a high death rate, and then subsides: "Cholera reached *epidemic* proportions that winter." The word can be applied to anything that is temporarily prevalent to a large degree: "An *epidemic* of laughter greeted his joke." "Rioting reached *epidemic* levels in Northern Ireland."

Pandemic describes a disease that occurs over a wide area and affects an exceptionally high proportion of the population: "Malaria was *pandemic* among the settlers until the introduction of quinine." It also can describe anything that affects the majority of people in a large area: "the *pandemic* fear that gripped Europe during the days of Hitler."

Note: A technical point of usage would reserve *epidemic* to refer to diseases that affect humans, not plants or animals. According to precisionists, plants are said to wither and die from *epiphytotic* diseases; animals are said to perish from *epizootic* diseases. This distinction is debatable. Surely if you say that "an *epidemic* of potato blight attacked the crops," people will understand you, and they will probably think you are trying to impress them if you use *epiphytotic*. And to some people, *epizootic* is not an adjective that modifies any disease but specifically a noun that stands for equine influenza.

energize, enervate, innervate. *Energize* means to give energy or vigor to: "Throwing the switch *energizes* the circuits." "His stirring speech *energized* the audience." *Enervate* means to lessen the strength or vigor: "Hot, humid, sleepless nights *enervate* people." *Innervate* means to supply with nerves or to stimulate a nerve or muscle to action: "The injection *innervated* the heart muscle and revived the patient."

engine, motor. An *engine* is a machine for converting energy into mechanical force or motion. So is a *motor*. Some people insist that an *engine* burns a fuel such as gasoline, and a *motor*, such as an electric *motor*, produces power without consuming fuel. Dictionaries do not support this distinction, and the words can be used interchangeably. Therefore, it is all right to say that your car has a *motor* even though mechanics like the word *engine*.

In addition, the respected *Jane's Aerospace Dictionary* says that a rocket *engine* burns liquid propellants, and a rocket *motor* burns solid propellants. Therefore, *engines* and *motors* can burn fuel, despite the opinions of purists.

engineer, scientist. The traditional distinction is that a *scientist* studies natural phenomena to develop knowledge, and an *engineer* puts that knowledge to practical uses, as in the designing and making of structures and devices. This definition excludes the glorification of work by the use of *engineer* in job titles, as in locomotive *engineer* for locomotive operator (or driver), sanitation *engineer* for garbage collector, and building *engineer* for custodian.

England, Great Britain, United Kingdom. *Great Britain* is an island occupied by *England*, Scotland, and Wales. *England*, Scotland, and Wales are part of the nation known as the *United Kingdom* of *Great Britain* and Northern Ireland. Northern Ireland is on the island of Ireland, which is separated from *Great Britain* by the Irish Sea.

enhance. *Enhance* means to add to or to intensify. What starts out as good and is *enhanced* becomes better: "The pretty girl used a little makeup to *enhance* her beauty." What starts out as bad and is *enhanced* becomes worse: "An increased crime rate *enhanced* the deplorable conditions in the ghetto." This last usage is deplorable itself and should be avoided. Because *enhance* is strongly connected to *improve*, all sorts of confusion can arise. It would be better to say, "A lowered crime rate improved conditions in the ghetto" or "An increased crime rate worsened conditions in the ghetto."

enormity, enormousness. *Enormity* denotes a considerable departure from the expected or the normal. The *enormity* is often a moral transgression: "He was condemned to death for the *enormity* of his crimes." However, the *enormity* need not be a crime or a sin: "Water pouring into the ship's cabins thrust upon the passengers the *enormity* of their situation." In addition, *enormity* may be used to refer to something of huge or colossal size: "The *enormity* of the solar system is hard to grasp."

Enormousness is restricted to describing something that is immense or huge: "The *enormousness* of Cyrano's nose struck people as hilarious."

Some people insist that *enormity* should not be used in place of *enormousness* to refer to physical size. Dictionaries do not support this contention, and *Webster's Ninth* says, "*Enormousness*, however, is simply not a popular word."

When faced with conflicting advice, the best thing to do is write your way around the problem. Instead of trying to choose between *enormity* and *enormousness,* recast the sentence: "The *enormous* size of Cyrano's nose struck people as hilarious."

enthrall, thrill. *Enthrall* means to hold in a spell, to fascinate: "The magician's act *enthralled* his audience." *Thrill* means to cause sharp excitement: "The roller coaster ride *thrilled* the children."

enthusiasm, zeal. *Enthusiasm* implies strong feelings in favor of something, an eagerness to pursue a cause: "The crowd noisily expressed *enthusiasm* for Long's proposals." "His reading habits showed an unmistakable *enthusiasm* for suspense novels."

Zeal implies a stronger feeling than *enthusiasm,* along with vigorous and untiring activity: "No one could match the *zeal* shown by Columbus in his repeated voyages to the New World." "Missionary *zeal* became the black African's burden."

SEE ALSO   élan, verve; vigor, vim, vitality; zeal, zest.

entomology, etymology. *Entomology* is the scientific study of insects. *Etymology* is the history of a word or the study of the history of words.

envelop, envelope. *Envelop* is a verb meaning to enclose, encircle, or surround. *Envelope* is a noun, the thing that encloses or *envelops:* "The letter was mailed to me in an shocking-pink *envelope.*"

enviable, envious, jealous. The starting point here is the definition of *envy:* to resent a person's advantage and to wish to have the same advantage.
Enviable describes something that arouses envy or is highly desirable: "Her recent promotion placed her in an *enviable* position."
Envious describes the feeling or showing of envy: "Her former coworkers were *envious* of her promotion."
Jealous describes fear of and hostility toward a rival: "He was so *jealous* that he wouldn't let her dance with anyone else."

épée, foil. An *épée* is a fencing sword. It has a bowl-shaped guard to protect the hand, a rigid 35-inch blade with no cutting edge, and a blunted point on the end of the blade. A *foil* resembles an *épée* except that the guard is flat, the blade is more flexible, and the blade is tipped with a button.
SEE ALSO **saber, sword.**

epigram, epigraph, epitaph, epithet. An *epigram* is a short, witty statement or poem that pointedly treats a single subject: "Man proposes, but God disposes" (Thomas à Kempis). And John Wilmot, Earl of Rochester, said this of Charles II:

> Here lies our sovereign lord the King,
> Whose promise none relies on;
> He never said a foolish thing,
> Nor ever did a wise one.

An *epigraph* is an inscription on a building or a quotation at the beginning of a chapter or a book.
An *epitaph* is an inscription on a gravestone. The French

poet Nicolaus Boileau is credited with composing this epitaph:

Beneath this stone my wife doth lie;
Now she's at rest, and so am I.

Benjamin Franklin, some sixty years before his death, suggested this epitaph for himself:

The body of Benjamin Franklin, Printer (like the cover of an old book, its contents torn out and stripped of its lettering and gilding), lies here, food for worms; but the work shall not be lost, for it will (as he believed) appear once more in a new and more elegant edition, revised and corrected by the Author.

An *epithet* is a characterizing word or phrase. "Alfred the Great" is an *epithet* as are expressions such as "Stonewall Jackson," "rosy-fingered dawn," "wine-dark seas," "man's best friend," "sweet silent thought," and "dazzling immortality."

An *epithet* can be used as an uncomplimentary label, as in "narrow-minded person."

epoch, era.   *Epoch* and *era* are close synonyms for periods of time that are marked by radical change or great development. However, a distinction can be made. *Epoch* emphasizes the starting point: "The incarnation of Christ signaled the start of what is known as the Christian *epoch*." *Era* emphasizes the period itself: "We live in an *era* of global communication."

equable, equitable.   *Equable* means steady, uniform, not easily upset: "John's *equable* temperament helped him through troubled times." "A warm, *equable* climate attracts many people to the islands."

Equitable means fair and equal to all concerned: "He administered justice in an *equitable* manner to all who came before the court." "Management and labor deemed the raise *equitable*."

equinox, solstice.   These terms refer to the travels of the sun throughout the year.

The *equinox* is either of two days each year when the sun is at the equator, and day and night are of equal length in all parts of the world. The vernal *equinox* occurs about March 21, and the autumnal *equinox* occurs about September 22.

The *solstice* occurs on the days when the sun is at its northernmost or southernmost point. The summer *solstice* in the northern hemisphere (winter *solstice* in the southern) occurs about June 22, and the winter *solstice* in the northern hemisphere (summer *solstice* in the southern) occurs about December 22.

erotic, exotic. *Erotic* pertains to sexual desire, love, or pleasure: "The author's idea of an *erotic* novel meant nothing more than sex on every page."

Exotic means from another country, excitingly out of the ordinary, or intriguingly beautiful: "*exotic* fish"; "*exotic* birds"; "*exotic* plants."

error, mistake. These two terms refer to any straying or deviation from truth, accuracy, a standard, or whatever is assumed to be right.

Error implies a wrong opinion, judgment, perception, reasoning, expression, or belief. With the word *error* goes the implication that correct performance of the act was often within conscious control of the individual: "Profits and losses on the balance sheet did not check out because of numerous *errors*." "Flight 207 strayed off course because of a navigational *error*."

Mistake implies carelessness, misunderstanding, or inadvertent wrong action: "It was easy to *mistake* one twin for the other." "They didn't know at the time that their marriage was a big *mistake*."

Of the two, *mistake* is weaker than *error* in laying blame, and *mistake* implies less criticism than *error*.

SEE ALSO **failing, fault, foible.**

especial(ly), special(ly). In short, *especial* is more special than *special*. That is, both words apply to what is distinctive or unique, but *especial* may suggest a preeminence or preference over *special*. A house that "has an *especial* charm" would be more appealing than a house that "has a *special* charm."

estimate, estimation. Dictionaries and people tend to treat these two as synonyms. However, a useful distinction is to use *estimate* for an opinion or judgment, and *estimation* for the process of getting to that opinion or judgment: "The value of his art collection is beyond *estimate*." "After careful *estimation*, I do not know what his art collection is worth."

eternity, infinity.   *Eternity* is everlasting or infinite time. By way of contrast, *infinity* refers to anything that lacks limits or boundaries.

SEE ALSO   **immeasurable, immense; innumerable, numerous.**

euphemism, euphuism.   A *euphemism* is an inoffensive word or phrase that is substituted for one that might be offensive. "Pass away" is a *euphemism* for "die." "Restroom" is a *euphemism* for "toilet." Some people believe the more direct term is offensive, but lovers of direct speech say that the *euphemism* is evasive.

Euphuism refers to an affected and elegant style of speech and writing that flourished in sixteenth-century England. The word *euphuism* comes from John Lyly's prose romance *Euphues,* which popularized the style.

eve, evening.   "Union contracts were signed on the *evening* of March 8." Contracts being what they are, an important legal point could arise over whether *evening* means the night before or the night of.

Evening is the latter part of the day that extends from some vague time in the afternoon until dark. When *evening* is over, night begins. *Eve* is the *evening* or night before a day of the period before a major event: "the *eve* of the Civil War."

every day, everyday.   *Every day* (two words) is a noun phrase that means each day. The test is to substitute *each day:* "A newspaper that is delivered *each day* means that it is delivered *every day.*"

Everyday (one word) is an adjective that refers to whatever occurs typically or routinely: "an *everyday* occurrence."

evoke, provoke.   *Evoke* means to call forth a memory or mental image by stimulating the emotions: "The photo album *evoked* memories of her childhood."

Provoke means to arouse or stir up some action, thought, feeling, or image: "The instructor liked to ask thought-*provoking* questions."

SEE ALSO **excite, incite.**

examine, inspect, investigate. *Examine* suggests a detailed questioning or scrutiny in order to determine condition or quality: "As part of being judged physically able to withstand the rigors of basic training, each recruit is thoroughly *examined* by a doctor."

Inspect suggests a careful search for flaws or errors: "Quality control personnel *inspect* each unit before allowing it to be shipped."

Investigate suggests a searching, systematic, probing inquiry. As compared to *examine* and *inspect*, *investigate* indicates a more time-consuming and more thorough process: "Federal agents spend months *investigating* people for security clearances."

SEE ALSO **scan, skim.**

example, sample. Both of these refer to a representative part from a group or larger whole. *Sample* is the broader of the two, generally taken to mean any part that is typical of the whole. *Example* may imply that part which is to be imitated (a good *example*) or not imitated (a bad *example*).

exceed, excel. *Exceed* means going beyond a limit. One may *exceed* in a good or bad direction. That is, the driver who *exceeds* a speed limit is violating the law; however, the salesperson who *exceeds* the expected quota could be due for a bonus.

Excel implies superiority: "Tarkinov *excelled* at chess." "This car *excels* all others in its ability to climb hills."

exceedingly, excessively. *Exceedingly* implies whatever is better than expected; *excessively* implies too much: "The chocolate cake was *exceedingly* tasty, but—oh my!—it was *excessively* rich." Something can also be *exceedingly* worse than expected: "The scores were *exceedingly* lopsided for professional ballplayers."

except, exempt. *Except* means not including: "All the apples *except* one were rotten." "Our delicatessen is open every day *except* Sunday."

Exempt means excluded from some requirement: "Taxpayers who submit returns by April 15 are *exempt* from paying late charges."

SEE ALSO **accept, except.**

exceptionable, exceptional. Anything that is *exceptionable* is open to debate, question, or objection: "This term paper needs a lot more work, for it has an unproven, *exceptionable* thesis."

Anything that is *exceptional* is out of the ordinary, rare, or uncommon: "This term paper is excellent, for it has a well-proven, *exceptional* thesis." "Because of his learning difficulty, he was placed in a program for *exceptional* children."

excite, incite. *Excite* means to stimulate, to agitate, to stir up: "Speakers harangued a rather placid crowd in an attempt to *excite* them about their civil rights." *Incite* means to initiate, to start: "Rabble rousers worked on the fringes of the crowd to *incite* a riot."

SEE ALSO **evoke, provoke.**

exhausted, exhaustive. *Exhausted* means tired; *exhaustive* means thorough: "The graduate student was mentally *exhausted* after finishing the *exhaustive* bibliography of his thesis."

expect, suspect. *Expect* means to look forward to an occurrence with confidence and anticipation; the implications of *expect* are generally positive: "I *expect* your report on my desk by noon tomorrow." "She *expected* her date to arrive at seven." "The boy *expected* a reward for finding the lost dog." Also, "The boy *expected* that he would be spanked for breaking the cookie jar."

Suspect means to have doubt about a person or about the probability of an occurrence; the implications of *suspect* are generally negative: "I *suspect* him of robbing the bank." "She *suspected* that her date, always unreliable, would be late." "Mother *suspected* that it was Timmy who broke the cookie jar." Also, "Because I know that he is honest, I *suspect* that he is faithful."

explicit, express. Both of these words apply to actions or statements that are as clear and as unmistakable as possible. *Explicit* suggests the basic ideas of clarity and distinctness: "an *explicit* sex scene that left no doubt in moviegoers' minds." *Express* carries those ideas further by referring to actions or statements that carry with them a sense of urgency, positiveness, or directness: "Hitler's *express* purpose in invading the Low Countries . . ."

exploit, feat. An *exploit* is a notable or heroic act: "Rescuing the fair damsel in her moment of distress was his most gallant *exploit*." "The *exploits* of Columbus in the New World were the envy of many explorers."

The word *feat* refers to an *exploit* that requires unusual strength or daring: "the *feats* of an acrobat"; "the *feats* of soldiers in combat."

extemporaneous, impromptu. Long-standing distinctions separated these two until recently. That is, an *extemporaneous* speech was one that was carefully prepared but delivered without referring to notes or text, and an *impromptu* speech was one that was made up or improvised on the spur of the moment. Current usage, however, treats the two as interchangeable.

extract, extricate. "Dentists *extract* teeth." "Heroes *extricate* heroines from fates worse than death." The distinction is that *extract* indicates forcible removal, and *extricate* indicates the setting free or the disentangling of someone or something.

extravert, extrovert, introvert. The *extravert* (or *extrovert;* either spelling will do) is the person with the outward-directed personality. The *extravert* is characterized by sociability and an interest in others and in the social and physical environment.

The *introvert* is the inward-directed personality. The *introvert* is characterized by interest in personal thoughts and feelings and a tendency toward self-centeredness.

F

fable, tale. A *fable* is a brief *tale*, in either prose or verse, told to show a moral. *Fables* often deal with unusual or supernatural incidents. A *fable* in which the characters are animals is a beast *fable*. Rudyard Kipling's *Jungle Books* are beast *fables*, as is George Orwell's *Animal Farm*.

As a form of literature, a *tale* is a simple recital of a series of events, in either prose or verse, without a complicated plot. Otherwise, a *tale* can be any recitation of fact or fiction: "The *tale* of corporate failure is the usual one of lack of leadership." "The story about Paul Bunyan and Babe, the blue ox, was just another tall *tale*, told to amuse people around the campfire." "She dried the boy's tears while listening to his *tale* of woe."

fact. The word *fact* is overworked and frequently misused. Because *facts* are called into play so much, it is relatively easy to become confused about just what a *fact* is.

Therefore, correct use of the *fact* depends upon knowing what a *fact* itself is: "A *fact* is an objective statement of reality; a *fact* can be verified by observation or judged reasonably likely because of documentary evidence.

The street address of the house in which you live is a *fact*. This address is visible and real to any number of observers at any time. In addition, the address is recorded at the county seat and on many documents, such as the mortgage, the deed, insurance papers, and utility bills.

That the house is comfortable, spacious, airy, large,

small, or just right—these are not statements of *fact*. These are opinions, and it is highly possible that no two observers would hold the same opinion.

An aid to identifying *facts* is to classify them as historic or scientific:

Historic: the assassination of President Kennedy on November 22, 1963; the armistice terminating World War I on November 11, 1918; Napoleon's evacuation of Moscow in 1812. A historic fact can be verified by checking records written by observers then living.

Scientific: the temperature at which water freezes; the speed of light; the terminal velocity of a falling body in a vacuum. A scientific fact can be rechecked at any time and its validity established.

factious, factitious, fictitious. The word *factious* is related to *faction*. A *faction* is a party or clique that is often contentious and self-serving: "a political *faction*." Therefore, someone who is *factious* is one who produces *faction* or causes dissension: "The *factious* approach of the Speaker and his followers immobilized the House."

Factitious describes that which is not genuine, natural, or spontaneous: "Advertising has created a *factitious* need for many products." "Hired demonstrators produced a *factitious* enthusiasm for the candidate." *Factitious* is a seldom-seen word; *artificial* is more commonly used.

Fictitious applies to the fabrication of a story as the product of one's imagination, often without any intent to deceive: "As a novelist, everything he wrote was *fictitious*." When used figuratively, *fictitious* applies to anything that is invented: "a *fictitious* promise to balance the federal budget"; "*fictitious* reasons why she was late every morning."

faculties, senses. A person's *faculties* are that person's abilities or powers whether inherent or cultivated: "She had a *faculty* for leaving lovers in the lurch." "He has a *faculty* for being in the right place at the right time." "My aunt's *faculties* dimmed as she grew older."

Broadly speaking, the word *sense* refers to judgment and intelligence: "common *sense*"; "horse *sense*." Compared with *faculties*, the *senses* are those of hearing, sight, smell, taste, and touch.

faggot, fagot. A *faggot* is a derogatory term for a male homosexual. A *fagot* is a bundle of sticks or branches to be used as fuel, or a bundle or heap of iron or steel pieces to be worked into bars. *Fagot* is sometimes also spelled *faggot*.

failing, fault, foible. *Foible* is the mildest of these three terms, meaning an idiosyncrasy or character weakness that is minor, harmless, and perhaps even amusing or endearing: "Wearing a baseball cap to bed was one of the small boy's *foibles*."

A *failing* is a minor *fault* or weakness: "Not shining his shoes is one of his *failings*."

In general, a *fault* is any flaw or defect in quality. When speaking of people, a *fault* is an imperfection in character that is slightly more serious than a *failing* but not necessarily condemnatory: "His biggest *fault* is his tendency to be a perfectionist."

SEE ALSO **error, mistake.**

fake, fraud. A *fake* is any person or thing that is not genuine: "The so-called lawyer was a *fake*." "The latest fashion includes pants with *fake* pockets." The implication of *fake* is that no one need necessarily suffer from it.

Fraud is deliberate deception or trickery in order to cheat someone out of something: "The con man worked a big *fraud* on the widow."

fallacious, fallacy. *Fallacious* refers to errors in reasoning: "Because of a failure to consider all the evidence, the committee reached *fallacious* conclusions."

Fallacious reasoning can occur because of a *fallacy*. Generally speaking, a *fallacy* is any false or mistaken idea: "He believed in partying and staying out late every night, embracing the *fallacy* that there's no tomorrow."

The word *fallacy* also refers to statements that violate the rules of formal argument as established by logicians. This type of *fallacy* is known by the self-contradictory term *logical fallacy*.

One of the most common of logical *fallacies* is the *post hoc fallacy*, which is short for *post hoc ergo propter hoc:* "after this therefore because of this." The term applies to a statement in which cause and effect are scrambled. One of the most oft-cited *post hoc fallacies* is that of Chanticleer, the fictional rooster who thought that his crowing brought about the sunrise. Another case of scrambled cause and effect is this one: "Married men live longer than single men. Therefore, men, if you want to die a slow death, get married."

Another common logical *fallacy* is the *non sequitur,* in which one point of an argument does not follow from the previous point. This following passage contains a *non sequitur;* that is, the first idea is not tied to the second: "I'm not for moratoriums. All they do is scare people." This *non sequitur* could be connected by saying why moratoriums scare people.

SEE ALSO **deduction, induction.**

familiarity, intimacy. *Familiarity* suggests closeness of an informal nature: "His *familiarity* with insider trading made him the ideal investigator for this case." "She missed the *familiarity* of family meals taken together." *Familiarity* can imply *intimacy:* "He displayed an affectionate *familiarity* with her, even in public."

Intimacy suggests very close association, perhaps of a very private or personal nature: "Their love letters were of an *intimacy* too personal to be made public." *Intimacy* may be other than personal or physical: "His *intimacy* with the history of Europe showed through in his writings."

famished, ravenous. To be *famished* is to severely lack food or other necessities: "The escaped prisoner of war was filthy and *famished* for food and sleep."

Ravenous implies unusually great hunger along with violent means of satisfying the hunger: "It was a nation gone wild with war and a *ravenous* desire for more territory." "He groped around inside the bin, a child with a *ravenous* appetite for the cookies he hoped to find."

farther, further. *Farther* is used to express literal, physical, measurable distance or time: "*farther* down the road"; "to walk *farther* west"; "a folder *farther* back in the files"; "go back still *farther* to the time of Cleopatra."

Further is used for anything else that means in addition or more: "*further* from the truth"; "a soil *further* enriched by organic fertilizer"; "found himself *further* into debt"; "harbored no *further* illusions"; "was unable to *further* her education."

Because usages overlap, the best general advice in this case comes from the *Oxford English Dictionary:* "In standard Eng. the form *farther* is usually preferred where the word is intended to be the comparative of *far,* while *further* is used where the notion of *far* is altogether absent; there is a large intermediate class of instances in which the choice between the two forms is arbitrary."

fashion, style, vogue. *Fashion* is the most general of these three terms, referring broadly to any conventional custom or practice that is favored at a time or place: "The *fashion* these days is the increased wearing of casual clothing in a business environment." "Poetry is no longer in *fashion,* having given way decades ago to more easily readable forms."

Style is a distinctive *fashion* from the point of view of elegant, affluent society: "All of her clothing was purchased from the best shops and was in the latest *style.*" "They furnished their home in the Victorian *style.*"

Vogue may be interchangeable with *fashion,* or it may emphasize the great popularity of something for a given time: "*Vogue* words come and go." "Among lovers of rock music, his work enjoyed a great *vogue* a few years ago."

fatal, fateful. *Fatal* refers to death or destruction—the causes or inevitability of either: "a *fatal* blow to the head"; "a *fatal* gunshot wound to the abdomen"; "a *fatal* earthquake in 1906"; "a *fatal* moment in which the passengers knew that the ship had struck an iceberg"; "a *fatal* policy that spelled out genocide."

Fateful refers to whatever is ominous or prophetic, whether for good or evil: "a *fateful* conference at which the truce was arranged"; "studied all night for a *fateful* examination"; "a *fateful* decision that determined his future."

fatigued, tired, weary. To be *fatigued* is to experience physical or mental exhaustion; rest or sleep is essential. To be *tired* is to experience a draining of one's strength and patience. To be *weary* is to be at the point of being unable to bear more of the same.

faze, phase. *Faze* means to disturb or disconcert: "The insults didn't seem to *faze* him one bit."

Phase refers to an aspect or stage of a course or path: "At this *phase* in his career, he considered changing jobs." "Primitive people became restless during certain *phases* of the moon."

feasible, possible, probable. *Feasible* means that something can be done: "It is *feasible* to design a car that will get forty miles per gallon."

Possible means that something can happen: "Rain is *possible* by tomorrow night."

The word *probable* means that something is likely but is not a certainty: "Until proof was established, investigators suspected arson as the *probable* cause of the fire."

SEE ALSO **practicable, practical, pragmatic.**

feckless, reckless. A *feckless* person is one who lacks effect—is weak, feeble, incompetent, or inefficient: "As a so-called leader, he was a *feckless* figurehead."

A *reckless* person is one who lacks caution or is not concerned with the consequences of an act: "He openly criticized his superiors, *reckless* of the consequences."

fecund, fertile. *Fecund* and *fertile* both refer to the ability to reproduce, to bear fruit or offspring. *Fecund* emphasizes abundance or rapidity in reproducing, while *fertile* refers to the power to reproduce. Both are used to refer to biological or botanical reproduction ("a *fecund* civilization"; "a *fertile* garden"), or to refer to intellectual ability ("the *fecund* mind of Leonardo da Vinci"; "a *fertile* novelist who had published more than fifty books").

felonious, nefarious. In general, *felonious* is an adjective that refers to a felony, which is a grave or serious crime. As a technical word in law, *felonious* means that something was done with the intent of committing a crime, that is, criminal intent.

Nefarious means evil, wicked, vicious, or villainous, but not necessarily having anything to do with crime or the law.

female, lady, woman. *Female* should be used primarily in scientific or technical senses: "The main reproductive organs of the *female* consist of a pair of ovaries." "Our dog had puppies last night, one male and three *females*." In addition, police jargon often contains references to "*female* suspects" and "male suspects" when referring to humans, but, again, this is technical language and not the words of ordinary speech.

Woman refers to an adult *female* human being, and *lady* refers to a *woman* of refinement and culture. However, *lady* has taken on shadings of the trivial, while *woman* remains a strong, positive term. Casey Miller and Kate Swift observe in the *Handbook of Nonsexist Writing*, "*Woman* is the most useful all-around word for referring to an adult female person."

SEE ALSO **gentleman, male, man.**

ferment, foment. *Ferment* means to excite, to stir up, to agitate: "He is a restless person, full of ideas that are in constant *ferment*." "I would like to get a novel *fermenting* in that creative brain of yours."

Foment means to incite, to urge or stimulate into action, and is usually used in an unfavorable sense: "*foment* a riot"; "*foment* a rebellion."

fervent, fervid. Both of these terms refer to the showing of strong feelings.

Fervent implies a steady and sustained deep and glowing feeling: "Over the decades he demonstrated a *fervent* loyalty to the crown." "She was a popular teacher, *fervent* in her desire to see students succeed."

Fervid implies an intense, perhaps spontaneous, feverishly expressed emotion: "Jealousy drove him to a *fervid* hatred of her husband." "In the Golden Age of Oratory, he was the most *fervid* of all the speakers."

festival, festive. *Festival* is the occasion, and *festive* applies to whatever is appropriate to the occasion: "The jazz *festival* ended Monday." "Her wedding was a *festive* affair."

feud, vendetta. A *feud* is a bitter, prolonged, and sometimes violent quarrel or hostility between individuals or factions: "The rival parties carried their political *feud* well into the twentieth century." "The *feud* existed between the two families for years."

Vendetta refers to a bitter act of vengeance that is **part** of a *feud*: "It was a typical *vendetta* in which the Johnsons, whose daughter was attacked by the McCrory boy, killed him in retaliation." Not all *vendettas* are bloody: "Because the critic was unsuccessful in having his own work published, he went on one literary *vendetta* after another, lashing out at those who had rejected him."

SEE ALSO **avenge, revenge.**

fewer, less.   *Fewer* refers to number: "*fewer* eggs in the basket"; "*fewer* people at the park"; "*fewer* cars on the road"; "*fewer* chances for employment."

Less is a comparative of *little* and refers to matters of degree: "took *less* time to do the work"; "a plan *less* likely to succeed"; "*less* opportunity to succeed"; "was *less* mad than confused."

When numbers are used in a collective sense, *less* is used in place of *fewer:* "earned *less* than $5,000 last year"; "on vacation for *less* than two weeks"; "a room *less* than ten feet wide."

SEE ALSO **above, greater than, more than, over.**

fiancé, fiancée.   *Fiancé* is the man who is engaged to be married; *fiancée* the woman.

field, meadow.   A *field* is any open expanse of level land. A *meadow* is grassland, either natural or a pasture for growing hay.

figurative(ly), literal(ly).   *Figurative(ly)* means representative of and not in the exact or factual sense: "This part of the problem is *figuratively* the tip of the iceberg."

The opposite sense is conveyed by *literal((ly)*, which means word for word, factually, and not imaginatively: "The building *literally* burned to the ground."

Literally is often misused. Statement such as these, in which the meaning isn't *literal* at all, are common: "The band *literally* blew me away!" "I was *literally* coming apart!" "She was *literally* climbing the walls!" And think about what kind of picture this one creates:

"I've had it with rotten kids. They are *literally* coming out of my ears!"

filet, fillet. A *filet* is a pattern done in lace, or a shorter way of saying "*filet* mignon." A *fillet* is a thin ribbon or strip; a boneless, lean piece of meat or fish; or a wood or metal fairing or molding.

Filipino, Philippines. A *Filipino* is the person, a native of the *Philippine* islands; also a citizen of the *Philippine* nation.

firmware, hardware, software. Computer equipment is divided into three categories. *Hardware* consists of physical equipment such as the display screen and the electronic circuits. *Software* consists of the programs, procedures, and documentation that pertain to the operation of the computer. *Firmware* is *software* that has been programmed into the circuitry of a computer.

first, former. What is *first* comes before all others, while what is *former* occurs earlier but is not necessarily *first*. A much-wed woman could speak of her *former* husbands, only one of whom would have been *first*. When only two are in the series, *first* and *former* could be the same: "Suzie and Joan are sisters, the *former* (*first*) being the taller."
   SEE ALSO **last, later, latest, latter.**

fiscal, monetary. *Fiscal* has to do with administering the financial affairs—debt, taxation, revenues, and expenditures—of a public or private organization: "The company's *fiscal* year is not the same as the government's."
   Monetary pertains to the money itself, the coins and currency in use: "Increasing the amount of paper money was a sharp change in *monetary* policy."

fission, fusion. *Fission* is the act of splitting or dividing; organisms can undergo *fission*, as can atoms, families, and nations.
   Fusion is the act of bringing together, often by using intense heat; in fact, a technical definition of *fusion* allows the word to be used as a synonym for *melting*: "Welds are commonly accomplished by *fusion*."

flack, flak.   *Flak* is an acronym for the German word *Fl(ieger)a(bwehr)k(anone)*—antiaircraft artillery; more particularly the word stands for shells fired by the guns. *Flak* also stands for intense criticism: "The President caught a lot of *flak* for his plans to increase taxes."

Flack is a synonym for *press agent.* Dictionaries give no reason for this origin, but Stuart Berg Flexner, in *I Hear America Talking,* suggests that the word "came to mean one whose work is to put out a barrage of words, as in advertising or public relations."

flair, flare.   A *flair* is a natural or instinctive ability or talent: "She is one of Washington's most popular hostesses, always showing a *flair* for hospitality."

A *flare* is a bright, unsteady flame: "A signal *flare* arced across the sky to show that the lost boy had been found."

flammable, inflammable.   Both of these words mean that something can burn; the prefix *in* does not mean negative, as in "not able to burn."

To avoid confusion, use *flammable* for whatever can burn and *nonflammable* for whatever cannot.

flat, level.   A *flat* surface is any surface that is smooth, even, on one plane, and without curves. A *flat* surface may be at any angle—horizontal, vertical, or somewhere between. A *level* surface is one that is parallel to the horizon.

flaunt, flout.   *Flaunt* implies an ostentatious, boastful, or even defiant display: "*He flaunted* his superiority among his employees." "Ever the snob, she delighted in *flaunting* her wealth in public."

Flout means to mock or scoff at, to regard with contempt: "Career criminals make a profession of *flouting* the law." "The political profession has no method of chastising its practitioners who *flout* the public faith."

fleece, fur.   *Fleece* is the coat of wool from a sheep. *Fur* is the hairy coat of a mammal or an article of clothing made from the same.

flier, flyer. A *flier* (or *flyer;* either spelling is shown in dictionaries) is anyone or anything that flies; also a handbill or advertising circular.

flinch, wince. To *flinch* is to draw back from anything that is painful or threatening; to *wince* is to do almost the same. Any difference exists in the implication that a *wince* involves more immediate pain and sensitivity than does a *flinch;* that is, "You may *flinch* at the thought of going to the dentist, but you will probably *wince* at the pain of the needle (or at the sight of the bill)." In addition, a *flinch* may be a whole-body effort, while a *wince* may be a grimace or some other facial contortion.

flotsam, jetsam, ligan. These words apply to debris in the water. *Flotsam* is whatever floats, such as cargo or wreckage that is left after the ship sinks. *Jetsam* is any cargo or equipment that is jettisoned overboard from a ship during a storm or emergency. The difference between these two confusables can be sorted out by linking *flotsam* to *float* and *jetsam* to *jettison.*
    Ligan is anything jettisoned and tied to a buoy to allow for recovery.

flounder, founder. *Flounder,* other than the fish, is to struggle awkwardly or to thrash about: "The horse *floundered* in the deep mud, unable to obtain a footing." In the figurative sense, "He *floundered* as a painter but succeeded as a photographer."
    Founder means to become disabled, to grow lame, or to sink: "His horse caught a hoof in a gopher hole and *foundered* while still eight miles from home." "The tanker began to *founder* after hitting the reef."

fluid, liquid. A *fluid* is a substance that flows—undergoes a continuous change of shape. *Fluids* include two of the three forms of matter, *liquids* and gases, the third being solid. *Water* is a *fluid* and a *liquid.* Air is a *fluid* and a gas.

foam, froth. *Foam* is the mass of bubbles formed in or on a liquid by a process such as agitation or fermentation: "the *foamy* head on a glass of beer." *Foam* also exists as the spongy or rigid mass known as packing *foam.*

Froth is a whitish mass of bubbles: "*frothing* at the mouth like a mad dog." *Froth* also pertains to light, trivial ideas: "The chatter at the cocktail party was nothing but *froth.*"

SEE ALSO **spray, spume.**

fog, mist. *Fog* is condensed water vapor in cloudlike masses on or near the ground. *Fog* is less transparent than *mist,* the latter consisting of fine droplets of water floating or falling at or near the ground.

foolhardy, foolish. "Was the attractive young blond *foolhardy* or *foolish* for stopping at the dimly lit waterfront bar?"

Unless she was going to meet a friend there, she was *foolhardy,* for she was unwisely bold and venturesome. Even if she was to meet a friend, she was *foolish,* for she lacked good sense and judgment in agreeing to such a meeting place.

forage, foray. *Forage* means to search for food. *Foray* refers to a sudden attack or raid to steal or seize things.

forceful, forcible. Literally speaking, *forceful* means full of force and applies to abstract concepts: "A strong-willed suitor, he impressed her with his *forceful* personality." "She won an Oscar for her *forceful* acting."

Forcible applies to physical concepts and refers to the use of force: "The police had to resort to *forcible* entry to get into the apartment." "The coup was accomplished by bloody, *forcible* means."

forego, forgo. *Forego* means to go before: "The tales of his exploits will *forego* him on his wanderings."

Forgo means to give up or abstain from: "He said he would *forgo* his corporate salary while serving as an adviser to the government."

forest, woods. Both of these stand for a dense growth of trees and underbrush; a *forest* covers more land than *woods.*

formally, formerly.   Careless pronunciation makes these words confusing. *Formally* pertains to whatever is formal: "He was *formally* introduced to the prime minister at high tea." *Formerly* means previously, at a former time: "He had been *formerly* introduced to the prime minister at high tea."

fort, fortress.   A *fort* is a military installation that is fortified with troops, weapons, and barricades. A *fort* is smaller than a *fortress*, and many *forts* of the American West were nowhere near as impressive as shown in the movies.

Howard R. Lamar says, in the *Reader's Encyclopedia of the American West:* "The military presence in the West came largely in the form of small installations (variously called posts, forts, camps, cantonments, or barracks), which were built at strategic sites along the lines of communication or in areas of Indian disturbances. They were frequently no more than log palisades with blockhouses at the corners, similar to the defenses thrown up by the frontiersmen themselves, but a few of the more permanent posts became imposing structures of brick and stone."

A *fortress* is a large, permanent, military stronghold that sometimes includes a town. A *fortress* may also be a region: "*Fortress* Europe."

forthcoming, forthright.   *Forthcoming* means about to appear: "This matter will be examined in the author's *forthcoming* book."

Forthright means frank, direct, or free from ambiguity: "He was honest, and provided a *forthright* appraisal of the project's chances for success."

fortuitous, fortunate.   *Fortunate* refers to good fortune or favorable luck: "He became wealthy by virtue of *fortunate* investments."

A *fortuitous* event is one that occurs by luck or chance and is not necessarily *fortunate:* "She saw these meetings as strictly *fortuitous*, occurring as they did without any planning or prearrangement."

foyer, lobby.   A *foyer* is an entranceway or transitional area from the exterior of a building to its interior. A *lobby* is a space inside the entrance to a building, theater, or auditorium.

fraternal twins, identical twins. *Fraternal twins* are developed from two egg cells, and may be easy to tell apart. *Identical twins* are developed from one egg cell and usually are more difficult to tell apart than *fraternal twins*.

frequently, intermittently, occasionally, periodically, sporadically. These words classify the repeated occurrence of an event:

Frequently means that the event occurs often, at short intervals.

Intermittently means that the event does not occur often; *intermittently* tends to emphasize pauses and interruptions, not occurrences.

Occasionally means now and then, at random, and not necessarily important.

Periodically implies predictability; that is, the event occurs at regular intervals.

Sporadically means that the event occurs at scattered, irregular, and unpredictable intervals.

frog, toad. *Frogs* and *toads* look a lot alike, and both are amphibians—creatures that can live on land or in the water. The majority of *frogs* favor water; the majority of *toads* favor land.

frown, scowl. A *frown* is a wrinkling of the brow. A *scowl* is a threatening look, a look of anger; all of the face is involved in a *scowl*, not just the brow.

SEE ALSO **glare, glower.**

frugal, thrifty. These two words emphasize careful management of money, time, or other resources.

Frugal implies self-denial and abstention from luxury: "They are members of a *frugal* farm family who eat and dress simply."

Thrifty applies to the person who is hardworking and who saved and conserves: "Like any *thrifty* housewife, she always watched for sales."

furor, furore.   These both refer to excitement or confusion. *Furore* is the British spelling.

fuse, fuze.   A *fuse* is an electrical device for protecting circuits or a combustible material used to set off explosives. In military terminology, a *fuze* is the device for detonating explosives.

G

gale, storm. In general usage, a *gale* is a strong wind, and a *storm* is an atmospheric disturbance marked by any of the following: strong wind, rain, sleet, hail, snow, thunder, or lightning.

A precise definition for *gale* or *storm* is contained in the Beaufort scale, which was devised by British Rear Admiral Sir Francis Beaufort (1774–1857). On the Beaufort scale, numbers indicate wind speeds.

Beaufort Scale

Beaufort number	Description	Speed (mph)
0	Calm	less than 1
1	Light air	1–3
2	Light breeze	4–7
3	Gentle breeze	8–12
4	Moderate breeze	13–18
5	Fresh breeze	19–24
6	Strong breeze	25–31
7	Moderate gale	32–38
8	Fresh gale	39–46
9	Strong gale	47–54
10	Whole gale	55–63
11	Storm	64–72
12	Hurricane	73 +

SEE ALSO **hurricane, typhoon.**

gamble, gambol. *Gamble* means to play games of chance for money, while *gambol* means to frolic or skip about while having fun.

game, sport. *Games* and *sports* are similar in that they are diversions, forms of recreation, or contests; both are conducted according to rules. The difference is that a *sport* is a *game* that usually requires athletic ability and physical exertion. Thus chess, golf, and football are all games, but only the later two are *sports*.

A clear-cut distinction can't always be made. Children's *games* frequently require physical exertion, as do war *games,* yet the word *sport* is not used with either kind.

gantlet, gauntlet. These two are easily confused, and dictionaries allow either spelling for either meaning. However, many people prefer to separate the two according to these usages:

Gantlet refers to a former military punishment in which the person being punished was forced to run between two rows of men who struck the runner with sticks and clubs as he passed. From this usage came the expression "run the *gantlet.*" The word is sometimes used in a figurative sense: "Her actions placed her in the unenviable position of having to run the *gantlet* of criticism from all sides." Also seen as "run the *gauntlet.*"

A *gauntlet* is a heavy glove with a flared cuff. The *gauntlet* was part of medieval armor and was used to protect the hand and lower arm. The expression "throw down the *gauntlet*" refers to a challenge. In the Middle Ages, when one knight challenged another, the custom was for the challenger to throw his *gauntlet* on the ground. If the challenge was accepted, the person toward whom the *gauntlet* was thrown picked it up.

gargantuan, gigantic. *Gargantuan* indicates tremendous size and immense appetite, especially for food and pleasure: "The hotel's Sunday brunch is truly a *gargantuan* feast." The word and its meaning come from two sources. One is *garganta,* the Spanish word for throat. The other is the Rabelais satire *Gargantua and Pantagruel,* the story of two stupendous and genial kings.

Gigantic describes anyone or anything that is large for its kind: "Wind hurled the trees with *gigantic* force." "The attacking armies suffered a *gigantic* setback." "The *gigantic* force of his personality overwhelmed his opponent." "Oil tankers are *gigantic* ships."

garish, gaudy. Both of these words refer to the showing of loud colors, excessive ornamentation, or both. However, a *garish* dress is not the same as a *gaudy* one, for *gaudy* implies a greater lack of taste than does *garish*. Here, everything depends on taste—and who can define taste?

gas, gasoline. *Gas* is a state of matter that is neither liquid nor solid. *Gas* is not the fuel for your car; the fuel is *gasoline* and is a liquid. The distinction is a technical one that is observed in the laboratory but not in everyday use. Even scientists talk about "putting *gas* in the car" or "filling up the *gas* tank."

gem, jewel. A *gem* is a precious or semiprecious stone that has been cut and polished to serve as an ornament. A *jewel* is a precious stone or metal worn as an accessory of dress.

SEE ALSO **jewelry, jewels.**

gentleman, male, man. *Male* should be used primarily for technical references: "Fourteen *male* guinea pigs were used in the second part of the experiment." "The *male* population of the colony outnumbered the female." "He recommended planting *male* holly plants upwind of the female plants."

The restricting of *male* to this usage is not always done, for popular speech and writing contain expressions such as "a *male* chorus" and "a deep, *male* voice." In addition, it's hard to describe as technical or scientific the expressions "*male* chauvinist pig" and "fragile *male* ego." Incidentally, you have to wonder who coins such expressions, for has anyone ever heard of a "fragile female ego"?

Nevertheless, *male* is primarily a technical word, with *gentleman* and *man* reserved for more personal contexts.

Gentleman was once limited to referring to a *man* born into the aristocracy or into a family of high social standing. More broadly, *gentleman* means a *man* of refinement who subscribes to a certain standard of conduct: "Despite the emphasis on equality of the sexes, he still considered himself a *gentleman* and always rose when a woman entered the room." In addition, there is the all-encompassing "ladies and *gentlemen*" to refer to everyone in the room.

Man is the word used in most cases to refer to an adult human *male*. This usage is not questionable, but the generic *man* is.

The generic *man* is the use of the word *man* to refer to both men and women. This broad meaning is recognized by dictionaries, which allow *man* to stand for the human race, all of mankind, or any human being.

Unfortunately, use of the generic *man* ignores the fact that women participate too. And as Rosalie Maggio says in summarizing research in her *Nonsexist Word Finder: A Dictionary of Gender-Free Usage,* "Both men and women reported that they usually pictured men when they read or heard the masculine 'generic.' "

Among replacements for the generic *man* are these choices: *person(s), people, human(s), human being(s), humankind, the public, citizen(s), worker(s).* Other options that have come into use are:

Generic man	Gender-free
man-made	synthetic, artificial
manpower	workforce
man-hours	working hours, staff hours
gentleman's agreement	informal agreement
chairman	chair, chairperson
businessman	executive, entrepreneur
foreman	supervisor
salesman	sales representative

The words *human* and *person* are not sexist, even though gender-specific syllables—*man* and *son*—appear in them. Throughout their history, *human* and *person* have been used as generic references to all people, men or women, and men and women. The same cannot be said for the gender-specific words *female, male, man,* and *woman.*

SEE ALSO   **female, lady, woman.**

German measles, measles, rubella.   *German measles* and *rubella* are contagious diseases with rashes of short durations. The signs and symptoms or *rubella* resemble those of *measles* but are milder except for the harm that *rubella* can do to a fetus in the early months of pregnancy. *Rubella* is also known as three-day *measles*.

Measles is a highly communicable disease that is characterized by a fever, symptoms resembling a cold, and a rash. The complications of *measles* can be severe and can include pneumonia and permanent damage to the central nervous system. *Measles* is also known as *rubeola*.

gesticulate, gesture.   *Gesticulate* refers to the act of making *gestures*, especially with the hands or arms when speaking. *Gesture* is the motion itself.

In some cases, the two can be used interchangeably: "She ranted and raved during her fiery speech, *gesticulating* (*gesturing*) wildly with her hands and arms."

Gesture, however, is the better word when the motion is not overly involved: "He shrugged his shoulders in a *gesture* of despair." "She *gestured* to the waiter for the check." *Gesture* is also used in the figurative sense: "a gift given as a *gesture* of friendship"; "a *gesture* of peace."

ghost, phantom, specter.   For people who like to write or read spooky stories, creatures that go bump in the night can be one of these:

A *ghost* is the disembodied spirit or soul of a dead person, sometimes said to appear as a pale, shadowy apparition in the haunting of houses or cemeteries.

A *phantom* is something seen, heard, or sensed in some way but having no substance or physical existence. A *phantom* can be a *ghost*, an optical illusion, or a figment of the imagination.

A *specter* can be a *ghost* or a *phantom*, especially one that is horrid and inspires fear, dread, or terror.

gibe, jibe.   To *gibe* it to jeer at, taunt, or ridicule: "Their cruel *gibes* hurt him visibly." "The other players *gibed* him for his repeated errors."

To *jibe* is to match, agree with, or be in accord: "The witnesses' accounts *jibed* with each other." "Ellen's boyfriend did not *jibe* with her mother's expectations of what her young man should be like."

glance, glimpse.   A *glance* is a brief, quick look. A *glimpse* is a brief, incomplete view of whatever is seen by a *glance:* "He was an incurable girl-watcher, and his numerous *glances* provided him with more than an occasional *glimpse* of a well-turned leg."

glare, glower.   To *glare* is to present a fierce, angry stare, the basic dirty look: "She *glared* at him for beating her to the parking place."

Closely related is the *glower;* to *glower* is to show anger and annoyance, often with a sullen and brooding expression: "He *glowered,* making it apparent that his pride had been grievously hurt."

SEE ALSO **frown, scowl.**

gleam, glimmer.   *Gleam* implies a fleeting flash of light or view of something as seen through another medium or a background of darkness: "The white sand of the beach *gleamed* at them through the swirling fog." "Streetlights *gleamed* in the night." "He stood on the bank, studying the silvery *gleam* of trout in the brook."

Glimmer implies a feeble or flickering light or reflection: "He saw the first *glimmer* of dawn in the east." "Her satiny gown *glimmered* as she moved across the floor."

A *gleam* is stronger than a *glimmer,* and both can be used figuratively. Thus "a *gleam* of hope" is more powerful, if not by much, than "a *glimmer.*" And a person who possesses "a *gleam* of intelligence" is smarter than one who possesses "a *glimmer* of intelligence," although that's not saying very much for either one.

glider, sailplane.   A *glider* is an airplane having no engine and designed to glide. A *sailplane* is a *glider* designed for soaring. Soaring is the maintaining of flight by seeking rising warm air currents or updrafts near mountains.

gloss, luster, sheen.   *Gloss* refers to a superficial, glowing shininess: "The groom took pains to brush the horse's coat to a rich *gloss.*"

Luster (or *lustre*) refers to the glow of reflected light: "The dining-room table was polished to a high *luster.*"

Sheen is a broad word that implies beautiful, bright, glittering, radiant, resplendent, or splendid.

good, well. The expression "I feel *good*" is correct if you are describing your health. Also correct are expressions like "The food tastes *good*"; "The bread smells *good*"; "You look *good* today"; and "The music sounds *good*."

They are correct because words such as *feel, taste, smell, look,* and *sound* are linking verbs. A linking verb functions chiefly as a connection between the subject and the predicate of a sentence; it does not fit the ordinary definition of a verb as a word that specifies action. In these cases, each linking verb is followed by an adjective that describes a condition—*good* health, *good* food, and so on. An adverb would be out of place.

However, if you use a verb in its sense of specifying action, the rule changes. Then you have to use an adverb, in this case, *well.* Therefore, in the rare instance when you want to describe your sense of touch, you'd say "I feel *well*." Other correct uses of *well* include "She dances *well*" and "My car runs *well*."

SEE ALSO **bad, badly.**

gorilla, guerrilla (guerilla). A *gorilla* is a large ape. A *guerrilla* (or *guerilla;* both spellings are allowed) is a warrior—a member of an independent and perhaps loosely organized force that carries out raids and often functions behind enemy lines.

gourmand, gourmet. A *gourmand* is a person who eats well and heartily. A *gourmet* is an epicure, a connoisseur of food and drink, and not necessarily a greedy, ravenous eater.

graceful, gracious. *Graceful* refers to the displaying of grace in movement, form, composition, or expression: "The stairway ended in a *graceful* curve at the landing." "Her dancing was marked by a *graceful* and delicate style."

Gracious refers to the showing of charm, courtesy, or kindness: "A *gracious* host, he made certain that all his guests were properly introduced." "She thanked him with a *gracious* letter that encouraged him to write to her again."

graduate, martriculate. People *graduate*—successfully complete a course of study—from college, high school, junior high school, or elementary school. Even kindergartens and preschools hold *graduation* ceremonies for those who are moving onward and upward.

Getting into school is something else. Unless you are going to a college or a university, you simply enroll or enter the school. But at a college or university, you don't enroll, you *matriculate.*

Anyway, the short answer is that *graduate* means to receive a diploma; *matriculate* means to be admitted.

graduate, postgraduate, undergraduate. These three words refer to college or university students. Lowest in order of rank is the *undergraduate,* the student who has not yet received a bachelor's degree. In the middle is the *graduate* student, the person who has received a bachelor's degree and is studying for an advanced degree. A *postgraduate* student can also be one who is working for an advanced degree. In some cases, the term *postgraduate* refers to a person who has received the highest degree that the school awards but has not yet been weaned from academe and is still on the campus participating in studies beyond degree requirements.

grapple, grope. To *grapple* is to struggle with the hands, as in wrestling or hand-to-hand combat: "They *grappled* for a few minutes before commencing wrestling in earnest." *Grapple* can also refer to any form of struggle: "*grapple* with a problem"; "*grapple* with the tribulations of being a teenager"; "*grapple* with proposals to provide food to starving people in the Third World."

To *grope* means to reach about blindly or uncertainly: "He *groped* for the light switch in the dark." "She *groped* for his arm as they walked into the darkness of the cave."

grave, tomb. These hold corpses. A *grave* is a hole in the earth, while a *tomb* can be a *grave,* a crypt, or a vault partly in the earth or entirely above the ground.

SEE ALSO **crypt, vault.**

gravitation, gravity. *Gravitation,* one of the fundamental forces of nature, is the force of attraction between all matter. The *gravitational* attraction of the sun keeps planets in their orbits, and *gravitation* holds the universe together.

Gravity is much more broadly defined. "The force of *gravity*" refers to *gravitation*. Otherwise, the word *gravity* refers to the state of being grave or serious: "The judge informed the defendant of the *gravity* of the charges." "As a scholar, he gave the impression of being a man of *gravity* and learning."

SEE ALSO   **levitation, levity.**

Gregorian Calendar, Julian Calendar.   Today we use the *Gregorian Calendar,* which is a modification of the *Julian Calendar.*

The *Julian Calender* was an attempt to straighten out problems with the calendar used by the Romans. In particular, the length of a year had become a rather slippery item. It was, and still is, difficult to reconcile lunar and solar cycles so that every year is the same length; in this day and age, we take care of that problem by adding an extra day every fourth year.

That was a solution that the Romans hadn't arrived at, and years were of varying lengths. Worse, the length of a year could be fixed by ruling politicians. As a consequence, a year was at times shortened to reduce the length of an official's term. By the time Julius Caesar came to power, the calendar was so abused that January was falling in autumn.

To put an end to the confusion, Caesar decreed a calendar with a year of 365 days and six hours. That length of year, as established by the *Julian Calendar,* is a little too long. Therefore, by the sixteenth century, the first day of spring was March 11, not March 21.

In the 1580's, Pope Gregory XIII rectified the error by decreeing the calendar that came to be named after him. Roman Catholic countries quickly accepted the new calendar, but England and the English colonies in America delayed changing their calendars for almost two centuries. Therefore, by 1752 the English calendar was eleven days off from the calendar being used on the continent. In that year, England and the Colonies adopted the *Gregorian Calendar,* which has now become the standard for reckoning the passage of years throughout the world.

grieve, mourn. *Grieve* refers to feelings of deep sorrow or mental suffering that is related to loss or distress: "They *grieved* over their mother's death." "Trifles are not worth *grieving* over." "He devoted himself to his work, for he did not want to *grieve* over his misfortunes."

Mourn implies a demonstration of grief. In other words, some people keep their grief to themselves over the death of a loved one, but the *mourner* is the one who wears black.

In addition, the word *grieve* applies to any misfortune, but *mourn* particularly pertains to feelings of sorrow over death.

grill, grille. A *grill* is a cooking grate or surface. A *grille* is any metal grating meant to serve as a barrier or for decorative purposes.

grisly, grizzly. *Grisly* means gruesome, horrifying, repugnant, or terrible: "In a brutal and *grisly* attack, he hacked her body to pieces."

Grizzly is the bear, and a word meaning grayish or flecked with gray, also often seen as *grizzled:* "Whenever he took off his beret, his *grizzled* hair gave away his age."

guarantee, guarantor, guaranty, warranty. In law there exists a three-party contract known as a *guaranty*. The first party, the *guarantor,* agrees to see that the performance of a second party, the *guarantee,* is fulfilled according to the terms of the contract. If the *guarantee* does not meet obligations made under the contract, the *guarantor* becomes responsible for the obligations; these obligations could include being responsible for the *guarantee's* debts. The third party, the creditor, is the one who will benefit from performance of the contract.

Another form of *guarantee* is a written statement that an item is as represented or that it will perform as advertised for a stated period. Some *guarantees* promise return of all or part of the purchaser's money if the item fails to meet the terms of the *guarantee*. This form of *guarantee* is also known as a *warranty*.

H

hail, hale. *Hail* is a greeting, salute, or shout: "To welcome the president, the Marine Corps Band played 'Hail to the Chief.' " "Let's *hail* a cab." "His people *hailed* him as a hero."

Hale, under one definition, refers to good health, as in "*hale* and hearty"; "a *hale* body and a clear mind."

Hale also means to haul, pull, draw, or compel in some manner: "The embezzler was *haled* into court." *Haul* is probably more commonly seen in this context.

Centuries ago there came into being the greeting "*Hail* fellow well met." The expression still shows up occasionally in print, sometimes as "*Hale* fellow well met." However, the spelling "*Hail* fellow well met" is shown in all the dictionaries used as references for this book, and that spelling should be regarded as the standard.

hail, sleet. *Hail* consists of balls of ice, and *sleet* consists of frozen or partially frozen pellets of rain. *Hail* is often associated with thunderstorms and can occur at any time of the year; *sleet* is primarily a wintertime phenomenon.

half-mast, half-staff. These are not confusing. A *mast* can be any pole, whether on land or sea. Consequently, a flag can be flown at *half-mast* or *half-staff*.

harbinger, herald. A *harbinger* can be a person or thing that comes before, an omen or sign to foreshadow what is yet to occur: "Frightened, wounded soldiers fleeing the battle were *harbingers* of a major defeat." "The first robin is a *harbinger* of spring."

A *harbinger* can also be a trailblazer, one who causes

or pioneers a major change: "The 'Brain Trust' was a *harbinger* of Roosevelt's New Deal." "Jesuits were *harbingers* of Catholicism in the Pacific Northwest."

A *herald* is a person or thing that announces what is to come: "*Heralds*, blowing on trumpets, warned of the approach of the king." Or as a verb: "The rooster *heralds* the dawn."

harbor, port.   A *harbor* is a sheltered body of water where ships can anchor. A *port* is a city with a *harbor*. "The *port* of Rio de Janeiro has a natural *harbor*."

hare, rabbit.   *Hares* have longer hind legs and longer ears than *rabbits*, and move more by hopping rather than running as *rabbits* do.

hay, straw.   *Hay* is food for cattle and horses. *Hay* is made up of dried grasses, alfalfa, barley, or oats.

Straw is used for bedding for animals and in hats, baskets, and other products. *Straw* consists of the dried stems of threshed grain.

he, she, her, him, I, me, them, they, us, we, you.   What's confusing about these pronouns is whether to use them as subjects or objects in statements. The rules are:

*   *He, she, I, they,* and *we* specify the subject of a statement, the doer of the action in that statement. In grammatical jargon, we are talking about the subjective (or nominative) case.
*   *Her, him, me, them,* and *us* specify the object in a statement. In grammatical jargon, we are talking about the objective case.
*   *You* is used for subject or object.

1. Pronoun in a simple subject. A simple subject contains one noun or pronoun. The pronoun is written in the subjective case:

I am Tarzan.
You are Jane.
He is Boy.
We live in the jungle.

This rule is pretty simple, and anything's better than Tarzan's greatest line, "Me Tarzan. You Jane."

2. Pronoun in a compound subject. A compound subject contains two or more nouns or pronouns. The pronouns are written in the subjective case:

He and *I* were late for work.
We and *they* were on time.

3. Pronoun to restate all or part of a subject. The subjective case is used to restate all or part of the subject:

Jones appears to be *he* who robbed the bank.
Many of those present, at least *we* in the bleachers, felt that the game was lopsided.

Of course, one of the best rules to follow is that if something sounds stilted or awkward, rewrite the sentence. For instance, if you don't like the sound of "Jones appears to be *he* who robbed the bank," other options exist: "Jones appears to the be man who robbed the bank" or "Jones appears to be the one who robbed the bank."

4. Choice of pronouns when the subject is incomplete. We often construct sentences that contain incomplete statements. In each of the following examples, the incomplete statement takes the subjective case; if the statement were completed, it would be written as shown in the parentheses:

She is prettier than *I* (*I* am).
He is a better dancer than *she* (*she* is). (We wouldn't say "*her* is a dancer.")

5. Pronoun with the verb *to be*. The verb *to be* exists in forms such as *am, be, is, was, are,* and *were.* When any form of the verb *to be* is used, the same pronoun case is used before and after the verb.

This next set of examples shows the use of the subjective case with the verb *to be*:

If *we* were *they, we* would have bought that house.
If *you* were *she,* would *you* go and live with Tarzan?
It is *he* who swings from the trees in the jungle. (*It* is a pronoun that can be used in the subjective or objective case.)

This same rule applies when pronouns are in the objective case. That is, the same pronoun case is used before and after any form of the verb *to be*:

> The leader took *him* to be *me*. Not "*he* to be *I* ."

But what about "*It* is *I*"? Or "*It* is *me*"? Which is correct?

In this case (no pun intended), your interpretation of the doctrine of grammatical correctness depends upon how formal you want your writing or speech to be. The grammatically correct form is "*It* is *I*," for the subjective case is used on both sides of the verb *to be*. However, many people don't like the sound of that and instead use "*It's me*."

Grammar books have come to recognize "*It's me*" as the standard in informal usage, but many people still expect to see "*It is I*" in formal contexts.

In all, some solace might be found in this little quotation from Harry R. Warfel's *Who Killed Grammar*?

> A candidate for Heaven rapped on the Pearly Gates.
> "Who is there?" asked St. Peter.
> "It is I," replied the candidate.
> "You go to Hell; you're a teacher of English."

6. Pronoun in a simple object. A simple object contains one noun or pronoun. The pronoun is written in the objective case:

> Margaret trusted *him*.
> Margaret trusted *us*.

7. Pronoun in a compound object. A compound object contans two or more nouns or pronouns. The pronouns are written in the objective case:

> Margaret trusted *him* and *her*.
> The store fired *them* and *us*.

8. Pronoun in an object with a clause or phrase attached. A pronoun in the objective case is used when the object begins a clause or phrase:

> Bill and Tom join *me* in wishing all employees a merry Christmas.
> I avoid *her* whenever I can.
> The boss invited *you* and *me* to the meeting.

9. Pronoun to restate all or part of the object. To restate all or part of the object, use a pronoun in the objective case:

The boss blamed *us*, both my partner and *me*.
The boss asked *us*—Jones, Smith, Rogers, and *me*—to be at the meeting.

10. Pronoun following an infinitive. An infinitive is a verb that begins with *to* (*to invite, to follow, to run*). The objective case is used after the infinitive:

The manager said to invite *you* and *him* to the meeting.
The new employee wanted us to meet *him* at the station.

However, a possessive pronoun that looks like a subjective pronoun is used after the infinitive:

He invited my wife but failed to invite *his*.

11. Pronoun following a preposition. Prepositions are words such as *to, into, through,* and *on*. The objective case is used after a preposition:

The success of this mission depends on *us*.
The governor wrote a nice letter to *him*.
The governor wrote a nice letter to *him* and *me*.
Everyone left except *me*.

SEE ALSO **its, it's; myself (and other compound pronouns); that, which, who; who, whom, whoever, whomever; you're, your(s).**

healthful, healthy. *Healthful* means helping to produce or maintain good health: "She considered jogging two miles every morning to be a *healthful* exercise." "The elderly couple attributed their longevity to the *healthful* climate."

Healthy means possessing good health: "She was *healthy* because of her diet and because of her two-mile jog every morning." "The elderly couple was *healthy* because of the climate in which they lived."

SEE ALSO **salubrious, salutary.**

hear, listen. *Hear* is the passive condition; *listen* is the active. That is, *hear* means to receive sounds through the ears, while *listen* means to pay attention, to make a conscious effort to hear: "As more than one parent will testify, children *hear* quite well, but they don't always *listen*."

heart attack, heart failure. A *heart attack* is caused by a blockage of the heart's arteries. The blockage produces heavy pressure or a squeezing pain in the chest. The pain may radiate to the shoulders, neck, jaw, teeth, back, and the fourth and fifth fingers of the left hand. Nausea, sweating, vomiting, or shortness of breath may accompany the pain. All of these symptoms may come and go, but one occurrence is enough warning to go and see a doctor without delay.

Heart failure is not as final as it sounds. In the jargon of the medical profession, *heart failure* refers to total or partial cessation of work by the heart muscle. When the heart stops beating altogether, the condition is known as cardiac arrest.

SEE ALSO **arteriosclerosis, atherosclerosis.**

heath, moor. *Heath*, or *heather*, is an evergreen shrub that grows on *moors* in Great Britain. A *moor* is an extensive area of open land that is usually covered with *heath*, coarse grass, sand, rocks, and moss.

Heath and *moor* have both come to stand for the piece of land. *Moor* is not used to refer to the shrub.

heathen, pagan. Both of these can apply to a person who has no religion. *Heathen* implies that the person is ignorant or unenlightened. *Pagan* implies that the person uninhibitedly seeks and enjoys sensual pleasures and material goods.

Hebrew, Israeli, Israelite, Jew, Yiddish. *Hebrew* refers to any of a group of peoples descending from Abraham (Abram), referred to in Genesis as "Abram the Hebrew." Abraham's grandson Jacob—who was also called Israel—was the father of twelve sons who became leaders of the Twelve Tribes of Israel.

Therefore, the terms *Hebrew* and *Israelite* have become somewhat synonymous when referring to the same group of people. Historical usage favors *Israelite*; modern usage favors *Hebrew* to avoid the religious and other associations sometimes attached to *Jew*. Neither *Hebrew* nor *Israelite* specifies a nation or a religion. *Hebrew* people live in Israel and other nations, and the religion of most *Hebrews* is Judaism.

Hebrew is also the name of one of the world's oldest living languages, dating back to at least 2000 B.C. Most of the Old Testament was written in *Hebrew*, and *Hebrew* is the official language of Israel today.

Israeli refers to anything or anyone from the modern state of Israel: "an *Israeli* newspaper"; "an *Israeli* diplomat."

Jews are members of a group held together for more than 3,000 years by a common history and a common belief in Judaism, the religion named after Judah, the fourth son of Jacob.

Yiddish is a language used by *Jews* in many parts of the world. *Yiddish* is about 1,000 years old and contains words from *Hebrew*, German and other languages.

SEE ALSO **Arab, Arabian, Arabic, Saudi, Saudi Arabian; Israel, Palestine.**

heir apparent, heir presumptive. The *heir (heiress) apparent* will inherit if he (or she) survives the death of the ancestor. In the English royal family, the eldest son is the *heir apparent*.

The *heir (heiress) presumptive* will inherit unless a nearer relative is born as *heir apparent*. That is, a niece could be *heiress presumptive* to the throne, but could be displaced from the succession by the birth of a son, males usually taking precedence over females in the line of succession.

These matters pertain not only to royal families but also to state laws that control the inheritance of property, and to any type of ladder-climbing: "Feathersmith is the *heir apparent* to the vice president's position." "At one time, England was the *heir presumptive* in the power struggles in Europe."

SEE ALSO **presumptive, presumptuous.**

helpmate, helpmeet. A *helpmate* is a helpful companion, usually a wife or a husband: "Benjamin Franklin wrote that his wife was a good and faithful *helpmate* for assisting him in attending his shop."

Helpmeet may be used, but it is based on an erroneous reading of Genesis 2:18. "I will make an help meet for him." Here *meet*, in one of its older usages, means suitable, and the Bible verse could be restated "I will make a helper suitable for him."

herb, spice.   An *herb* is a plant that does not develop persistent woody tissue as do shrubs and trees, and that dies down at the end of the growing season. A *spice* is an aromatic and pungent condiment made from vegetables.

Although modern usage implies that *herbs* and *spices* are used solely in food preparation, both are also used for medicinal purposes and in the making of perfume.

heritage, inheritance.   *Heritage* can refer to real property and physical assets, but it is frequently used in references to birthright and tradition: "He was well aware of his family's rich *heritage*, passed down through the generations, of taking care of their own regardless of the cost." "Orators boasted of the party's *heritage* of vision and boldness."

Inheritance refers to property which is to be inherited or was inherited: "Her *inheritance* included a brooch left to her by a favorite aunt." "They squabbled, bickered, and argued over a measly *inheritance* that included only a television set and some trashy old furniture—it wasn't worth it."

hernia, rupture.   A *rupture* is any tear or break: "A *rupture* in the levee caused serious flooding in the delta." "She tried hard to prevent their difficulties from leading to an open *rupture*." "A *rupture* of the heart muscle was listed as the cause of death."

In popular parlance, *rupture* means a *hernia* of the groin or testicles.

The term *hernia* is a precisely defined medical word that refers to the protrusion or projection of an organ through an abnormal opening in the wall of the cavity that contans the organ. One of the most common *hernias* is an inguinal *hernia*, which is a bulge in the groin. Some infants suffer from umbilical *hernias*. A umbilical *hernia* is a soft bulge of tissue around the navel of a newborn baby; it occurs when the abdominal wall is not fully developed.

high, highly; low, lowly.   *High* applies to that which is measurable: "The flag was placed on a pole *high* above the ground." "The airplane flew *high* in the sky."

Highly applies to that which is not measurable: "Zacado was *highly* prominent in the world of modern art."

Low and *lowly* are used in the same manner.

hill, mountain.   A *hill* is a well-defined, rounded, and elevated area that is smaller than a *mountain*. A *mountain* is higher than a *hill* and with steeper slopes.

These definitions are relative, and no precise difference exists. To someone from the Himalayas, the Ozark Mountains probably appear to be no more than a range of *hills*.

hippopotamus, rhinoceros.   A *rhinoceros* has a horn on its nose; a *hippopotamus* doesn't. On closer inspection, if you dare to get closer, a *rhino* has a thick skin resembling a coat of armor; a *hippo's* skin is smoother and resembles that of a hog, to which the *hippo* is related.

Both spend quite a bit of time in the water. *Hippos* come from Africa, while *rhinos* come from Africa and southeast Asia. Zoos are convenient places for observing either.

historic, historical.   *Historic* means famous or important in history: "The French Revolution was a *historic* event."

Historical means concerned with history or relating to it: "Scholars are concerned with the *historical* method of study when investigating events of the past."

This distinction exists between a *historic* novel and a *historical* novel: A *historic* novel is a book that makes history; a *historical* novel is a book with a plot based on history.

histrionics, hysterics.   The word *histrionics* pertains to acting or overacting, not always on the stage: "Her fits and tantrums were *histrionics* meant to draw attention to herself."

Hysterics are the signs of hysteria, which could be wild and emotionally uncontrolled behavior, or a psychiatric disorder.

hoard, horde.   A *hoard* is a supply, cache, treasure, or reserve that is kept stored away: "Baron Rothschild never admitted to keeping a *hoard* of bullion in an underground vault." "The elderly couple had spent their life *hoarding* money, and had never had any fun."

A *horde* is a swarm, crowd, or group: "The angry crowd turned into a *horde* of ruffians who charged the palace."

hobby, pastime.   A *hobby* is a specialized activity that is outside of a person's occupation and that is especially interesting to the person: "Stamp collecting is seen by many as a relaxing *hobby*." "The executive's only *hobby* was raising orchids."

A *pastime* is any pleasant means of passing time. A *pastime* can be a *hobby*, sport, game, or any recreational activity: "In the small towns of the Midwest, a favorite *pastime* was sitting on the front porch and talking to passersby." "To workaholics, work is a *pastime*."

SEE ALSO **avocation, vocation.**

hog, pig.   A *hog* is an adult *pig* that weighs at least 120 pounds.

home, house   A common distinction is that the word *home* implies a sentimental value—"*Home* is where the heart is"—while the word *house* simply refers to the structure.

That distinction doesn't always hold up. For instance, people do get *homesick* and long to be back at the family hearth, but would *housesick* refer to a bad case of cabin fever?

Simon and Garfunkel sang of "Homeward Bound," which is certainly more euphonious than "Houseward Bound." *Homework* isn't much fun, but, then again, neither is *housework*. You *housebreak* a puppy, but who or what do you *homebreak*? A *homecoming* is a warm welcome, but would a *housecoming* be a cottage moving up the street? And what of the *homebody*? Is a *housebody* a corpse assigned to be a permanent fixture in the place—the embalmed remains of Uncle Albert propped up on the living room couch as a form of macabre decor?

homicide, manslaughter, murder. These are primarily legal terms that are used with the following meanings: *Homicide* is the killing of another person; *manslaughter* is *homicide* without malice or premeditation; *murder* is *homicide* that is malicious and premeditated.

To be correct in the eyes of the law, a person should not be described as having committed *murder* or *manslaughter* until convicted of the charge.

homogeneous, homogenous. Both of these mean that something is similar to another thing in structure or quality. The difference is that *homogeneous* is the broader of the two terms in that it refers to similarity without cause, but *homogenous* is a more precise word that means similar because of descent from a common source. Therefore, *homogeneous* cells are similar to each other regardless of their sources, but *homogenous* cells are similar cells that come from a common organism.

homogenized, pasteurized. In *homogenized* milk the fat in milk is no longer separate but is part of the milk itself. *Pasteurized* milk has been subjected to a process that destroys disease-producing bacteria.

homograph, homonym, homophone. The difference between *homograph* and *homophone* is easy to keep track of if you'll remember that *graph* refers to what is written, and *phone* refers to what is heard.

That is, a *homograph* is a word that is written the same as another word but has a different meaning and sometimes a different pronunciation: *bow* (the front of a ship); *bow* (to bend from the waist); and *bow* (knot, as the knot in a ribbon).

A *homophone* is a word that sounds like another word but differs in spelling, meaning, or both: *Awl, all; right, rite, wright, write; too, two.*

The word *homonym* can mean either *homograph* or *homophone.*

homosexual, lesbian. *Homosexual* means one who relates sexually to the same sex, and *lesbian* means female
homosexual.

Confusion arises with these usages because the prefix
homo mistakenly is assumed to mean man, as it does
in *Homo sapiens*. In *homosexual* it means the same or
similar, as in *homogeneous* and *homonym*.

honorable, honorary. *Honorable* refers to a person who
deserves to be honored: "Supreme Court Justices are
honorable people because of their calling."

Honorary refers to something given as an honor only;
the person honored does not have to meet the usual
prerequisites and does not gain the usual rights and privileges: "Ah, 'tis spring again, the time when colleges give
honorary degrees to people who couldn't earn them the
regular way."

hoodoo, voodoo. *Hoodoo* and *voodoo* are different
names for a religion that originated among blacks in
Africa.

horrible, horrific. *Horrible* refers to that which directly
arouses dread or fear in the beholder: "To explorers, the
scattered skulls were *horrible* reminders that headhunters
had been in the area." "Hurricane Charles was a *horrible*
storm."

Horrific refers to a horror that is somewhat removed
from the observer. "Newspapers showed *horrific* pictures
of the bloodied bodies of students slaughtered during the
uprising in China." However, if you were on the scene,
the presence of the bloodied bodies would have been "a
horrible sight."

how ever, however. The two-word expression *how ever*
is an emphatic way of saying *how*: "*How ever* did you
manage that trick?" "*How ever* did Smith get that
promotion?"

As one word, *however* can mean *nevertheless* or *but*:
"*However*, conditions might improve by tomorrow." "I
would rather stay home; *however*, I find myself com-
pelled to go."

However can also mean in whatever way, degree, or

extent: "I will get there *however* I can." "*However* much money I give to you, you always want more." "Every trick, *however* small, was resorted to."

hull, keel. If you could turn a ship upside down and think of it as an animal, the *keel* is the backbone, and the *hull* is the body or trunk. In terms that are more nautical, the *hull* is the main part of the ship exclusive of masts, rigging, spars, and sails; the *keel* is the principal timber or piece of steel extending the length of the bottom of the ship.

humanist, humanitarian. A *humanist* is a person who enjoys studying or contemplating the humanities—history, language, literature, and philosophy.

A *humanitarian* is actively concerned with the state of humanity and the betterment of social reform and human welfare.

humiliation, mortification, shame. *Shame* is a good starting point here, for the word is basic to an understanding of the three.

Shame is a painful emotion or feeling based on the belief that a person has lost the respect of others because of improper behavior: "His dishonest acts put him to *shame*." "He suffered the *shame* of running from the battle." "His only feelings when reacting to criticism were feelings of *shame*."

Humiliation is the feeling of painful *shame*, often in public: "She experienced extreme *humiliation* when reprimanded in front of her classmates."

Mortification, in one sense, refers to a painful denial of bodily pleasures: "He fasted every Friday as an act of *mortification*."

In another sense, *mortification* refers to feelings of wounded pride or a loss of self-esteem; in this sense, *mortification* is almost synonymous with *shame*: "He suffered the *mortification* (*shame* would work just as well) of being stood up by his own wife." "The admiral's *mortification* (or *shame*) was unendurable as he watched his fleet sunk by the Spaniards."

If any difference exists, it exists in the minds of readers and listeners who will link *mortification* with its root words, which mean to kill. To these people, *mortification* alludes to the death of a person's self-respect, a condition that is far more serious than *shame*.

humor, wit.   *Humor* refers to anything that is amusing, comical, or funny. *Wit* refers to remarks that are clever or intellectual, often spontaneous, sometimes funny, and frequently cutting or sarcastic.

Any attempt to define either of these will be about as successful as saying that beauty is in the eyes of the beholder. For instance, here is an oft-quoted exchange between Lady Nancy Astor and Sir Winston Spencer Churchill:

Astor: Winston, if I were your wife, I'd put poison in your coffee.
Churchill: If I were your husband, Nancy, I'd take it.

Humor? Wit? Probably both, except perhaps in the mind of Lady Astor.

SEE ALSO **jape, jest, joke.**

Hun, Vandal.   The *Huns* were a warlike Asiatic people who invaded eastern and central Europe in the fourth and fifth centuries. The *Vandals* were a group of East Germanic people who ravaged Gaul, Spain, North Africa, and Rome in the fifth century.

hurricane, typhoon.   Both of these are cyclones that occur in the tropics. The word *typhoon* applies to storms occurring in an area near the Philippines or in the China Sea. *Hurricanes* occur in the Atlantic Ocean, the Gulf of Mexico, and the eastern part of the Pacific Ocean.

SEE ALSO **gale, storm.**

hyper-, hypo-.   The prefix *hyper-* refers to whatever is above normal or excessive; *hypo-* refers to whatever is below normal. A person with *hyperglycemia* has an abnormally high concentration of sugar in the blood, while a person with *hypoglycemia* has an abnormally low concentration of sugar.

This distinction applies only in part to *hypercritical* and *hypocritical.* A *hypercritical* person is one who is overly critical, but a *hypocritical* person is one who pretends to be who he or she is not.

hypothesis, theory.   *Hypothesis* implies that little evidence exists in support of a belief or principle; *theory* implies that considerable evidence exists.

I

icecap, ice pack. Under the heading of personal care, especially on the morning after, an *icecap* is a bag of ice shaped to fit the head. Still under the heading of personal care, an *ice pack* is a container of ice placed on a swollen body part.

On a much larger scale, an *icecap* (or *ice sheet*) is a vast field of glacial ice and snow that slopes outward and downward from a high central point: "Antarctica is covered by an *icecap* thousands of feet thick." "Except for its coastal areas, all of Greenland is covered by an *icecap*."

An *icecap* of glacial ice is not to be confused with an *ice pack*. An *ice pack* is a large, floating mass of ice floes or masses of ice: "Polar ice at the North Pole makes up the world's largest *ice pack*."

ideal, idyllic. The word *ideal* implies perfection, beauty, excellence, or the highest possible standard: "She was an *ideal* picture of charm and grace." "He saw Jefferson as the *ideal* statesman."

Idyllic refers to a scene of simple, rural, pastoral life: "He liked to relax on the bluff overlooking the Hudson, for the *idyllic* view was the perfect place to enjoy a few moments of respite after a frantic day in the city."

idiot, imbecile, moron. The terms *idiot*, *imbecile*, and *moron* are insults with the same meaning—a stupid, foolish person. At one time, the terms designated IQ (intelligence quotient) ranges for mentally deficient people: *moron*, 50-69; *imbecile*, 20-49; and *idiot*, below 20. Those designations are now obsolete.

Instead, *mental retardation* has become an umbrella

term under which four degrees of intellectual impairment are listed: mild, moderate, severe, and profound. As determined by IQ test scores, the degrees of severity are: mild, 50-55 to approximately 70; moderate, 35-40 to 50-55; severe, 20-25 to 35-40; profound, below 20 or 25.

These rankings are based solely on IQ test scores and do not take into account emotional, motivational, or social factors, all of which play a part in an individual's development.

idle, indolent. *Idle* means not in use, and can refer to people or machines: "The closing of the factories left thousands of workers *idle*." "The *idle* assembly line was a silent reminder of the fading power of industry."

Indolent means lazy: "Always energetic in her youth, she had grown fat and *indolent* with age."

if, whether. In many case, *if* and *whether* may be used interchangeably: "I haven't decided *if (whether)* I'll stay home." This usage has been standard for a long time.

However, *whether* (usually with *or*) should be used when expressing alternatives, and *if* when expressing conditions:

Alternatives: "He did not know *whether* to go or stay."
Conditions: "*If* the day is nice, we'll have a picnic."
SEE ALSO **provided, providing.**

illegal, illegitimate, illicit. These three terms are generally synonymous and refer to whatever is against the law, except that *illegitimate* is often used to describe a child born out of wedlock. From a moral standpoint, that last point isn't always important to some people. From a legal standpoint, especially when a large inheritance is involved, the question of *illegitimate* birth may be important.

illume, illuminate, illumine. *Illuminate* is the present way of saying "to shed light on" or "to give light to." *Illume* and *illumine* are poetic or outdated words with the same meaning as *illuminate*.

imaginary, imaginative. *Imaginary* means unreal or existing only in a person's imagination: "The drunkard's demons were *imaginary*, his only real foe being the devil in the bottle."

Imaginative refers to the use of imagination and creativity: "The artist's work was known for its *imaginative* use of color." "His *imaginative* manipulation of stock sales made the takeover a success."

immeasurable, immense. *Immeasurable* means that something cannot be measured: "Love is *immeasurable*, as are all abstract concepts."

Immense means that something is great or huge in amount, degree, size, scope, or significance. Unlike *immeasurable*, the word *immense* does not rule out the use of measurements: "The house was an *immense* one, with some 5,000 square feet of living space." "He is an *immense* man, weighing in at over 380 pounds."

SEE ALSO **eternity, infinity; innumerable, numerous.**

immerse, submerge. Both of these mean to place into the water so as to cover completely: "Submarines *submerge*, but Baptists *immerse*."

Otherwise, *immerse* means to become absorbed in, while *submerge* means to sink below a certain level: "Successful students *immerse* themselves in their studies." "The unfortunate are *submerged* in poverty."

immunity, impunity. *Immunity* refers to a whole string of freedoms, such as freedom from disease, obligations, duties, or hazards: "The metal had complete *immunity* to rust." "A balanced diet may be one step toward *immunity* from many diseases." "The court granted her *immunity* from prosecution."

Impunity refers to an exemption from punishment or penalty: "mere delay of punishment does not guarantee final *impunity*." "You can't kill someone and expect *impunity*."

impact. The problem with *impact* is that it has lost its *impact*. In the old days, *impact* was limited to meaning a blow or sharp contact. This meaning still exists, and so does a tendency on the part of some people—especially those who speak the wishy-washy subdialect of governmentese—to use *impact* to mean effect, or, as a verb, affect. Consequently, the word has become confusing and is often misused, just as *affect* and *effect* are.

The best way to prevent confusion over the meanings of *impact* is to use a substitute. *Collision, touch, bump, slam, press,* and *congest* will carry the thought of the original meaning. *Influence* and *consequence* easily replace the *affect* and *effect* meanings of *impact*.

SEE ALSO   **affect, effect.**

impair, impede.   *Impair* means to weaken, damage, or make worse or less; "Years of working around heavy equipment had *impaired* his hearing."

Impede means to obstruct, delay, or hinder the progress of: "Tight clothing *impedes* the circulation of blood."

SEE ALSO   **obstacle, obstruction.**

impeach.   *Impeach* does not mean to convict or to remove a government official from office. *Impeach* means to accuse or to bring charges against the official. The *impeached* official may continue to hold office until tried and found guilty of the charges. If the *impeached* official is found guilty, he or she is removed from office.

In the United States, a president can be *impeached* by Congress. The House brings charges, called articles of *impeachment*, against the president, and the trial is conducted by the Senate. Only one president, Andrew Johnson, has been *impeached*. He was acquitted, and remained in office until the end of his term. President Richard M. Nixon was threatened with *impeachment* but resigned before the House could vote on articles of *impeachment*.

Other federal officials can also be *impeached*, as can state government officials.

imperial, imperious.   *Imperial* pertains to kings, queens, emperors, empresses, and their empires: "The czar's view was not provincial but *imperial*."

Imperious means domineering and overbearing: "The sick woman's demanding and *imperious* manner drove her nurses wild."

impertinent, impudent, insolent.   These three terms apply to different degrees of rudeness.

Impertinent implies an overstepping of the bounds of

courtesy, propriety, or good breeding: "It's good manners on the part of children not to make *impertinent* remarks to their elders." *Impertinent* also refers to whatever is not relevant or not pertinent: "Her husband's excuses for tardiness were nothing more than *impertinent* arguments off the point."

Impudent implies boldness and a disregard for others: "He was an *impudent* young man given to insulting friends and strangers alike."

Insolent implies arrogant, defiant, or contemptuous behavior: "Because of his *insolent* and obscene gestures, he was thrown out of the lecture hall."

impetus, momentum. *Impetus* is a starting, impelling, or driving force: "The fear of parental punishment is often the *impetus* to do well in school."

Momentum is the property of a moving body to keep moving: "The racecar lost its power completely in the final yards, but its *momentum* carried it across the finish line."

impinge, infringe. *Impinge* means to hit, strike, or collide, whether in a literal or figurative sense: "Fine particles spin to the outside of the centrifuge, where they *impinge* upon the dust collector." "His liberal ideas *impinged* upon the Church's traditional ways and brought about his excommunication."

In one sense, *infringe* means to intrude or trespass, and is used with *on* or *upon*: "*infringe* on the privacy of others"; "*infringe* upon the civil rights of the individual." In another sense, *infringe* means to break or violate, as applied to an agreement or law: "*infringe* a contract"; "*infringe* a treaty."

imply, infer. These two words apply to the opposite ends of the same process. *Imply* refers to the sending end, *infer* to the receiving end. When you talk to someone, you may *imply* (suggest) a certain meaning, but that person may *infer* (derive) a different meaning. One device that may help in this instance is to remember that the last letter of *infer* is the same as the first letter of *receive*.

in, in to, into. You may tell someone to "Go jump *in* the lake" or "Go jump *into* the lake"; both forms may be used.

However, precisionists make a distinction between the two—*in* for position or location, and *into* for motion: "You are *in* a house because you went *into* it."

The two-word form *in to* is used in constructions such as "They dropped *in to* see us last night" and "We went *in to* dinner." An absurd usage is one that Roy Copperud shows in *American Usage and Style*: "A man wanted as an army deserter for fifteen years turned himself into the police last night." Should be *in to*; he certainly did not become a policeman.

inapt, inept, unapt. *Inapt* and *unapt* mean not apt, not suitable, or not appropriate: "Any comparison of water to electron flow is *inapt* because pipes spring leaks and wires do not."

Inept implies inadequate, incompetent, foolish, or clumsy behavior or speech: "Lorenzo's *inept* defense of the middleweight crown ended with his being knocked out in the third round." "Her sore toes were caused by her boyfriend's *inept* attempts at dancing."

incentive, motive. These two terms both mean a stimulus that prompts a person to act.

Incentive commonly applies to an external reward or punishment: "Promotion is a powerful *incentive* in the workplace." "Fear of heavy fines was the *incentive* for manufacturers to comply with regulations."

Motive commonly applies to an internal emotion or desire: "The *motive* for the crime was jealousy."

SEE ALSO **motif, motive.**

incidence, incidents. *Incident*, which stands for an event or an occurrence, appears in its plural form as *incidents*, a word that sounds a lot like *incidence*.

Incidence, however, refers not to the number of occurrences but to a range, degree, totality, or rate: "The country is experiencing a declining *incidence* of cancer."

Otherwise, an *incident* is one case of cancer; *incidents* are several or many cases.

SEE ALSO **accident, incident.**

incredible, incredulous. *Incredible* describes something unbelievable or seemingly not possible: "The federal budget increases by *incredible* amounts every year." "For a petite woman, she has an *incredible* appetite."

Incredulous describes a person who disbelieves or shows doubt: "She was stunned and *incredulous* when she heard of his demands for a divorce." "The *incredulous* look on his face gave away his distrust."

SEE ALSO **cynic, pessimist, skeptic.**

indict, indite. These words are alike in sound but not in meaning. *Indict* means to accuse of a crime; it usually refers to the action of a grand jury in finding a case against a person and in ordering that person to be brought to trial.

Indite is an old-fashioned way of saying *write* or *compose*.

indisposed, undisposed. *Indisposed* is a polite way of saying that someone is slightly ill: "Garanski's concert ended abruptly when the famed pianist became *indisposed* and had to leave the stage."

Indisposed can also mean that a person is unwilling: "The president was *indisposed* to send troops into the country."

Undisposed means that something is not settled, not sold, or not assigned: "Those goods remained *undisposed* of until just before closing time."

inequity, iniquity. *Inequity* refers to unfairness, inequality, or lack of justice: "Truman's speech dealt with the maladjustments and *inequities* of wages."

Iniquity refers to evil and wickedness: "The sermon's theme was that deeds of *iniquity* lead straight to damnation."

informant, informer. These are not confusing. Both can refer to the person who tells secrets or informs upon another person.

ingenious, ingenuous. *Ingenious* implies notable and brilliant cleverness, originality, or inventiveness: "The sewing machine is an example of an *ingenious* invention."

Ingenuous refers to someone who is childlike, naive,

candid, or frank: "he was so *ingenuous* and gullible that he fell for every swindler and con man who came to town."

inhuman, subhuman, unhuman. *Inhuman* describes someone who is cruel and who lacks the qualities associated with humans; an *inhuman* person is barbarous, brutal, unfeeling, or heartless. *Unhuman* is a rarely used word with the same meaning.

Subhuman means less than human or below the human race in development: "Explorers and colonizers in Africa treated the natives as *subhuman*." "No doubt exists that the intelligence of a dog is almost *subhuman*."

injure, wound. *Injure* refers to any harm or damage to appearance, comfort, health, feelings, or reputation: "He fell and *injured* his shoulder." "Slander *injured* her chances for success." "Increasing jealousy *injured* their relationship."

Wound implies physical *injury*, especially one in which the skin is broken by an outside agent such as a gun or knife: "The knife *wounded* him deeply, causing severe internal bleeding." "A gunshot *wound* to the head was the cause of death."

Wound can also imply a mental or emotional hurt: "*wounded* pride"; "*wounded* vanity."

innuendo, insinuation. *Innuendo* is an indirect and derogatory remark or expression: "His position was undermined by *innuendos*, anonymous accusations, and false rumors."

Insinuation refers to the process of gradual introduction: "Her *insinuation* into his favor took months." *Insinuation* also refers to the dropping of hints or suggestions to provoke doubt and suspicions about another: "Their *insinuations* about his personal life drove him to suicide."

innumerable, numerous. *Innumerable* means too many to count; *numerous* means many.

SEE ALSO **eternity, infinity; immeasurable, immense.**

inoculate, vaccinate. *Inoculate* is a broad term that refers to the introduction of microorganisms, serum, or other substances into living plants and animals. Some of what is introduced may be a *vaccine*. A *vaccine* consists of microorganisms used in the prevention or treatment of infectious diseases.

As far as the recipient is concerned, *inoculate* and *vaccinate* mean the same—a shot with a needle or high-speed jet, or a scarifying (scratching or cutting) of the skin.

insert, inset.   An *insert* is frequently thought of as printed material placed within other printed material: "The Sunday paper comes loaded with *inserts*."

An *inset* is something smaller placed within the border of something larger: "See the *inset* map for details of the downtown area."

insidious, invidious.   *Insidious* implies stealth: "He was the victim of an *insidious* plot." "He slowly wasted away, the victim of an *insidious* disease."

Invidious implies ill will and offensiveness: "The queen's *invidious* remarks drove her chambermaid to tears."

SEE ALSO   **denigrate, disparage.**

insipid, vapid.   *Insipid* pertains to anything that is dull of lifeless: "The retiree's farewell remarks were the least *insipid* of all the after-dinner speeches made that night."

Vapid pertains to something that has lost its freshness and sharpness: "Her poetry, lively in her youth, had become *vapid* as she grew older."

insoluble, unsolvable.   A crime or a mathematical problem that cannot be solved is either *insoluble* or *unsolvable*. Something that cannot be dissolved, in water for example, is only *insoluble*, not *unsolvable*.

instinct, intuition.   An *instinct* is an inborn, complex, and unlearned aspect of behavior: "An infant's first *instinct* is to suck." "Missionaries capitalized on the religious *instincts* of primitive peoples."

Intuition is knowing of something without the conscious, deliberate use of reasoning: "In the heat of battle, the hero relied on *intuition* rather than carefully thought-through actions."

instinctive, instinctual. These are not confusing, for both are adjectives that pertain to spontaneous and unlearned behavior: "She had an *instinctive* dread of mice." *Instinctive* is the more common of the two.

institute, institution. An *institute* can be a school or an organization that exists to promote some cause. "The *Institute* for Advanced Social Studies is supported by private funding." "Because his hearing was so severely impaired, he received most of his education at the state-operated *Institute* for the Deaf."

The word *institution* has broader meanings and can refer to any of the following:

An established custom, law, or system: "The family is a fundamental *institution* in any society."

A prominent organization, especially one with a public character: "The Smithsonian *Institution* is one of the must-see sights in Washington."

A well-established person: "Buckminster Fuller was an *institution* all by himself."

insufferable, intolerable, unbearable. These words refer to situations or persons that are not tolerable or not bearable: "*unbearable* pain"; "*intolerable* anguish"; "snobbish, *insufferable* social climbers at the party."

Dictionaries treat the three as synonyms, except that the unabridged *Webster III* says that the *insufferable* person is that way because of "pompous assurance or assumed superiority." By and large, however, the three may be used interchangeably.

intelligent, intelligible. *Intelligent* refers to a person's mental capacity, the ability to be alert, rational, perceptive, or informed: "He was so *intelligent* that the study of any new subject came easily to him."

Intelligible refers to whatever is clear and can be understood or comprehended: "For computer ads to be *intelligible* to the average person, the ads will have to be written in ordinary English and not jargon."

intense, intensive. *Intense* means high in degree, deeply felt, profound, violent, very strong, or extreme: "An *intense* light blinded him when he opened the door." "He is so *intense* about chess that he eats, sleeps, and breathes nothing else." "The experiment gave off *intense* amounts of radiation."

Intensive is occasionally used in those same senses, but perhaps with reference to a lesser degree of intensity. For instance, "an *intensive* training program" is one that is thorough but not as extreme as "an *intense* training program." Similarly, "an *intensive* course of study" may not be as highly concentrated as "an *intense* course."

Otherwise, *intensive* has acquired certain specialized meanings: Hospitals have "*intensive* care wards"; an *intensive* word such as *very* adds force to the word it modifies.

inter-, intra-.   The prefix *inter* means between or among: "*Inter*collegiate sports are played between colleges." *Intra* means within or inside of: "*Intra*mural sports are played by teams from within the same school."

interment, internment, internship.   *Interment* refers to burial or the placing of a body in a grave or tomb. *Internment* means confinement in a prison camp, as during a war.

It is true that medical students are interns during their advanced training. Although they may think of this period as *internment*, the correct term is *internship*.

interplanetary, interstellar.   An *interplanetary* journey is a trip among the planets. An *interstellar* journey is a trip among the stars.

inverse, reverse.   *Inverse* means directly opposite in order, nature, position, or relationship: "As he observed his commanding officers make a mess of the attack, the private speculated that rank was *inversely* proportional to intelligence."

Reverse applies more to direction or movement: "To back up, place the shift lever in *reverse* gear."

in vitro, in vivo.   *In vitro* means in a test tube or other artificial environment: "The *in vitro* fertilization process is sometimes referred to as making test-tube babies."

In vivo means in a living body: "natural synthesis of vitamin D occurring *in vivo*."

iridescence, luminescence, phosphorescence. *Iridescence* is a rainbow color effect as sometimes seen in soap bubbles, mother-of-pearl, oily water, and the feathers of some birds.

Luminescence is cool light, that is, light emitted by sources other than a hot, incandescent body. The typical household lamp produces light by using a heated filament. However, a fluorescent light is *luminescent* because its source of light consists not of a heated filament but of ultraviolet rays bombarding a phosphor coating. Fireflies are examples of *luminescence* caused by a biological source.

Phosphorescence is *luminescence* that persists after the source is removed. The glow may last for a fraction of a second or for a few days, depending upon the substance involved. Doctors can diagnose some diseases by analyzing the *phosphorescent* light given off by human tissue after it is exposed to ultraviolet rays.

iron, steel. *Iron* is a metallic element that is taken out of the ground as *iron ore*. *Steel* is a mixture that is made of *iron*, carbon, and often other metals such as nickel, chromium, or manganese.

irony, paradox. *Irony* applies chiefly to a manner of speaking or writing so that the meaning intended is contrary to what is stated on the surface. One of the most sustained pieces of irony is Jonathan Swift's essay "A Modest Proposal." On the surface, the essay is a witty, savage scheme to solve Ireland's problems by selling Irish babies to be cooked and eaten. The intended effect, however, was to call attention to the hardships the Irish were suffering because of English laws.

In this same category is dramatic *irony*, which exists when the audience knows something that is not apparent to the relevant actors. The impending death of the hero, obvious to the audience but not to the hero, is an example of dramatic *irony*.

Irony and *paradox* are both used to mean a situation in life where the result is the opposite of what was desired or worked for; "It was an *irony* of his life that success did not bring him the happiness he so eagerly sought." "It is a true *paradox* when hungry and impoverished people are found in such a rich land."

Otherwise, *paradox* refers to a statement that appears to be a contradiction in terms: "The pen is mightier than the sword" is a *paradox*. A pen wielded in combat against an opponent certainly is not mightier than a sword. However, the pen is an instrument used to sign treaties and write history. In the long run, the pen may well be mightier—more influential—than the sword.

SEE ALSO   **sarcastic, sardonic.**

irregardless, regardless.   *Irregardless* is nonstandard. The preferred form is *regardless*.

-ism, -ist, -ite.   The suffix *ism* refers to an act, process, or doctrine such as terror*ism*, pauper*ism*, social*ism*, alcohol*ism*, national*ism*.

An *ist* is a person who performs an act or is an expert in a field: terror*ist*, social*ist*, national*ist*, drugg*ist*.

An *ite* is a native or resident such as a Manhattan*ite*, or a believer or adherent such as a Hitler*ite* or McCarthy*ite*.

Israel, Palestine.   *Palestine* is a piece of geography that over the centuries has been controlled by Hebrews, Assyrians, Chaldeans, Persians, Arabs, and the British. At present, *Palestine* is divided into the State of *Israel* and the western part of the Kingdom of Jordan.

SEE ALSO   **Hebrew, Israeli, Israelite, Jew, Yiddish.**

itch, scratch.   An *itch* is what you *scratch*. An *itch* may be an irritation on the skin that is relieved by scraping or rubbing the skin—*scratching* it. An *itch* may also be an urge to do something, such as take a long trip. Figuratively speaking, taking the trip *scratches* the *itch*.

its, it's.   *Its* is a possessive pronoun and has no apostrophe: "The cat licked *its* paws." "Our new car? We're tickled pink with *its* smooth ride."

It's is a contraction for *it is* and takes the apostrophe: "*It's* (for *it is*) our new car." "*It's* going to be a nice day tomorrow."

SEE ALSO   **he, she, her, him, I, me, them, they, us, we, you; myself (and other compound pronouns); that, which, who; who, whom, whoever, whomever; you're, your(s).**

J

jail, penitentiary, prison.   A *jail* is a building designated by law to hold persons in lawful custody. The term *lawful custody* applies to persons who have been convicted of minor crimes and to persons who are legally held while awaiting trial. A *jail* is also considered to be more than a police station lockup.

The terms *penitentiary* and *prison* are used synonymously to designate institutions used for the imprisonment of persons convicted of more serious crimes.

jape, jest, joke.   *Jape* is an infrequently seen broad synonym for *joke* or *jest*, or for the playing of tricks on a person, or for the making of a fool out of a person.

Jest refers to anything that is said or done to provoke laughter; a *jest* is usually lighthearted: "His *jests* were more playful than caustic."

A *joke* is a funny story or anecdote, usually with a humorous or ridiculous twist at the end: "People had heard all of his *jokes* so often that they started to laugh before he got to the punch line."

SEE ALSO   **humor, wit.**

javelin, lance.   The *javelin* and the *lance* are descended from the spear, which is one of the oldest weapons of warfare. A *javelin* is thrown for distance at track and field meets. The *lance* is a weapon that is used by primitive peoples more for thrusting than for throwing.

jewelry, jewels.   *Jewelry* is a collective term that is applied to ornaments such as bracelets, necklaces, and rings: "A drawer in her dresser held her costume *jewelry*."

Jewels is a plural that is applied primarily to valuable gems: "The heiress kept her *jewels* in the hotel safe." "The Crown *Jewels* are on display in the Tower of London."

SEE ALSO **gem, jewel.**

job, position. Either of these words refers to any type of employment. *Job* is the less attractive of the two, often hinting at labor and exertion. *Position* implies intellectual skills as compared to hard work.

However, among executives who do the hiring, the old, old question is "Well, do you want a *job*, or do you want a *position*?"

SEE ALSO **avocation, vocation; career, job, occupation, profession, trade.**

jocose, jocular, jovial. A *jocose* person is one who is humorous or witty, whether the humor or wit is positive or negative: "She had the annoying habit of making *jocose* remarks about things that weren't at all funny."

A *jocular* person is one who tells jokes in an effort to keep others amused: "My uncle was such a *jocular* soul that he could always keep us laughing at dinnertime."

A *jovial* person is a merry, cheerful, happy soul: "Santa Claus is the perfect example of a *jovial* person."

SEE ALSO **humor, wit; jape, jest, joke.**

judge, magistrate. A *judge* is an appointed or elected official with the power to make decisions in a court of law. A *magistrate*, broadly speaking, is any civil officer with the power to administer the law. In practical terms, a *magistrate* has limited judicial power and is often a justice of the peace or *judge* of a police court.

judicial, judicious. *Judicial* pertains to the legal system—legal proceedings, courts of law, and the administration of justice: "His decisions while serving on the State Supreme Court set *judicial* precedents."

Judicious pertains to wisdom and sound judgment: "His decisions while serving on the State Supreme Court demonstrated a *judicious* understanding of social ills."

junction, juncture. Basically, these mean the same—a joining or the act of being joined. However, *junction* tends to refer to an easily measurable point such as the *junction* of two highways. *Juncture* implies larger circumstances: "at this *juncture* of human affairs . . ."

jurist, juror. A *jurist* is anyone—judge, lawyer, or scholar—who is an expert in the field of law. A *juror* is a member of a jury.

K

kilometer, nautical mile, statute mile. For measuring distances over land, the *kilometer* (1,000 meters) is a unit of length used in countries that have adopted the metric system; the *statute mile* is used in the United States. The *nautical mile* is used to measure distance for sea and air navigation.

The lengths of these units in feet are as follows: one *kilometer* equals 3,280.8 feet; one *statute mile* equals 5,280 feet; and one *nautical mile* equals 6,076.1 feet.

To describe speed over these distances, the terms are as follows: *miles per hour* (mph) when referring to *statute miles; kilometers per hour (kmph or kph) when referring to kilometers*; and *knots* when referring to *nautical miles*—not knots per hour.

kinetic energy, potential energy. *Kinetic energy* is the energy that a body possesses because of its motion. The up-and-down movement of a coil spring demonstrates *kinetic energy.*

Potential energy is energy ready to be released from a stationary body. A compressed spring contains *potential energy.*

kinky, kooky, quirky. As these words pertain to personality traits, the distinctions are: *Kinky* implies sexually bizarre or perverse actions; *kooky* implies silly or eccentric behavior; and *quirky* refers to any peculiarity of behavior.

L

labyrinth, maze. Both of these refer to a structure constructed of confusing passageways, or to any bewildering, tortuous situation. *Labyrinth* and *maze* can easily be used interchangeably: "a legalistic *labyrinth* (*maze*) of appeals and more appeals"; "a swamp that was a *maze* (*labyrinth*) of channels"; "a person who felt lost in a *labyrinth* (*maze*) of despair"; "the *maze* (*labyrinth*) that is the typical English garden."

laggard, sluggard. A *laggard* is a person who lags behind: "The hike leader was constantly nagging the *laggards* to keep up with the group."

A *sluggard* is a habitually lazy, slothful person: "He was such a *sluggard* that he could never hold a job."

lama, llama. *Lama* is a priest, a holy man of Tibetan Buddhism; *llama* is a beast, a pack animal in South America.

lamb, mutton, sheep. A *lamb* is a young *sheep*, especially one less than a year old. Besides being a source of wool, *sheep* also provide meat, either *lamb* or *mutton*. *Lamb* is more tender and more delicately flavored than *mutton*; *lamb* becomes *mutton* when the *sheep* is about a year old.

languid, limpid. *Languid* means weak, or lacking energy, vigor, or spirit: "Weakened by the disease, her arms were so *languid* that she could not lift them over her head." "He was so apathetic about the project that his interest in it could be described a *languid* at best."

Limpid refers to whatever is transparent and completely free of cloudiness: "The trout were easily visible in the *limpid* stream." *Limpid* also refers to a style that is clear and uncomplicated. It is a compliment to say that a writer has a *limpid* style.

lariat, lasso.   *Lariat* and *lasso* refer to the rope used by cowboys for catching large animals such as cattle and horses. Both terms come from Spanish words: *la reata*, the rope; and *lazo*, snare or loop. *Lariat* is sometimes used to mean a line on which horses are tethered.

SEE ALSO   **bridle, halter.**

larynx, pharynx.   *The larynx* is part of the air passage in the throat, located between the back of the tongue and the trachea (windpipe). It contains the vocal cords.

The *pharynx* is the cavity that connects the mouth to the esophagus. Part of the digestive tract, the *pharynx* also has openings from the nose and the *larynx* in the respiratory tract.

lascivious, lecherous, lewd, licentious.   *Lascivious* behavior is characterized by lust or lewdness: "His *lascivious* remarks offended guests and were the cause of his being asked to leave the party."

Lecherous behavior is characterized by excessive interest in sexual activity: He is a self-indulgent, *lecherous*, good-for-nothing gigolo."

Lewd refers to whatever is sexually unchaste or morally loose, especially in an obscene or offensive way: "The town's self-appointed censors automatically classified all girlie magazines as *lewd* and had them removed from the library shelves."

Licentious behavior is marked by disregard of rules or restraints: "Her *licentious* behavior only contributed to the harshness of her prison sentence."

SEE ALSO   **obscene, pornographic.**

last, later, latest, latter.   *Last*, of course, means final, occurring after all others: "took the *last* piece of candy"; "finished *last* in the race"; "happened *last* month"; "always the *last* person to get the word."

Latest means most recent, which could also be the

same as *last*: "Did you hear the *latest* (or *last*) news from Washington?"

Later and *latter* mean the same and are comparative forms of *late*: "the *later (latter)* stages of the revolution"; "the *later (latter)* chapters of the book"; "the *later (latter)* half of the seventeenth century."

SEE ALSO **first, former.**

latitude, longitude. Imaginary reference lines are used to locate positions on the earth's surface. These lines are known as parallels of *latitude* and meridians of *longitude*.

Latitude is measured in degrees north and south of the equator, the equator being zero degrees. *Latitude* lines run parallel to each other in 1-degree increments between the equator and the poles. The North Pole is 90 degrees north, and the South Pole is 90 degrees south.

Longitude is measured in degrees east and west of the zero-degree line, which runs through Greenwich, England. The line of 180 degrees longitude is located halfway around the world from Greenwich, and it passes through the Pacific Ocean. At the equator, the meridians of *longitude* are 60 nautical miles apart. Because of the earth's curvature, *longitude* lines converge at the pole; therefore, meridians of *longitude* do not run parallel to each other, although it is sometimes mistakenly said that they do.

laudable, laudatory. *Laudable* means deserving praise or commendation: "Clarity is a *laudable* feature of the new series of textbooks."

Laudatory means expressing or bestowing praise: "In a very *laudatory* speech, the chairman thanked employees for finishing the contract before the deadline."

lay, lie. The uses of these two words are complicated by the fact that the past tense of *lie* is also spelled *lay*.

Lay means to put something down. If *put* or *place* can be substituted, the correct verb is *lay*. The principal forms of the verb *lay* are:

Present: "He *lays (puts)* the fork down."
Past: "He *laid (placed)* the fork down."

Present participle: "He is *laying (placing)* the fork
                        down."
  Past participle: "He has *laid (put)* the fork down."

Lie means to recline. The principal forms of the verb
are:

              Present: "He *lies* on the couch."
                 Past: "He *lay* on the couch."
Present participle: "He is *lying* on the couch."
  Past participle: "He has *lain* on the couch."

leave, let.   *Leave* means to go away from: "She plans to
leave school before graduation."

Let means to permit or to allow: "*Let* me in. It's cold
out here."

These terms and their meanings are not interchangeable except in the combination "*leave (let)* alone," and
when *leave* or *let* is followed by a noun or pronoun:
"*Leave* John alone, and he'll do just fine." "*Let* her
alone, and she'll be happy."

lectern, podium.   A *lectern* is a rack or reading desk
with a slanted top used to hold a lecturer's notes. A
podium is a raised platform such as used by an orchestra
conductor.

SEE ALSO   **dais, rostrum.**

leeward, windward.   *Leeward* refers to the direction
toward which the wind blows, or the side or direction away
from the wind. *Windward* refers to the direction from
which the wind blows, or the side or direction toward the
wind.

If the wind is in your face, you are facing *windward*. If
the wind is at your back, you are facing *leeward*.

SEE ALSO   **offshore, onshore.**

legible, readable.   Handwriting is *legible*, that is, capable of being deciphered. Prose and poetry are *readable*,
that is, interesting to read or capable of being read.

lend, loan.   Confusion about these words exists because
some people insist that *loan* may not be used as a verb,
as in "*Loan* me some money." However, prevailing opin-

ion in dictionaries and usage books holds that *loan* is perfectly acceptable as a verb.

lengthways, lengthwise. Either *lengthways* or *lengthwise* may be used to refer to the direction of length: "*Lengthwise* (or *lengthways*) the ship measured 350 feet."

lesser, lessor. *Lesser* means smaller, less of, or less important: "the *lesser* of two evils"; "works of *lesser* known writers."

Lessor refers to the person, such as a landlord, who grants a lease.

levitation, levity. *Levitation* refers to the lifting or floating in air in defiance of gravitation: "Helium assisted the balloon in its *levitation*." "The finale of the magician's act was his *levitation* of a member of the audience."

Levity refers to being light in weight: "Some physical objects demonstrate a lightness known as *levity*."

Levity also implies a frivolous attitude: "The crew's joking behavior showed unwarranted *levity* for the seriousness of the situation."

SEE ALSO **gravitation, gravity.**

libel, slander. *Libel* and *slander* constitute damage to a person's reputation. *Slander* is spoken, while *libel* is expressed in forms such as print, writing, graphic means, recordings, or signs.

Libel is not to be confused with *liable*, the latter word referring to ability.

SEE ALSO **apt, liable, likely.**

lightening, lightning. *Lightening* means becoming or making less dark or less heavy: "After the tornado passed, occasional shafts of sunlight broke through, and the sky began *lightening* up." "The deckhands worked feverishly on *lightening* the sinking vessel."

Lightning is a flash of light in the sky caused by a discharge of electricity.

like, such as. *Like* and *such as* are both used when comparing. The difference is that *such as* lists similarities and is inclusive, while *like* lists similarities but is *not* inclusive.

In the following example, *such as* includes the items listed: "The car comes with numerous accessories, *such as* cruise control, air conditioning, and a cassette player." However, when *like* is used, the items listed are presented for comparison and are not necessary included: "The car comes with accessories *like* cruise control, air conditioning, and a cassette player."

SEE ALSO **as, like.**

linage, lineage. Both spellings are used to refer to the number of printed lines on a page. *Lineage*, however, is the only spelling for a person's descendants and ancestry.

linear, logarithmic. It's tempting to show off with words while revealing our ignorance about their meanings. This is the case when we speak carelessly of things that vary *linearly* or *logarithmically*. *Linear* simply describes anything that follows a straight line, while *logarithmic* involves the complicated use of exponents.

SEE ALSO **arithmetically, exponentially, geometrically.**

litany, liturgy. *Litany* was once limited to mean a prayer consisting of verses recited by a leader with responses given by a congregation: "The mournful *litany* of the funeral Mass hung heavily in the church." Today, a *litany* is any ritualistic repetition: "The problem with columnists today is that all they do is recite a *litany* of society's faults."

Liturgy is a system of rites and procedures that make up public worship, especially in the Christian faith: "the *liturgy* of the Eucharist"; "numerous Bible passages of modern *liturgy*."

loath, loathe. *Loath* means unwilling, reluctant, or disinclined: "I am *loath* to work today."

Loathe means to hate, detest, or feel intense dislike or disgust: "I *loathe* working this late at night."

locale, location. A *location* is a specific, marked, or established area, such as the site of a factory or a town. *Locale* may be used in place of *location*, but is also used to refer to the setting of a story or play.

lonely, lonesome.   A *lonely* person is one who is solitary, without company, cut off from others. A *lonesome* person is one who is sad or dejected as a result of being without the companionship of others.

long ton, metric ton, short ton.   Three weights exist for what we call a *ton*. The *long ton* weighs 2,240 pounds. The *short ton* weighs 2,000 pounds. In the United States, we are most familiar with the *short ton*, although some weights, such as those of coal and iron, are sometimes given in *long tons*.

The *metric ton* weighs 1,000 kilograms or 2,204.6 pounds and is used in nearly all other countries. The weight of a *long ton* in kilograms is 1,016, that of a *short ton* 907 kilograms.

loose, lose.   *Loose* means free, unrestrained, not tight: "When he hung up his pants, *loose* change spilled out of his pockets." "The punch to the jaw knocked a tooth *loose*." "She did not look good in *loose*-fitting clothing." As a verb, the meaning is the same: "They *loosed* the boat from its moorings." "The destroyer *loosed* a salvo from its main turrets." Dictionaries allow expressions such as "*Loose* the cows to avoid being trampled!" However, many people prefer "Turn *loose* of the cows."

Lose means to lack or mislay something: "Doctors said that she would *lose* a leg because of the accident." "He prayed that he would not *lose* his soul to the devil."

lucid, pellucid.   *Lucid* means clear, as applied to thinking or expression of ideas: "*lucid* prose"; "a *lucid* state of mind."

Pellucid suggests a sparkling clearness in reference to objects or the expression of ideas. Thus "*pellucid* writing" would be more admirable than "*lucid* writing," and there could exist such things as "*pellucid* windows" and "*pellucid* beakers of water."

lustful, lusty.   *Lustful* literally means full of lust, that is, excited or characterized by lust: "Her sensuous movements aroused his *lustful* nature."

Lusty implies vigor, power, strength, robustness, or heartiness—but not necessarily lust or sexuality: "All the brothers were tall, healthy, and *lusty* men." *Lusty* is frequently used as a synonym for *lustful*, a practice that will probably continue, given the powerful sexual implications of *lust*.

luxuriant, luxurious. *Luxuriant* means lush, abundant, vigorous, or flourishing: "The damp, mild climate produced *luxuriant* forests." "He took pride in his *luxuriant* beard."

Luxurious means rich, lavish, or extravagant: "The prince spared no expense and installed his lover in a *luxurious* suite of rooms." "It was a *luxurious* house, with every comfort imaginable."

M

machismo, macho. These are Mexican Spanish words that refer to the tough-guy, masculine, virile image. Neither word is necessarily derogatory, although they are often used in derogatory senses.

Macho is an adjective: "His girlfriend said he was a very *macho* guy." *Machismo* is a noun: "His prowess in the bullring demonstrated his *machismo*."

macro-, micro-. *Macro-* is a prefix that refers to things on a large scale. For example, a *macroclimate* is the general climate of a large area such as Florida.

Micro- is a prefix that refers to things on a small scale. For example, a *microclimate* is the particular climate of a separate area such as a valley or a forest, or even the different sides of a house—the south side will have a warmer *microclimate* than the north side.

madam, madame. *Madam* is a seldom-used form of address that could be losing its respectability because of its other meaning—the keeper of a brothel. *Ma'am* is the contraction for *madam*.

Madame is a title affixed to a name: "*Madame* Bovary was said to have that indefinable beauty that comes from happiness, enthusiasm, and success."

SEE ALSO **Miss, Mrs., Ms.**

magnificent, munificent. *Magnificent* suggests exalted or surpassing beauty, richness, splendor, or quality: "*Magnificent* red damask hangings set off the chancel and choir." "His *magnificent* bass voice could reach to the farthest rows of the largest concert hall." "Freedom was the most *magnificent* purpose expressed in the Declaration of Independence."

Munificent means very generous in giving: "She endowed her college with the *munificent* gift of $2 million."

majority, plurality.   These terms apply to votes garnered by candidates in an election.

A *majority* is more than half the votes. In an election with 200 votes cast, the *majority* would consist of at least 101 votes.

A *plurality* is the greatest number of votes received by any of three or more candidates; a *plurality* can be less than half the votes. If two candidates get 40 votes each and the winning candidate gets 41 votes, the *plurality* is 41 votes even though that number is less than half of the total of 121.

Majority and *plurality* are also used to refer to the winning margin. As an example, candidate A gets 100 votes, candidate B gets 70 votes, and candidate C gets 20 votes. In this case, candidate A could be said to have either a *majority* (more than half the votes cast) or a *plurality* (winning margin) of 30 votes.

malevolent, malignant.   *Malevolent* describes someone who wishes or does harm, or shows ill will toward others: "The old crone was disliked because she was gossipy and *malevolent*."

Malignant means evil, harmful, or dangerous: "Doctors have diagnosed a *malignant* tumor in the star's right arm." *Malignant* can also be used to describe the actions of a *malevolent* person or even the person: "*Malignant* gossip ruined their marriage." "He was extremely *malignant*, without a single redeeming feature."

malice, spite.   Both of these suggest hard feelings toward another person.

Malice is the stronger of the two, referring to a deep-seated and often unjustified desire to hurt others: "The critic enjoyed ruining reputations and did so with *malice* and not for the sake of art."

Spite suggests petty ill will, envy, and resentment: "She seemed a little cool when I called asking for her roommate, and I'm afraid she'll not pass the message along just out of *spite*."

mania, phobia. A *mania* is a fad, a craze: "a *mania* for designer jeans"; "the pet rock *mania* of several years back." *Mania* also refers to a mental state characterized by impulsiveness, high elation and excitement, rapid thought and speech, and violent and excessive motor activity.

A *phobia* is a exaggerated and illogical fear. The fear is insistent and intense, giving rise to panic and a compelling need to flee whatever causes the fear.

The word *phobia* is from a Greek word meaning fear or dread. In keeping with the Greek word roots, specific *phobias* are usually given Greek names: *agoraphobia*, fear of open space; *anthropophobia* (fear of human society); *hydrophobia* (fear of water); *nyctophobia* (fear of the night); *zoophobia* fear of animals).

An exception from the Greek roots is the well-known *claustrophobia* (from the Latin *claustrum* for confined space), fear of closed space.

mantel, mantle. A *mantel* is a shelf above a fireplace.

The word *mantle* applies to any cloak or covering such as a cape or robe. In this sense, *mantle* is sometimes used figuratively as in references to "the *mantle* of authority" or "hidden in the *mantle* of the night." A *mantle* is also a noncombustible meshwork hood used to contain the flame in a lantern.

marital, martial. A military newspaper said that "The base gym offers instruction in the *marital* arts." Readers are left on their own to decide what the "*marital* arts" are and if a gymnasium is the right place to learn about them.

Diligence is always needed to prevent typographical errors from appearing in published material. In this case, the source of embarrassment should have read "*martial* arts"—that is, warlike arts, such as kung fu and karate. *Marital* applies to marriage.

marshal, marshall. A *marshal* is an officer of the law or an official in charge of a parade. *Marshall* is a surname or a man's given name.

masochism, sadism.   Two men who have attached their names to the enjoyment of pain are Leopold von Sacher-Masoch (1836–1895) and Donatien Alphonse François, the Marquis de Sade (1740–1814).

Both were writers, which may account for the madness that afflicted them. Sacher-Masoch told of the pleasure to be had by experiencing pain; from his works we get the word *masochism*, pronounced "MASS uh kizem" or "MAZZ uh kizem." The Marquis de Sade described the pleasure derived from inflicting pain on someone else; from his works we get the word *sadism*, pronounced "SAD izem" or "SADE izem."

In general, the pleasure that is derived is either sexual or erotic; the pain may also by physical or psychic, as in debasement, humiliation, or exploitation. The literature of psychology and psychiatry mentions various forms of *masochism* and *sadism*.

mass, weight.   Technically speaking, *mass* is not *weight*. *Mass* is the resistance of a body to acceleration or the amount of matter in a body. *Weight* is the heaviness of a body. *Mass* exists independent of gravity, but *weight* doesn't.

masterful, masterly.   *Masterful* means commanding, domineering, or able to impose one's will upon others: "Without a doubt, Rommel was an imperious and *masterful* field officer."

Masterly refers to expert ability or skill: "He did a *masterly* job of building cabinets."

material, matériel.   *Material* refers to matter or substance. *Matériel* refers to the weapons, equipment, and supplies of armed forces.

maudlin, mawkish.   Both of these describe people or situations that are overly sentimental.

Maudlin implies drunkenness, excess emotions, or unwarranted weeping: "Fans touring Graceland often become *maudlin* at the thought of the departed Elvis."

Mawkish implies a sickening, objectionable, or grossly insincere form of sentimentality: "When you consider that all she wanted was to be written into her uncle's will, her behavior at his sickbed was totally *mawkish*."

SEE ALSO **sentiment, sentimentality.**

maunder, meander. In American English, *maunder* and *meander* mean to move, act, or talk in a vague, aimless, or rambling way; *meander* is probably the more frequently seen of these two. In British English, *maunder* has an added meaning: grumble or complain.

may be, maybe. The two-word form of *may be* is a verb combination that indicates possibility: "You *may be* right." As one word, *maybe* is a substitute for *perhaps*: "*Maybe (perhaps)* it'll rain tomorrow." "*Maybe (perhaps)* those boring guests will go home early." The test is whether you can substitute *perhaps*. If the substitution sounds awkward, the two-word *may be* is called for: "There *may be* a chance that the boring guests will go home early." It would be grossly incorrect English to say "There *perhaps* a chance that the boring guests will go home early."

As one word, *maybe* sometimes serves as a noun: "She took the job after she got all the *maybes* out of her mind." "We could never pin Dad down. All we got out of him was *maybes*."

SEE ALSO **can, could, may, might.**

mean, median, mode. These three terms have to do with different types of averages.

Mean (also called the *arithmetic mean*): obtained by dividing the sum of numbers in a set by the amount of numbers in a set. In the set of 3, 4, 5, 5, 8, the sum of 25 is divided by 5 (because there are five numbers), giving a mean of 5.

Median: obtained by taking the middle value, above and below which lie an equal number of values. In the set of 3, 4, 6, 7, 8, the *median* is 6.

Mode: obtained by taking the value that occurs most frequently. In the set of 3, 4, 4, 4, 6, the *mode* is 4.

meaningful. *Meaningful* literally means full of meaning, which doesn't say whether the meaning is good or bad, positive or negative.

As a consequence, statements such as these are vague:

"Lessons are learned more easily when they are *meaningful*." Yes, but what kind of meaning? Tending toward some idealistic value? Some criminal value? "What is needed is a *meaningful* high school course in science." What kind of science would be *meaningful*? The kind that builds guns or bombs? Or the kind that cures cancer and the common cold?

However, *meaningful* is extremely useful when indicating things that do not have meaning: "Pollsters said the early returns were not *meaningful*."

SEE ALSO **significant.**

meantime, meanwhile. The distinction given here is not critical, and many good writers interchange the usages and the meanings.

Meantime is a noun that refers to the intervening time: "In the *meantime* she had satisfied her appetite for reading all that she could about James Joyce."

Meanwhile is an adverb that refers to the intervening time or to two things happening at the same time: "The children were *meanwhile* left in the orphanage until homes could be found for them." "He neglected his crops, *meanwhile* paying attention to his horses and cattle."

medication, medicine. *Medication* was once the process of taking or administering *medicine*. However, the fascination that many people have for saying or writing extra syllables has made *medication* a synonym for *medicine*: any drug or substance used in treating disease or for relieving pain.

meet, pass. Cars on the highway *meet* or *pass*. They *meet*, and hopefully do not collide, when they come at each other from opposite directions. When one car traveling in the same direction overtakes and goes around another, the overtaking car is said to have *passed* the other.

melodic, melodious. These two adjectives pertain to the noun *melody*, a pleasant or agreeable sequence of musical sounds.

Melodic is a general reference to the presence of melody: "*melodic* tones of the woodwinds"; "the *melodic* nature of Greek music."

Melodious describes something pleasing and agreeable to the ear: "The *melodious* voices of the choir were a blessed relief after the minister's hellfire-and-brimstone sermon."

ménage, menagerie. A *ménage* is a group of persons living together as a household or domestic establishment. A *menagerie* is a collection of wild or strange animals kept in cages. Given the nature of some families, it is possible to say that a *ménage* could also be a *menagerie*.

meretricious, meritorious. Sir Francis Bacon in 1626 wrote, "The Delight of Meretricious Embracements (where Sinne is turned Art) maketh Marriage a dull thing." Bacon used *meretricious* to indicate prostitution, a definition retained by dictionaries today.

However, in modern usage *meretricious* mainly describes whatever appears to possess merit but lacks it, that which is superficially and falsely attractive: "What counts in a good movie is a substantial story with human appeal, not the *meretricious* catering to cheap taste."

Meritorious describes whatever does possess merit and is worthy of reward or honor: "Her *meritorious* performance earned her an Academy Award."

metaphor, simile. A *metaphor* is a figure of speech in which the literal meaning of a word or phrase is changed or adapted to convey an idea more vividly:

Time is but the stream I go a-fishing in.
—Henry David Thoreau
A few hair shirts are part of the mental wardrobe of every man.
—Herbert Hoover
In the evening of my memory, I come back to West Point.
—Douglas MacArthur

Not nearly so grand is the *mixed metaphor*, which conjures up an illogical, confused image. An example is this comment: "When you take the clothes off the body, all you've got left is the fight for the turf."

A *simile* is a figure of speech that compares unlike things by using the words *like* or *as*:

Venice is like eating an entire box of chocolate liqueurs at one go.
—Truman Capote

As welcome as a letter from home.
—Anonymous

Like the *metaphor*, the *simile* can also be botched: "Women know that getting a man to wear a condom is like pulling teeth."

meteorology, metrology. *Meteorology* is the study or science of weather, including forecasting. *Metrology* is the science of weights and measures.

method, methodology. There is a difference, although it's ignored by people who like long words. A *method* is a way of doing something, which some people also refer to as *methodology*. Actually a *methodology* is more properly a study or collection of *methods*.

mildew, mold. *Mildew* and *mold* are fungi that attack different forms of matter. *Mildew* is generally associated with damage to crops, plants, clothes, and bookbindings. *Mold* is generally associated with the aging or spoiling of foods such as cheeses and breads.

militate, mitigate. *Militate* is usually used with *against*, meaning to operate or work against: "His age *militated* against his keeping his job."

Mitigate means to make milder: "Air pollution control regulations are written to *mitigate* the emissions of hazardous pollutants."

minimal, minimum. Both mean the smallest in number, size, or degree. Both are used as adjectives, but *minimum* is the only noun form: "a *minimal*(or *minimum*) pay raise"; "reduces expenses to an absolute *minimum*."

minister, pastor, priest. Broadly speaking, a *minister* is any person, such as an agent, who acts in place of another.

In religious matters, a *minister* is a person authorized to conduct worship services, preach the gospel, and administer the sacraments.

The duties of a *priest* may be the same as those of a *minister*, except that the title *priest* implies a greater attention to ritualistic and interpretative functions.

A *pastor* is the person in charge of a church and its parish.

minstrel, troubadour. A *minstrel* was a medieval professional entertainer who traveled around reciting poetry, singing songs, playing musical instruments, and spreading the news of the day. The typical *minstrel* was a combination of actor, poet, journalist, and orchestra. In America during the nineteenth and early twentieth centuries, the term *minstrel* came to stand for the blackface performer in a musical show.

The word *troubadour* is sometimes used as a synonym for *minstrel*. However, *troubadour* is more narrowly defined as a special type of entertainer that flourished in the south of France and in the north of Italy during the twelfth and thirteenth centuries. The *troubadours* were aristocratic poets and poet-musicians who composed romantic songs in complex metrical forms.

minute, moment. A *minute* is sixty seconds; a *moment* is some vague period of time, usually of a very short duration.

Miss, Mrs., Ms. *Miss* and *Mrs.* are social titles that indicate the marital status of women. For men, no such indication exists, and married and single men alike are known as *Mr*.

Accordingly, the *Handbook of Nonsexist Writing* and the *Nonsexist Word Finder* offer *Ms.* (pronounced "miz") as the feminine counterpart of *Mr*. However, both sources, along with common courtesy, say that a woman's preference should be respected. If the preference is not known, modern practice allows the use of *Ms.*, or the person may be addressed by name with no social title shown.

Many people feel strongly that the titles *Miss* and *Mrs.* should be retained. As evidence, Jan Mollman, who likes to be known as Mrs. J. Peter Mollman, composed this little poem, which appeared in the *Handbook of Nonsexist Writing*:

> In typing *Ms*. for *Mrs*.
> Your Smith Corona slipped.
> I am a wife and mother
> And not a manuscript.

SEE ALSO **madam, madame.**

model, paradigm.   A *model* can be a copy on the same scale ("a *model* home") or on a different scale ("a *model* airplane"). A *model* can also be a person or thing worthy of emulating: "a *model* of success."

A *paradigm* is a *model*, example, or pattern that is effective in explaining or demonstrating a complex process: "Pavlov's dogs were a *paradigm* of the conditioned-response theory."

SEE ALSO **copy, replica; paradigm, paragon.**

morbid, moribund.   *Morbid* describes an unhealthy condition or the characteristics of disease: "His heavy drinking had given him a *morbid* appearance." *Morbid* is also used to refer to gloomy or dismal feelings: "His *morbid* outlook on life makes him one of the dreariest people around." "Many people respond to accident scenes with a *morbid* fascination."

Moribund means at the point of death or extinction: "Her weak pulse and all of her other vital signs indicated that she had become *moribund*." "Declining membership and a loss of faith had placed the commune in a *moribund* condition."

morgue, mortuary.   *Mortuary* is the most general of these two terms, referring to a place, such as a funeral parlor, where dead bodies are kept awaiting burial. The more specific term is *morgue*, which is a *mortuary* that specializes in holding unidentified bodies or bodies of people who have died from violent or unknown causes.

mortgagee, mortgagor(er).   The *mortgagee* is the person or institution, such as a bank or savings and loan association, that receives the mortgage. The *mortgagor* is the person who mortgages property.

If you wish to buy a home and are like most people, you borrow the money to pay for the home. When you do, you then become the *mortgagor*, and the lending institution is the *mortgagee*. The mortgage itself is a pledge to pay, and gives the lending institution the right to take the house if you can't make the payments.

motif, motive.   A *motif* is the main theme in a book, piece of music, or design. A *motive* is the inner drive or reason that causes a person to do something or to act in a certain manner.

SEE ALSO   **incentive, motive.**

mucous, mucus.   *Mucous* is an adjective, as in "*mucous* membranes." *Mucus* is a noun, the secretion that comes from the *mucous* membranes.

myself (and other compound pronouns).   The compound pronouns are *herself, himself, itself, myself, ourselves, themselves,* and *yourself.* They are used as intensives and reflexives.

As an intensive, a compound pronoun adds emphasis: "I *myself* will pay the bill." "They *themselves* caused the accident."

As a reflexive, a compound pronoun expresses action turned back upon the subject: "She will hurt *herself* if she continues in this manner." "You have apparently convinced *yourself* that this madness will work."

A lot has been written and said about whether a compound pronoun can stand in place of a personal pronoun such as *I* or *me*. The answer is generally no. According to that answer, these usages are wrong: "give the book to Tom and *myself*" (should be *me*). "Dick, Jane, and *myself* ran up the hill" (should be *I*). The best advice is: Don't use *myself* where *me* or *I* will do.

SEE ALSO   **he, she, her, him, I, me, them, they, us, we, you; its, it's; that, which, who; who, whom, whoever, whomever; you're, your(s).**

N

nadir, zenith. *Nadir* and *zenith* are opposite points that are frequently used when talking about astronomy and the celestial sphere. If you could stand at the center of the earth and look straight up—that is, look straight north—the north celestial pole would be at your *zenith*, and the south celestial pole would be directly below you at your *nadir*.

The figurative use of these terms applies to high and low points: "In my opinion, the *nadir* of the movie was reached in the melodramatic scene where Scarlet said, 'As God is my witness, I'll never go hungry again.' " "His appointment to the board of directors marked the *zenith* of his career."

SEE ALSO **apogee, perigee.**

nauseated, nauseous. *Nauseated* or *nauseous* means suffering from nausea: "The constant rolling of the ship made many passengers *nauseated*." "I feel *nauseous*."

Nauseous also means causing nausea: "The *nauseous* taste of the herbs began to make me feel sick to my stomach."

Nauseated and *nauseous* can both be used to exaggerate emotions of disgust and loathing: "His *nauseous* portrayal of Hamlet left me *nauseated*."

SEE ALSO **queasy, squeamish.**

naval, navel. *Naval* pertains to the navy: "The *naval* bombardment lasted until the invasion started."

Navel pertains to the belly button or to the *navel* orange.

need, want. *Need* pertains to the necessities of life: "Food, clothing, and shelter are three basic *needs*."

Want pertains to what is desired: "Like many young men, he *wanted* a powerful car."

Some crossover exists in constructions such as "the *wants* of the poor" or "the *wants* of the homeless." In those constructions, *wants* is used as a synonym for *needs*, although *needs* would be the more powerful word.

SEE ALSO **perquisite, prerequisite; requirement, requisite.**

neglectful, negligent. Neglectful and *negligent* both imply failure to attend to duty or business properly.

Neglectful implies laziness or deliberate inattention: "Having won reelection, the mayor ignored the voters' wishes and became *neglectful* of his campaign promises."

Negligent implies inattention that may not be deliberate: "Our son is so busy with his career and family that he's *negligent* in writing home."

neuralgia, neuritis. All pain is conducted by nerves, but *neuralgia* is pain that originates within a nerve. *Neuritis* is an inflammation of a nerve.

neurosis, psychosis. Because of vagueness and disagreement concerning the meanings of these words, the mental health profession favors the terms *neurotic disorder* and *psychotic disorder*. By any name, both apply to personality or mental disorders. Various classifications of these disorders exist, but the general distinctions are that a *neurotic disorder* is not rooted in any demonstrable organic disorder, but a *psychotic disorder* is perhaps rooted in or accompanied by an organic disorder.

niche, nook. A *niche* (pronounced to rhyme with *rich*) is a recess or a hollowed-out spot in a wall where a statue or other work of art may be placed. A *niche* is also a place in life that is particularly suitable to the person occupying it: "He eventually found his *niche* as a househusband."

A *nook* is a corner of a room or a quiet, secluded spot: "When she wanted to read, she retreated to her favorite *nook* in the attic."

noise, sound. *Noise* is unwanted *sound*. This is a subjective definition that varies from individual to individual. In general, *noise* is any *sound* that is annoying, damages the ears, reduces concentration, or impairs work efficiency.

Sound is a measurable physical phenomenon expressed in waves or cycles per second (hertz). *Sounds* that humans can hear occur in the range of 20 hertz to 20 kilohertz.

noisome, noisy. *Noisome* is based not on *noise* but on an old word meaning annoyance. It means harmful, noxious, disgusting, destructive, or offensive: "The flophouse was a *noisome* environment." "His morning breath was *noisome* to all around him."

Noisy indicates the presence of *noise*: "a *noisy* party last night."

notable, noticeable. *Notable* describes whatever is remarkable, outstanding, or worthy of notice: "He demonstrated the *notable* characteristic of being despised by all." "Geologists found *notable* deposits of limestone throughout the area."

Noticeable pertains to whatever is conspicuous or easily observed: "He talks with a *noticeable* lisp." "The vermouth gave the martini a *noticeable* but not unpleasant taste."

nourish, nurture. *Nourish* means to provide with food or other substances necessary for life: "She helped *nourish* the sick puppy."

Nurture shares that meaning, but also has a broader sense—the act or process of providing upbringing, training, education, and development: "After being released from the orphanage, he was raised in a very *nurturing* environment."

nourishment, nutrition. Both of these refer to the act of providing or receiving nutriment, that is, healthful food. *Nutrition* specifically refers to all the processes by which an animal or plant takes in and uses food; these processes involve ingestion, digestion, absorption, and assimilation. This definition runs counter to the popular idea that *nutrition* applies only to the content of the food itself.

O

O, oh. In traditional usage, *O* is a form of direct address, and *oh* is an exclamatory interjection.

O is always capitalized, and punctuation is not used to separate it from the expression it comes before: "Hear me, *O* Israel." "Have mercy, *O* Lord!"

Oh is capitalized when it is the first word of a sentence. *Oh* is usually followed by a comma; an exclamation mark is used for stronger emphasis: "*Oh*, waiter! Come here please." "*Oh*! Think what you will of me!" "I don't know, *oh*, what to say." Omitting the comma is acceptable: "*Oh* John!" "*Oh* Mary!"

However, Roy Copperud's *American Usage and Style* says that the forms are becoming interchangeable, and *Webster's Ninth* treats *Oh* as the principal form. Not all references agree, and the venerable *Chicago Manual of Style*, the editor's bible, requires the forms given here.

Accordingly, the safest recourse is to stick with the traditional usages.

obdurate, obstinate. Both of these words refer to the person who is unyielding and inflexible.

Obdurate suggests a hard attitude toward persuasion or softening influences: "He was an *obdurate* old grouch, untouched by the joys of life."

Obstinate suggests unreasonableness or perversity: "Despite overwhelming evidence presented during the trial, one juror *obstinately* refused to vote for acquittal."

obligate, oblige. Both of these terms refer to constraint or restraint.

Obligate is the more forceful and implies responsibility,

duty, or legal or moral requirements: "He was *obligated* to pay alimony." "Citizenship *obligates* a person to pay taxes."

Oblige implies the return of a favor or a sense of gratitude, or the doing of something that is pleasing or helpful to someone else; "The children felt *obliged* to pay their father's debts." "He liked to *oblige* his neighbors by doing odd jobs for them."

SEE ALSO **constrain, restrain.**

obliqueness, obliquity. *Obliqueness* refers to a deviation from a straight line, a turning aside, or an indirect approach: "The *obliqueness* of the angle would have to be precisely measured."

Obliquity suggests confusing statements or thinking, or a deviation from moral rules: "The *obliquity* of his approach to money matters makes me suspect that he can't be trusted."

Exception: Astronomers use the term *obliquity of the ecliptic*, which is an angle pertaining to a planet's equator.

SEE ALSO **acute angle, oblique angle, obtuse angle, right angle.**

obscene, pornographic. *Obscene* applies to anything that is strongly objectionable or offensive to accepted standards of decency, especially in sexual matters. The courts have been busy defining and redefining *obscene* for a number of years. No firm standard exists, and possibly none ever will exist. Involved are concepts such as sexual impurity; appeal to the beholder; community standards; interpretation of terms such as *immoral, indecent,* and *insulting;* offensiveness to chastity or modesty; and whether the material has any redeeming social value.

Pornographic applies to material that is meant to stimulate immoral thoughts, cause sexual excitement, incite sexual desire—and that has no serious literary, artistic, political, or scientific value.

SEE ALSO **lascivious, lecherous, lewd, licentious; profane, vulgar.**

observance, observation. *Observance* pertains to a holiday: "The *observance* of Lent is meant to impose a period of sacrifice." *Observance* also pertains to the act of following a custom or law: "*observance* of the speed limit."

Observation pertains to seeing or noticing: "Numerous *observations* of the sun with a sextant proved that they had reached the North Pole." It can mean a comment or conclusion. "His *observation* on her performance was that she needs a lot more practice."

obsolescent, obsolete.   *Obsolescent* means that something is becoming *obsolete*. *Obsolete* means something is no longer in use or fashion. Airplanes become *obsolescent* before they become *obsolete*.

obstacle, obstruction.   *Obstacle* is a broad term that applies to anything that figuratively or literally is in the way: "Lack of education is an *obstacle* to promotion." "Soldiers must complete the *obstacle* course in the minimum time." "His negative attitude is an *obstacle* that he will have to learn to overcome."

Obstruction implies anything that physically blocks passage: "President Eisenhower entered the hospital to have an *obstruction* removed from his intestines." "*Obstructions* such as rocks and rapids are part of the thrill of white-water rafting."

SEE ALSO **impair, impede.**

ocean, sea.   The *ocean* is a saltwater body that covers some 71 percent of the earth's surface. This body of water is divided into these named areas: Atlantic *Ocean*, Antarctic *Ocean*, Arctic *Ocean*, Indian *Ocean*, and Pacific *Ocean*.

Sea is a word loosely applied to the *ocean*. *Sea* more correctly stands for a saltwater body that is part of an *ocean* or that opens into an *ocean*: Black *Sea*, Mediterranean *Sea*, Red *Sea*, Sargasso *Sea*. The Caspian *Sea* and the Salton *Sea* are not true *seas* in that they are landlocked saltwater lakes. Neither is the *Sea* of Galilee, which is a freshwater lake.

oculist, ophthalmologist, optician, optometrist.   *Oculist* is an early term for a physician who treats diseases and defects of the eyes. The medical profession now uses the word *ophthalmologist*. *Ophthalmologist* is worthy of note because it is frequently misspelled or erroneously keyboarded: The first *h* is usually omitted.

An *optician* is a technician who makes eyeglasses; in some states, *opticians* also fit contact lenses.

An *optometrist* examines the eyes and prescribes glasses or contact lenses.

Neither an *optician* nor an *optometrist* is licensed to treat diseases of the eyes.

odious, opprobrious. *Odious* describes someone or something that deserves to be loathed or hated: "His cruelty to animals made him an *odious* person." "The executioner loved his *odious* profession."

Opprobrious describes whatever brings disgrace: "His palace was an *opprobrious* monument to human greed."

odometer, speedometer. An *odometer* measures the distance traveled; a *speedometer* measures the speed of travel.

official, officious. *Official* pertains to an office or a position of authority: "*official* duties"; "*official* business"; "governor's *official* representative."

Officious pertains to being meddlesome, frequently in an overbearing way: "Bureaucrats sometimes forget that they are supposed to be public *officials* and not *officious* nuisances."

offshore, onshore (wind). An *offshore* wind blows from shore to sea; an *onshore* wind blows from sea to shore.

SEE ALSO **leeward, windward.**

Olympian, Olympic. *Olympian* refers to Mount Olympus and the Greek gods, a resident of any place called Olympia, and anything majestic and lofty. *Olympian* can also refer to the *Olympic* games—although that event is usually referred to as the *Olympic* games, the *Olympics*, or the *Olympiad*, and not the *Olympian* games.

Olympic is used with reference to the games only.

Both *Olympian* and *Olympic* begin with capital (uppercase) letters.

omnipotent, omniscient. *Omnipotent* means all-powerful; *omniscient* means all-knowing.

on, on to, onto, up on, upon.   You may place something *on* a table, *onto* it, or *upon* it; usage allows each form. However, *on* emphasizes a position of rest, while *onto* and *upon* emphasize movement. Therefore, *on* is best used in constructions such as "The cat lay *on* the roof," and *onto* or *upon* is best used to show movement; "The cat jumped *onto* (*upon*) the roof." In these examples, *on*, *onto,* or *upon* function as prepositions, and each is written as one word.

When used as a verb or as part of a verb, *on to* or *up on* is written as two words: "Let's move *on to* the next topic." "If the AUTO light is lit *up on* the front panel, go to step 7."

The next question is, Do you "depend *on* someone," or do you "depend *upon* someone"? Answer—either way.

opaque, translucent, transparent.   *Opaque* material is material through which light cannot pass and through which you cannot see. *Translucent* material allows some passage of light; images are unclear when seen through *translucent* material. *Transparent* material allows the passage of light without diffusing it; things seen through *transparent* material are distinctly visible.

Opaque also describes a person who is thickheaded, or an argument that is hard to understand: "Economists are noted for their *opaque* attempts at explaining the actions of money and the marketplace."

Translucent is occasionally used to describe a person or argument that is straightforward and easy to understand: "Her *translucent* dissertations on linguistics made the subject seem simple."

Transparent may be used in the above sense, but it further implies that the person or argument is readily seen through so that faults or deceptions are easily detected: "He was so *transparent* in his swindles that it's hard to see how he stayed out of jail."

optimal, optimum.   *Optimal* and *optimum* may be used as adjectives: "*optimal* performance" or "*optimum* performance." *Optimum* is the noun form: "Temperature soon reached the *optimum* for this experiment."

Optimal and *optimum* are casually used as synonyms

for *best*. More precisely, they mean best under the conditions or circumstances.

oral, verbal.   *Oral* means of the mouth; an *oral* message is a spoken one. *Verbal* pertains to words whether spoken or written; a *verbal* message can be a spoken one or one put down on paper.

Confusion over these terms arises with statements like this: "We will need your *verbal* permission to excuse your child early from school." Can the permission be spoken, as over the phone, or must written permission be presented? A more precise form of expression would be "Before we can excuse your child early from school, we must have your written permission."

ordinance, ordnance.   An *ordinance* is a law, a municipal statute that is enacted by a city, county, or similar body. *Ordnance* means military weapons and equipment.

oscillate, undulate.   *Oscillate* means to swing back and forth like a pendulum, whether literally or figuratively: "Temperature *oscillated* 6 degrees above and below the mean." "He is so timid, always *oscillating* between choices and never making a decision."

Undulate means to move in a wavelike way: "Every cheap thriller has a sexy heroine whose hips *undulate* when she walks."

ostensible, ostentatious.   *Ostensible* means apparent or seeming to be: "The *ostensible* purpose of this law is to aid the plight of welfare babies, but a close reading shows that the real purpose is to restrict eligibility for family assistance."

Ostentatious means showy, pretentious, or conspicuous: "The *ostentatious* entertainer wore a diamond ring on every finger." "The mansion on the hill north of town was the most *ostentatious* building in my home town."

outlaw, scofflaw.   An *outlaw* is a habitual criminal who is a fugitive from the law. A *scofflaw* is a person who shows contempt for the law by habitually breaking minor laws, such as parking regulations, or ignoring court orders, such as an order to pay child support.

oven, stove.   *Stove* applies to the complete cooking unit, of which the *oven* is a part.

overlook, oversee.   An *overlook* is a point from which people may look down: "an *overlook* at the Grand Canyon." *Overlook* also means to ignore or to fail to notice: "The secret of a successful marriage is to *overlook* your spouse's faults."

Oversee means to manage, supervise, or superintend: "State law gives the agency the authority to *oversee* operations of the local districts."

oversight.   *Oversight* is one of those curiosities of the language in that it is a word that has acquired two considerably different meanings: (1) surveillance or supervision, or (2) mistake or omission. Therefore, the meaning of this sentence is unclear: "A few problems existed because of management *oversight*." Did the problems exist because of the way that management supervised the work? Did the problems exist because of a management mistake? Or are they both one and the same?

The sentence could have been worded more precisely: "A few problems existed because of management's lack of supervision."

P

palate, palette, pallet. The *palate* is the roof of the mouth. The bony part, the hard *palate*, occupies the front part, and the soft *palate* makes up the back part. *Palate* is also used to refer to a person's intellectual taste or liking: "My literary *palate* is just not suited to the refined, subtle nuances of Japanese poetry."

Palate is sometimes used to refer to a person's physical sense of taste. This reference has to be a figurative one, not literal, for the taste buds are located not on the *palate* but on the tongue.

A *palette* is a board on which an artist mixes different colors of paints; the board frequently has a hole for the thumb.

The word *pallet* means a small, hard bed; a portable platform on which goods are stacked for storage or transportation in a warehouse; or any of a number of specialized items in different fields.

papyrus, parchment. *Papyrus* is an Egyptian water plant. In ancient times, the Egyptians crushed *papyrus* stems and matted the crushed stems into paper. *Papyrus* fibers were also used in mats, sandals, and sailcloth.

Parchment is material made from the skins of sheep, goats, or other animals. *Parchment* paper is a durable, high-quality paper. It replaced the weaker *papyrus* paper of antiquity, and is occasionally used today for important documents.

parade, promenade. A *parade* is an organized public procession conducted in honor of an occasion: "Fourth of July *parades* are big events in small-town U.S.A." "Closure of the base was marked by a *parade* and other military festivities."

A *promenade* is a leisurely walk taken in a public place as a form of social activity, and often done to display one's finery: "He liked to dress up and *promenade* through Central Park every afternoon." "An Easter *Parade* is usually nothing more than a *promenade*."

paradigm, paragon.   A *paradigm* is any model, example, case, or instance that is effective in explaining or demonstrating a complex idea or process, or that is typical or representative: "For years, the exploration of space was a *paradigm* of the unattainable." "The freeway system has become a *paradigm* of California life, with its emphasis on the single-occupant vehicle along with a disregard for the benefits of mass transit."

Paragon refers to a model of perfection or excellence: "a *paragon* of virtue"; "a *paragon* of beauty."

SEE ALSO   **model, paradigm.**

parameter, perimeter.   *Parameter* was originally a specialist's word to which mathematicians attached highly technical definitions. Somewhere along the way, people began adding other definitions. Consequently, *parameter* is broadly used these days to stand for limit, range, scope, or boundary.

Because language does change, the addition of these definitions is unavoidable. Nevertheless, specialists' terms are best left to specialists. Moreover, words such as *limit, range, scope,* or *boundary* have well-established usages, all of which convey meaning a lot more accurately than *parameter*.

In addition, *parameter* does not mean *perimeter*. A *perimeter* is the boundary around or outer limits of something.

pardon, parole.   A *pardon* exempts or releases a person from the entire punishment prescribed for the offense: "He spent not one day in jail, for he was *pardoned* by the governor."

Parole releases a person from jail before the person's sentence is completed: "He was *paroled* after serving five years of his seven-year sentence."

partially, partly. In general, these words are not confusing, and either may be used to refer to some amount or degree that is less than the whole: "Her story is *partly (partially)* true." "Attempts to scale Everest were only *partially (partly)* successful."

However, *partially* may imply favoritism because of its apparent relationship to *partial to*. Any ambiguity in this respect can be avoided by using the most precise form: "He was *partial to* baked beans," not "He was *partially (partly?)* favorable to baked beans."

particular, peculiar. *Particular* and *peculiar* are both associated with a single, definite person or thing. The difference is that *particular* emphasizes individuality, while *peculiar* emphasizes strangeness: "A *particular* approach" to solving a problem is an exclusive approach; "a *peculiar* approach" is an unusual and odd one.

pastry, pasty. A *pastry* is a sweet baked good such as a pie or sweet roll. A *pasty* (pronounced "PASS tee" or "PACE tee") is a pie filled with a mixture of meat and vegetables.

peaceable, peaceful. *Peaceable* means inclined toward or promoting peace: "He hated quarrels, for he was a quiet, *peaceable* person."

Peaceful can be used in the same sense as *peaceable*, but *peaceful* also means calm, undisturbed, or tranquil: "The *peaceful* valley gave them their sought-after escape from civilization."

pedal, peddle. You *pedal* a bicycle, and you *peddle* (sell) goods.

pedigreed, purebred, thoroughbred. A *pedigree* is a known list of ancestors and line of descent; *pedigreed* is used mainly when referring to dogs.

A *purebred* animal is one in a strain established through generations of breeding unmixed stock.

The word *thoroughbred* refers in one usage to a *purebred* horse. In another usage, the capitalized *Thoroughbred* is a racing breed obtained by mating Arabian stallions with English mares.

penultimate, ultimate. *Penultimate* is next to last; *ultimate* is last.

people, persons. *People* is used with indefinite numbers or masses: "the *people* of South America"; "the Jewish *people*"; "We, the *people*"; and "*People* will talk."

Person or *people* is used with definite numbers: "The crime was witnessed by four *persons (people)*."

Peoples is the plural of *people*: "The *peoples* of Africa live in many nations."

perceptive, perspicacious. There isn't much difference between these two. *Perceptive* means capable of keen insight; *perspicacious* means *perceptive* carried to a somewhat higher degree. Compared to *perspicacious, perceptive* is shorter and sounds less formal; its obvious relationship to *perceive* makes its meaning easier to grasp. These factors may account for its being the more common of the two.

peremptory, perfunctory. *Peremptory* indicates the final and absolute shutting off of debate, action, or questioning: "His *peremptory* dismissal of his staff ended the discussion." "The airborne invasion of Grenada was a *peremptory* strike that prevented any further action."

In law, a *peremptory* challenge is the challenging of a juror without giving a reason for the challenge. The other kind of challenge is a challenge for cause, in which a reason must be given for the challenge.

Perfunctory indicates something done routinely and perhaps superficially with little interest or care: "Although she had the IQ of a genius, her *perfunctory* approach to studying left her buried in the inconspicuous middle of her class." "He gave a *perfunctory* smile and once again became engrossed in his book."

permeate, pervade. These two terms suggest in common the idea of spreading or diffusing.

Permeate implies spreading through the total or all the pores or spaces of a substance or entity: "The pleasant smell of fresh-brewed coffee *permeated* the shop." "The dye *permeated* the fabric."

Pervade implies spreading through all the parts of the

whole: "A deathly silence *pervaded* the place." "Excellent insight *pervades* his writings."

perpetrate, perpetuate. *Perpetrate* means to do or to perform; the word is usually used in reference to an act that is criminal or at least shocking: "Con men are notorious for *perpetrating* hoaxes on the elderly." "He *perpetrated* one bad pun after another." "The massacre, at first blamed on Indians, was in fact *perpetrated* by white men."

Perpetuate means to cause something to continue or to endure: "A gravestone *perpetuates* the memory of the deceased." "His edicts were meant to *perpetuate* his absolute control."

perquisite, prerequisite. A *perquisite* is a special privilege in conjunction with a job, over and above regular pay and benefits: "The *perquisites* of the college president included a home and a car."

A *prerequisite* is a requirement: "A high school diploma is a *prerequisite* for admission to college."

SEE ALSO **prerogative, privilege; requirement, requisite.**

persecute, prosecute. *Persecute* means to annoy and harass constantly: "Classmates *persecuted* him because of his strange accent."

Prosecute refers to a legal procedure that is carried out against a person accused of a crime: "The district attorney decided not to *prosecute* because of a lack of evidence."

persevere, persist. Both of these refer to efforts made to reach a goal despite difficulty or opposition.

To *persevere* implies effort that is continued, patient, and usually looked upon favorably: "*Persevere* and you will be promoted." "Anyone who sets out to write a five-hundred-page book had better know how to *persevere*."

Persist implies stubborn, dogged effort that may be looked upon as annoying or unreasonable: "He *persisted* in inflicting needless punishment in the form of excessive homework on his pupils." "He *persisted* long after I said I would not marry him."

persona, personality. *Persona* is the role played by a person. On a stage, the *persona* is the part taken by the actor. In real life, the *persona* is the role played by a person because of the pressures of society. The *persona* is public, the face or facade that is presented to others.

Personality is a very broad word that refers to all of the qualities that make up an individual. As of a half century ago, the literature of psychology listed nearly fifty different definitions of *personality*, and there is no way of counting how many exist today.

pertinacious, tenacious. *Tenacious* means able to hold firm, to be stubborn: "The dog had a *tenacious* grip on his leg." "She had a *tenacious* memory for names and faces." "He showed *tenacious* courage in the ring."

Pertinacious means obstinate, *tenacious* in an unfavorable or perverse way: "*Pertinacious* creditors hounded him to the grave." "The child's fever was *pertinacious* and of unknown origin."

physical, physiological.   In referring to the human body, *physical* pertains to the body as distinguished from the mind and spirit, while *physiological* pertains to life processes and functions.

Pilgrim, pilgrim, Puritan, puritan.   Any attempt to sort out the confusion attached to these terms begins with the capitalized form of *Puritan*.

The *Puritans* were English Protestant reformers who flourished in the sixteenth and seventeenth centuries. *Puritans* sought to purify the Church of England by removing any remaining touches of Roman Catholicism. *Puritans* advocated strict religious discipline and wanted to do away with the wearing of wedding rings, kneeling to receive sacraments, and all forms of religious images, statues, and pictures. Because of persecution, many *Puritans* fled to Holland and America. *Puritans* who came to America founded the colony called Plymouth Plantation.

Since then, this particular group of people has been known as *Pilgrims*. In the broader sense, the lowercased *pilgrim* refers to a foreigner or wanderer, or to a religious devotee who travels to a shrine or sacred place: "Every Easter, thousands of *pilgrims* journey to the Holy Land."

And that brings us to the lowercased *puritan*—a person with severe and narrow views on sex and luxury: "Her *puritanical* views ruined whatever pleasure her husband felt himself entitled to."

SEE ALSO **purist, puritan.**

pistol, revolver. A *pistol* is a small firearm meant to be held and fired with one hand. One form of *pistol* is the *revolver*. In a *revolver* the cartridges are held in a revolving cylinder behind the barrel.

SEE ALSO **bullet, cartridge, round, shell.**

piteous, pitiable, pitiful. *Piteous* stresses the object that calls for pity instead of how the object influences the observer: "The injured dog gave off *piteous* groans."

Pitiful emphasizes sadness on the part of the observer: "The injured dog was a *pitiful* sight."

Pitiable mingles sadness with contempt as felt by the observer: "No one approached the injured dog, and only a *pitiable* few even glanced at it as they passed by."

plain, plane. *Plain* refers to a flat stretch of ground ("the Great *Plains* of the American West"); something that is easily understood ("insurance policies written in *plain* English and not legalese"); freedom from obstruction ("came into *plain* view"); something that is simple and not ornate ("a *plain* dress"); whatever is pure or unmixed ("a *plain* glass of water"); or an ordinary person ("a *plain* man").

Plane refers to a level of development, a real or imaginary surface that is absolutely flat, or an *airplane* or an airfoil such as the wing of an airplane.

plait, pleat. A *plait* is a braid of hair. A *pleat* is a fold in cloth.

plan, scheme. As verbs, both of these mean to devise a method to reach an end. The difference is that *plan* implies a method that is well thought through and perhaps placed on paper, while *scheme* implies a method motivated by craftiness or for underhanded purposes. Therefore, engineers *plan*, while villains *scheme*.

plat, plot. A *plat*, or *plat map*, is a map of a real estate development. The *plat* shows items such as individual lots, streets, alleys, and easements.

A *plot* is a small piece of ground marked off for special use: "a garden *plot*"; "a cemetery *plot*." A *plot* also is the outline or plan of action of a story, or a secret and usually evil scheme.

poetry, verse. *Verse* is a term applied to rhythmical and often rhymed composition. The word *verse* implies nothing about the merits of the composition.

Poetry, on the other hand, indicates *verse* of high merit. *Poetry* implies a rhythmic expression of a writer's most imaginative and most intense perceptions. Any definition of *poetry* contains terms such as *emotion, imagination, depth of thought, beauty, dignity, sentiment, passion, power, freshness of expression,* and *pleasure.*

Any number of people have tried to define *poetry*. Here are a couple of samples:

> If I read a book and it makes my body so cold no fire will ever warm me, I know that is poetry. If I feel physically as if the top of my head were taken off, I know that is poetry.
> —Emily Dickinson

> When power leads man toward arrogance, poetry reminds him of his limitations. When power narrows the areas of man's concern, poetry reminds him of the richness and diversity of his existence. When power corrupts, poetry cleanses, for art establishes the basic human truths which must serve as the touchstone of our judgment.
> —John Fitzgerald Kennedy

SEE ALSO **rhyme, rime.**

populated, populous. *Populated* means that an area has inhabitants: "After weeks in the desert, they were glad to be back in the *populated* area of Egypt."

Populous means that an area is thickly *populated* or crowded: "Parts of the rapidly growing Southwest are ten times more *populous* than they were a decade ago."

pore, pour. As verbs, *pore* means to read carefully and studiously, and *pour* means to cause to flow. Thus you "*pore* over a book" but you "*pour* drinks for everyone."

port, starboard. *Port* is the left side of a ship when looking forward, and *starboard* is the right. These can be kept sorted out by remembering that *port* has as many letters as *left*.

Early Teutonic ships were steered with a large oar or a paddle—literally a steering board—on the right side; from steering board we get *starboard*. Because the steering board on the right side prevented loading or unloading at a port from the right side, ships approached docks from the left. For a time, the left side was the *larboard*, a word that sounded confusingly like *starboard*. When *port* replaced *larboard*, the confusing sound was eliminated.

postulate, stipulate. *Postulate* means to demand or require; it quite often means to require that something be accepted as true without proof so that reasoning can proceed: "Rosinski's argument *postulates* that a process can generate as much energy as it expends."

Stipulate means to include a requirement as part of a contract or agreement: "The union wanted the contract to *stipulate* that raises would be tied to the cost-of-living index."

Lawyers use *stipulate* to refer to an agreement as to the conduct of legal proceedings: "Counsel for both sides will *stipulate* to the admission of the gun as evidence."

practicable, practical, pragmatic. *Practicable* and *practical* refer to whatever can be done, accomplished, used, or put into practice. *Practicable* implies that the idea has not yet been tested, and *practical* implies proven success: "At one time, only a few people thought that computers were *practicable*; now most people acknowledge that computers have many *practical* uses."

Pragmatic is closely related to *practical* except that *pragmatic* places greater emphasis on matters of fact and actual everyday practice rather than on matters of theory, intellect, or art: "The Modoc Indians were a *prag-*

matic people because they adapted to change without worrying why."

SEE ALSO **feasible, possible, probable.**

precede, proceed. *Precede* means to go before in time or status: "Careful exploration *preceded* settlement." "The English language *precedes* others in the rate of adaptation for business and diplomatic purposes." "She *preceded* her address with a brief prayer."

Proceed means to start or to continue: "After offering a brief prayer, she *proceeded* to deliver her prepared speech." "In his restless state, he *proceeded* to pace the hall hour after hour."

precedence, precedent. *Precedence* refers to the establishment of a priority or the act of going before: "The lodge's officers were seated at dinner according to *precedence* based on their titles." "The old saying 'Ladies first' means that ladies have *precedence* over men when going through doorways."

Precedent refers to an example that is based on principles and facts established in earlier, similar situations: "In winning the case, defense lawyers cited *precedents* going back to the seventeenth century." "*Precedents* indicate that subversive activity increases several months before summit conferences."

precipitate, precipitous. *Precipitate* refers to whatever is hurried, rash, abrupt, or impetuous: "Without even thinking about what he was going to say, he *precipitated* himself prematurely into the debate on creationism."

Precipitous refers to a slope that is steep or sheer: "*Precipitous* limestone walls line both sides of the gorge." "To the old man, the angle of the stairs seemed quite *precipitous*."

predecessor, successor. A *predecessor* is the person who comes before another; a *successor* is the person who comes after another.

preeminent, prominent. *Preeminent* means eminent above all others: "Mozart, whose music and name survive today, was *preeminent* among court composers of his time."

Prominent means easily noticeable or conspicuous: "The Leaning Tower of Pisa is a *prominent* landmark." "He is easy to recognize because of his *prominent* nose."

premise, premises. A *premise* is a basis for reasoning: "My *premise* is that history repeats itself." Or, in the plural form: "My *premises* are that historical events foreshadow the future." The word *premiss* is sometimes used in this same sense, but American usage today favors *premise(s)*.

The word *premises*, always used as a plural, refers to a piece of land: "These *premises* are posted against trespassing." "On the *premises* are a store, bar, gas station, and lodge."

premonition, presentiment. These two terms mean a feeling or belief that something bad is about to happen.

Premonition implies warning or indication: "Colder nights offered a *premonition* of winter." "The general staff's bungling was a *premonition* of disaster."

Presentiment refers mainly to an intuitive, perhaps mystical, perception of a coming event: "She claimed a dream had given her a *presentiment* of the accident that would kill her nephew."

SEE ALSO **prescience, presence.**

prerogative, privilege. A *prerogative* is an exclusive or peculiar right, or a distinctly superior advantage; a *prerogative* is a special *privilege*: "One of the royal *prerogatives* is that the Queen of England is not to be photographed while she is eating." "It is a *prerogative* of the president to grant pardons."

A *privilege* is a particular benefit enjoyed by a few persons and beyond the common rights allowed to other persons: "Newspaper reporters always plead the *privilege* of confidentiality of sources." "Diplomatic *privilege* usually means freedom from arrest."

A *privilege* can also be a fundamental right that is guaranteed by government: "The Constitution gives Americans the *privilege* of living in a free society.

SEE ALSO **perquisite, prerequisite.**

prescience, presence. Does a person have *prescience* of mind or *presence* of mind?

Prescience is the human attribute, quality, or talent of possessing foresight: "Mothers seem to have great *prescience* of the dangers that their children will face." The expression "*prescience* of mind" is a misnomer.

Presence has many meanings, but "*presence* of mind" is limited to referring to self-control in the face of an emergency or crisis: "Mothers have great *presence* of mind when treating bloody noses and other ailments of childhood."

SEE ALSO   **premonition, presentiment.**

prescribe, proscribe.   *Prescribe* means to instruct, order, advise, or direct: "*prescribe* medicine for a patient"; "qualifications *prescribed* for the practice of law"; "a witness *prescribed* to take an oath"; "self-*prescribed* shot of whiskey each day for the prevention of stress."

Proscribe means to forbid, denounce, banish, or deprive: "a truce that *proscribes* the development of new weapons"; "censorship that *proscribes* freedom of the press."

presently.   *Presently* has two contrasting meanings—now or soon. The announcement "We will *presently* hear from our guest speaker" means either (1) "We will now hear from our guest speaker," or (2) "We will soon hear from our guest speaker."

Therefore, if by *presently* you mean *at present*, use *now, currently*, or simply *is* or *are*. If you mean the near future, use *soon* or *in a little while*.

presumptive, presumptuous.   *Presumptive* refers to the establishment of grounds for reasonable opinion, belief, or probability: "*Presumptive* evidence was strong enough to convict him."

Presumptuous refers to the overstepping of bounds or to the assuming of an unjustified prerogative or privilege: "It was *presumptuous* of him to think that I would ever go out with him again!"

SEE ALSO   **heir apparent, heir presumptive.**

pretense, pretext.   These are used interchangeably to refer to the act of pretending. Either one stands for a claim, assertion, reason, motive, or appearance that may not be supported by fact: "They kept up the *pretext* (*pretense*) of being a civilized nation." "Mother was such a domineering woman that the idea of father being head of the family was only a *pretense* (*pretext*)." When the intent is to hide the real motive, the better word is *pretext*: "She used any *pretext* to stay home from school."

preternatural, supernatural. *Preternatural* refers to anything that is irregular, exceptional, or extraordinary: "A self-imposed reading program had honed his intellect to a *preternatural* acuteness."

Supernatural refers to anything outside of nature or observable existence, especially the occult, gods, spirits, the devil, or something eerie: "the *supernatural* character of a person's soul"; "*supernatural* rustlings and whirrings of a ghost in the attic"; "to fulfill our *supernatural* destiny after death."

preventative, preventive. These mean exactly the same—acting or serving to prevent. What is confusing here is why people would use the longer form.

prim, prissy. *Prim* means stiffly formal, proper, decorous, or demure: "He was very *prim* for a man, and easily shocked." "Even though endless social events pained her, she endured them with a *prim* smile."

Prissy refers to being fussy, prudish, and perhaps sissified; also, a higher degree of being *prim*: "Truly *prissy* tea drinkers elevate their pinkies."
SEE ALSO **prudent, prudish; sedate, staid.**

primeval, primordial. *Primeval* refers to the first or earliest age, while *primordial* refers to the first in order.

The two are used interchangeably to refer to the earliest ages of the world or human history: "the *primeval* state of the wilderness"; "origins of the world traced to a *primordial* explosion." Either word is also used to refer to anyone or anything that is primitive or crude: "a *primeval*, rustic man of the mountains"; "a *primordial* hellfire-and-brimstone preacher."

The uses of *primordial* extend to whatever is first: "the *primordial* instincts of the newborn child"; "the *primordial* cells of life."

principal, principle. *Principal* refers to whatever is chief, main, or leading; *principle* refers to a rule, law, or fundamental axiom. If you want to avoid confusing the spellings of them, keep in mind that both *principle* and *rule* end in *le*.

procedure, proceeding(s). A *procedure* is a deliberate way of doing something: "Adherence to parliamentary *procedure* ensures that a meeting is conducted in an orderly manner." A *procedure* often gives a sequence of steps to be followed: "Our office *procedure* manual lists six steps that must be followed when making airline reservations."

Proceeding, in its singular form, emphasizes the carrying on of a course of action: "His journey over the mountains was not as reckless a *proceeding* as it might seem."

As a plural word, *proceedings* are the written records of a meeting: "A bound copy of conference *proceedings* is available for $10." *Proceedings* also refers to action taken under the law: "Legal *proceedings* have been instituted to seek compensation for those injured in the accident."

proclivity, propensity. *Proclivity* implies a strong natural inclination to do something, especially something objectionable: "a *proclivity* for telling lies"; "the criminal *proclivity* for violence"; "a *proclivity* for spreading gossip."

Propensity implies an intense, almost uncontrollable inclination or tendency: "a *propensity* for breaking out in song at odd moments"; "a *propensity* for heavy drinking"; "a *propensity* for going shopping."

procure, secure. *Procure* means to get or obtain by active care, effort, or contrivance, sometimes over a period of time: "They *procured* a settlement of the lawsuit." "He made his living by the unsavory practice of *procuring* women for prostitution."

Secure can also be used to mean get or obtain, but in this usage *secure* implies difficulty: "Diplomats discussed the problems encountered in *securing* a lasting peace." "Detectives *secured* a confession from Smith, but only after long and arduous hours of questioning."

prodigy, protégé. The primary meaning of *prodigy* is an amazing event or thing. When referring to a person, *prodigy*'s only application is to the young. Therefore, "child *prodigy*" is a well-established expression, even though it is redundant: "child, young wonder."

A *protégé* is a person guided or helped in a career by a more influential person: "As an undergraduate, he became a *protégé* of the most famous historian on the faculty." *Protégée* is the feminine form.

profane, vulgar. A *profane* person is irreverent and not concerned with religious matters. Literally speaking, *profane* language (*profanity*) is not swearing or cursing in general, but instead language that is directed against God or religion.

A *vulgar* person was originally one of the common folks as opposed to educated or cultivated people; today a *vulgar* person is usually thought of as being coarse and crude. Obscene or otherwise coarse language is sometimes called *vulgar*.

SEE ALSO **obscene, pornographic.**

profligate, prolific. *Profligate* means immoral, dissolute, wasteful, or extravagant: "*Profligate* aristocrats gambled away their days and their inheritances in the island's casinos."

Prolific means fertile or fruitful: "A *prolific* author, he wrote more than forty books in his short life." "Cats are notoriously *prolific* animals capable of producing large litters throughout much of their lives."

Prolific also means occurring in large numbers: "The book contained *prolific* references."

prone, supine. *Prone* means lying facedown; *supine* means lying face up.

prophecy, prophesy. *Prophecy* is a noun that means prediction: "The medicine man's *prophecy* was that rain would soon come."

Prophesy is a verb that means to predict: "The medicine man *prophesied* that rain would soon come."

proportional, proportionate. Generally speaking, these two are not confusing, and they may be used interchangeably as adjectives when referring to proportion. However, certain usages have become standard: "*proportional* representation," "*proportional* dividers," and "*proportional* tax."

proposal, proposition. Both of these refer to something put forward for consideration.

Proposal has a slightly more formal sense in that it may refer to a plan ("a *proposal* to provide cable television for the community"), while *proposition* may refer to a theory ("the *proposition* that all persons are created equal.")

That distinction is not infallible, for *proposal* and *proposition* are sometimes used interchangeably in business deals. Nevertheless, it's worth mentioning that people speak of a "*proposal* of marriage," while *proposition* is used when soliciting sexual intercourse. Certainly, marriage is more formal than a caper in bed.

prostate, prostrate. *Prostate* is the male gland, while *prostrate* means lying facedown, as to demonstrate humility or abject subjection.

provided, providing. In *Modern American Usage*, which was published in 1966, Wilson Follett sorted *provided* and *providing* into two neat categories. According to Follett, only *provided* should be used to mean *if*, while *providing* was to be used to mean *giving* or *furnishing*. In this respect, Follett was echoing Henry W. Fowler's *Modern English Usage*, which first came out in 1926.

Both books are still around, still popular, perhaps reasonably modern as their titles say—but not necessarily contemporary with current usage. Roy Copperud's review of usage books and dictionaries in *American Usage and Style* (1980) shows that *provided* and *providing* are interchangeable when you want to mean *only if*. A more recent work, the *Harper Dictionary of Contemporary Usage* (1985), says, "Where certain conditions or requirements are stated, either *provided* or *providing* (each followed by 'that') is acceptable."

Therefore, when a proviso is established or when substituting for *only if*, the following is correct in either form: "You may leave early, *provided* (*providing*) that your work is done."

Providing retains its meaning of giving or furnishing: "She was arrested for *providing* food to the homeless but not having a license to do so."

SEE ALSO **if, whether.**

prudent, prudish. *Prudent* means careful, wise, and judicious: "*Prudent* leaders write *prudent* laws, and the entire nation benefits." "He was too *prudent* a commander to waste his troops in such a poorly defined plan."

Prudish means excessively modest or demure: "His poetry was so *prudish* that it was almost sterile." "A vivacious girl, she longed to escape from the home run by her *prudish* foster mother."

SEE ALSO **prim, prissy; sedate, staid.**

pseudo-, quasi-. The prefix *pseudo* identifies whatever is a sham: "A *pseudonym* is a fictitious name or a pen name." "He was nothing more than a quack using a limited knowledge of anatomy to pronounce his *pseudomedical* advice."

The prefix *quasi* means to some degree: "The court's investigative arm was a *quasijudicial* body." "The private operation of municipal services would establish *quasipublic* organizations."

psychiatrist, psychologist. A *psychiatrist* is a licensed physician who specializes in the treatment of mental and behavioral disorders.

A *psychologist* is a person who has a graduate degree in psychology and who is licensed by the state to provide counseling services to patients with mental and behavioral disorders.

punctilious, punctual. A *punctilious* person is very attentive to the fine points of behavior and ceremony: "A *punctilious* host, he gave flawless parties."

A *punctual* person is one who is on time, neither early nor late: "She attracted notice by the *punctual* accomplishment of her duties."

pupil, student. The word *pupil* is applied to a person in elementary school, or to a person under the personal supervision of a teacher: "He was a *pupil* of the only piano teacher in the small town."

The word *student* is applied to a person in high school or college, or to one who studies a particular subject: "a *student* of social reform."

purist, puritan. A *purist* is a person who insists on the strict observance of precise, formal, and sometimes pedantic rules: "Scholarly *purists* don't feel happy unless they see dissertations in which the pages are bottom-heavy with footnotes." "As a fisherman, he was such a *purist* that he would never use live bait, only dry flies."

A *puritan* is a person with narrow-minded sexual or moral views.

SEE ALSO **Pilgrim, pilgrim, Puritan, puritan.**

purposeful, purposely. *Purposeful* means having a purpose or aim: "*Purposeful* activities are good therapy." "He is a *purposeful* man, determined to succeed."

Purposely means that something was done on purpose: "He *purposely* yawned in the hope that the speaker would notice and conclude his remarks."

quaint, quixotic.   Thank God for Miguel de Cervantes Saavedra! Cervantes gave us the magnificent Don Quixote, and writers ever since have seized upon *quixotic* to add a new dimension to whatever is strange or odd.

Quaint, after all, is limited to describing only what is old-fashioned and unusual in a pleasing sort of way—the emphasis being on the out-of-date. *Quixotic* (pronounced "kwik SOT ik") adds to that by emphasizing the oddball touch that can only be a product of the imagination. In addition, *quixotic* usually applies to some kind of naive heroism or advocacy—the tilting at the windmills of modern dilemmas.

Therefore, if your neighbor down the street starts studying medieval poetry, you could say, "My, how *quaint*." If that same person writes a letter to the editor suggesting that teachers' salaries be tripled, you could say "Good grief! How *quixotic*!"

quake, quaver, quiver.   *Quake* means to shake or tremble: "The building *quaked* as if struck a mighty blow."

Quaver and *quiver* mean to vibrate with a slight tremulous motion or sound. *Quaver* is used primarily for abstract ideas or sounds: "He *quavered* inwardly at the thought of proposing marriage." "His voice *quavered* and broke when he proposed." *Quiver* is used primarily to refer to visible vibration: "The branches *quivered* in the wind."

queasy, squeamish.   Both of these can refer to the feeling of being nauseated: "The rough flight over the mountains made my stomach *queasy* (*squeamish*)."

However, *squeamish* also means overly fastidious or oversensitive: "Dirty fingernails bother some people who are *squeamish*." "Politics is not for the *squeamish* person."

questionable, questioning.   That which is *questionable* is open to doubt and invites being questioned: "Cold fusion experiments conducted with little scientific rigor are highly *questionable*."

Questioning is the act of asking questions: "*Questioning* of the witness continued into the afternoon." "We live in a skeptical, *questioning* age." "She shot him a *questioning* look."

quiescent, quiet, quietude.   *Quiescent* means inactive or still: "Like many ghost towns of the Old West, Bodie is melancholy and *quiescent*."

Quiet refers to silence, the absence of noise: "What with ghetto blasters and boom boxes everywhere, it's hard to find a *quiet* place these days."

Quietude is the quality or state of *quiet* and tranquillity: "In the high mountains, the *quietude* is broken only by the whisper of the wind."

R

racket, racquet. *Racket* is the prevailing word for the light bat used in tennis or badminton. Even in references to the game of *racquetball*, the bat is usually spelled *racket*.

rancid, rank. *Rancid* and *rank* both refer to unpleasant smells, tastes, or impressions.

Rancid is usually associated with decomposing matter or stale oil, fat, or grease: "the unpleasant taste of *rancid* butter"; "the *rancid* smell of a filthy diner."

An obnoxious person can be called *rancid* in a figurative sense: "a *rancid* psychopath who thrived in the gutters of human existence."

Rank applies regardless of source: "air made foul by smoke from a *rank* cigar"; "the *rank* odor of the murder scene."

rant, rave. When a person "*rants and raves*," are two different actions involved, or only one?

Both *rant* and *rave* refer to loud, wild, or extravagant speech; with *rave*, however, a touch of insanity or irrationality is involved, and the speech may be incoherent. If self-control is present, a sentence such as this would be appropriate: "Anger at their laziness drove the headmaster to *rant* at boys who did not do their homework." Otherwise, if the headmaster has gone off the deep end, a sentence such as this would be more appropriate: "Uncontrolled anger at their laziness drove the headmaster to a frenzy of screaming in which he *ranted* and *raved* at boys who did not do their homework."

Rave is also used to indicate excessively enthusiastic

commendation or compliment: "She *raved* about what a great hairdresser John was." "You could tell that she was their first baby because of the way they *raved* about her."

rapacious, voracious. *Rapacious* means taking by force, plundering, or preying: "More than one Khan was a *rapacious* tyrant, invading, seizing, and looting countries throughout Asia." "She is a *rapacious* divorcée on the prowl."

Voracious means gluttonous, very greedy, or very eager: "After a month of barely existing on survival rations, he had a *voracious* appetite for anything that was placed before him." "She is a *voracious* reader."

rascal, rogue, scoundrel. In a hierarchy descending toward total villainy, the downward order is *rascal, rogue,* and *scoundrel*.

In current usage, the word *rascal* refers to a person or animal that is pleasingly mischievous: "a *rascal* of a child"; "a pet cat called *Rascal*."

In older uses, *rascal* was a synonym for *rogue* or *scoundrel*.

A *rogue* is an unprincipled or dishonest person: "a *rogue* who swindled the elderly."

The word *rogue* also applies to an animal that breaks from the herd and becomes fierce and wild: "a *rogue* elephant."

A *scoundrel* is an immoral, mean, or wicked person: "a crew of pirates made up of the worst *scoundrels* on the face of the earth."

ravage, ravish. *Ravage* means to destroy or devastate; *ravage* also implies violent and severe depredation that can occur over time: "Fires *ravaged* the forest for weeks." "Disease and drought *ravaged* the tiny nation and left its people helpless and starving."

Ravish is a unique word because of the diverse nature of its meanings. It can be used as a synonym for *rape*; it can mean to seize and carry away by force; or it can mean to enchant or enrapture.

The use of *ravish* makes this sentence totally unclear: "The village's women were *ravished* by the invading soldiers." Did the soldiers rape the women, carry them away, or enchant them? Maybe all three? Talk about confusing!

Anyway, as you have guessed by now, the thing to do is use the most accurate form of expression, even if it isn't very *ravishing* (enchanting).

raze, razz. *Raze* (pronounced to rhyme with "haze") means to tear down or demolish: "Crews *razed* the old theater to make room for an office building."

Whether a building is *razed* or *raised* poses no problem in writing, for readers can see the spellings and pick out the meanings. Spoken English is something else again, especially when two words have such vastly different meanings. Therefore, in speech it's best to either "build" a structure or "tear it down."

Razz (pronounced to rhyme with "jazz") means to heckle or tease: "Classmates *razzed* her about her new hairdo until she broke down in tears."

rebuff, rebuke. When you *rebuff* someone, you snub the person or deliver a blunt refusal or a setback: "In the pecking order of our town, newcomers are *rebuffed* by 'old money.' " "The tiny outpost *rebuffed* the attackers four times during the night."

When you *rebuke* someone, you scold them sharply: "It may seem that the chief duties of a sergeant are to *rebuke* privates and to bring them into line."

rebuke, reprimand, reproach, reprove. These four verbs refer to different degrees of adverse criticism.

Rebuke implies a sharp and severe expression of disapproval: "His commanding officer *rebuked* him for not saluting."

Reprimand may refer to a severe, official, and formal criticism: "The commanding officer *reprimanded* him for falling asleep at his post and took away his corporal's stripes."

Reproach implies a mild scolding: "Although glad to see me, she *reproached* me for not telling her I was coming."

Reprove implies a kindly intent to correct a fault: "It was better to spare the rod and simply *reprove* the child, so infrequently did he misbehave."

recalcitrant, reluctant. *Recalcitrant* describes a person who is deliberately hard to handle or who refuses to obey authority or custom: "The Church simply does not need any more *recalcitrant* heretics." "Child-rearing books never deal well with the problem of controlling the *recalcitrant* misbehaving youngster."

Reluctant describes a person who is unwilling because of distaste or indecisiveness: "He was *reluctant* to accept the promotion because doing so meant working longer hours."

recant, retract. These two words apply to the withdrawing or taking back of statements.

Theories and beliefs are *recanted*: "They were to be spared if they *recanted* Christianity, and executed if they persisted in their faith."

Promises, offers, and accusations are *retracted*: "She *retracted* her confession after she talked to her lawyer." "In order to avoid a lawsuit, the paper had to *retract* charges made on its editorial page."

receipt, recipe. A *receipt* is a written acknowledgment of payment for something received. A *recipe* is a formula for cooking ("a *recipe* for cherry pie") or, loosely, any kind of formula ("a *recipe* for success"; "a *recipe* for a great party"). However, *receipt* still exists as another word for *recipe*.

recoup, recover. *Recoup* pertains to recovering financial losses or compensation: "He *recouped* his losses in the stock market."

Recover pertains to getting back something that was lost in any manner: "Police *recovered* jewels and furs stolen from the Witherby mansion last night." "She took a year off from work in an attempt to *recover* her health." "He paused in his speech to let the hecklers finish while he tried to *recover* his self-possession."

recourse, resource. *Recourse* is the act of turning to someone or something for help: "Citizens have *recourse* to the law to settle disputes." "She had *recourse* to her sister in her time of grief."

A *resource* is the thing or person turned to for help:

"The law is a *resource* for citizens needing to settle disputes." "During her grief, her sister was a precious *resource*."

recur, reoccur. *Recur* is the preferred way of saying "occur again"—literally *re-occur*. *Re-occur* or *reoccur* is a word that editors and teachers disapprove of and that not all dictionaries even acknowledge the existence of. Such are the vagaries of English usage. Here we turn our backs on a spelling that makes sense both literally and visually. Instead we adopt a spelling that causes people to ask, "I wonder why it's spelled that way?"

redundant, repetitious. When repetition becomes boring, it is *repetitious*, and when repetition becomes superfluous, it is *redundant*.

Redundant is often used to label the unnecessary repeating of words: "We were snowed in by the snows of the night before." The expression is *redundant* because there is only one way to be snowed in, and "snows" is not needed.

reflection, refraction. Pertaining to what happens to a ray of light, *reflection* is the throwing back of a ray, while *refraction* is the bending of a ray.

When light strikes a mirror, the rays are thrown directly back, and you can see your *reflection*. *Refraction* can be demonstrated by placing a pencil in a glass of water. Light rays bend as they pass from the air and go through the water; where the light rays bend, the pencil appears to be broken. Eyeglass lenses *refract* light to compensate for visual deficiencies such as nearsightedness.

refugee, renegade. A *refugee* is a person who flees oppression or persecution to seek safety: "The underground railroad provided an escape for *refugees* from slavery in the South." "A *refugee* government, operating in England, spoke for Free France during World War II."

A *renegade* is a person who abandons one allegiance to accept a hostile one; in this respect, *renegade* is very similar in meaning to *traitor, turncoat,* or *religious apostate*: "He was a *renegade* in the truest sense, having switched from the Loyalists to the Communists during the war."

Renegade also refers to a person who rejects lawful or conventional behavior: "The severity of his crimes, coupled with his complete lack of remorse, marked him as a *renegade* from the human race."

refurbish, remodel. *Refurbish* means to brighten or freshen up. *Refurbishing* a house stops short of *remodeling* it, for *remodel* means to make over again, to rebuild.

regal, royal. *Regal* is a general term that pertains to whatever is splendid, magnificent, or befitting royalty: "*regal* bearing"; "a *regal* estate."

As compared with *regal*, *royal* pertains more specifically to kings, queens, or matters of the crown: "the *Royal* Air Force"; "the *royal* family"; "the *royal* yacht."

regret, remorse. *Regret* refers to emotions that range from being disappointed over a declined invitation to experiencing intense sorrow over a wrong done or the loss of a loved one: "My *regrets*, but I will not be able to participate in the conference set for next May 15." "To be honest, I have learned to *regret* my mistakes but not to stop making similar ones." "In moments of *regret*, I realize how much I miss her."

Remorse implies deep *regret*, self-reproach, anguish, and guilt over one's past deeds: "She felt pangs of *remorse* for having been so brusque." "He carried with him to the grave his feelings of *remorse* for having been undutiful to his father."

regretful, regrettable. *Regretful* means feeling regret or full of regret: "I am *regretful* over your failure to pass the course."

Regrettable means deserving regret: "Your failure to pass the course is truly *regrettable*."

regulation, rule. One person's *rule* is another's *regulation*. The expression "*rules* and *regulations*" is redundant.

relation, relationship. *Relation* and *relationship* can be used interchangeably to specify an association between persons or things: "Her analyst discovered a *relation* (*relationship*) between her dreams and her fears." "Scholarly inquiry revealed a *relation* (*relationship*) between the first and last verses of the sonnet."

Relationship refers broadly to the condition of being related: "a married *relationship*"; "developed a good *relationship* with her employees."

reminisce, ruminate.   A television interviewer asked Nancy Reagan if she "would like to *ruminate* on her years as First Lady."

Sure she would, if she were a cow chewing on a cud, for that's what *ruminate* originally meant. True, the meaning of *ruminate* has broadened so that the word now means to reflect on or to meditate.

However, a better word for those purposes is *reminisce*, which means to remember or recall experiences, usually fondly: "They sat in the swing on the porch, *reminiscing* about the old days and telling tall tales until well after midnight."

Now, if *reminisce* and *ruminate* can be used to express the same idea, what difference does it make which word you use?

Well, many people know full well that *ruminate* is related to *ruminant*, a word that specifies a cud-chewing animal. Consequently, little good is done for a person's image to link that person to the picture of an animal that chews and swallows and regurgitates, only to chew again.

renaissance, renascence.   Renaissance and *renascence* both mean rebirth. *Renascence* is seldom seen, the preferred form being *renaissance*: "that great period of revival of art and literature, the *Renaissance*"; "a postwar *renaissance* of public confidence"; "a *renaissance* of classical literature."

repel, repulse.   These two words mean to beat back or to drive off. They may be treated as synonyms except that *repel* carries with it the sense of causing distaste or aversion. Therefore, "Armies can *repel* (or *repulse*) invaders," but "Bad breath can *repel* anyone."

repress, suppress.   *Repress* means to hold back, keep down, or restrain: "She could not *repress* a smile at the sight of the clown." "He had the remarkable ability to *repress* his worries about his large debts." "Devout grammarians always wish to *repress* the new, liberal theories about language."

Suppress means to subdue or to put down, sometimes by force: "Troops loyal to the dictator drove the rebels into the jungle and *suppressed* the rebellion." "She placed a handkerchief over her face to *suppress* a cough." "Martial law *suppressed* open debate."

Republican, republican. The capitalized form of *Republican* stands for someone who is a member of the Republican political party. When lowercased, *republican* refers to a person who believes in the *republican* form of government.

SEE ALSO **Democrat, democrat.**

requirement, requisite. *Requirement* is the broader of these two terms, and can imply that something is wanted, needed, or demanded, often as a condition: "the *requirements* for admission to college."

Requisite is a more narrowly defined term that pertains to something absolutely indispensable for some purpose or necessary to attain a goal: "the *requisite* supplies for an exploration of the Amazon."

SEE ALSO *need, want; perquisite, prerequisite.*

resin, rosin. *Resin* is a substance that is usually gummy and tacky when warm, yet as hard and brittle as glass when cold. *Resin* is transparent or translucent and yellowish to brown in color. *Resin* can occur naturally as a secretion from plants, or it can be manufactured. *Resins* are used in shellacs and varnishes, in medicine, and in molded products such as pipe mouthpieces and electrical insulators.

Rosin is a hard, brittle *resin*. *Rosin* is used on the bows of violins and other stringed instruments. Athletes use *rosin* in powdered form on their hands or on the soles of their shoes to prevent slipping.

resistant, resistive. *Resistant* and *resistive* both imply the act of resisting or the ability to resist; they are interchangeable and not confusable.

restive, restless.   *Restive* is sometimes loosely used as a synonym for *restless*, but *restive* is better reserved to mean contrary, balky, unruly, or hard to control: "Colonists became *restive* under the rule of King George."

Restless means impatient, nervous, or unable to rest or relax: "He always felt the need to be busy, so when he had nothing to do he became *restless*."

retire, retreat.   *Retire* means to go away or withdraw, and has a variety of applications: "They go to bed early, *retiring* every night at eight." "He *retired* from the military at an early age." "The government regularly *retires* crumpled and otherwise worn paper money from circulation." "In baseball, when the third out is made, the side is *retired*." "It's good business to *retire* outdated and worn machinery."

Retreat means to withdraw to a safe or quiet place: "Outflanked, and with his troops outnumbered, the general ordered his army to *retreat*." "Union officials refused to *retreat* from the gains they had made." *Retreat* also means to recede: "The slopes became bare as the glacier *retreated*."

review, revue.   A *review* is a written evaluation: "The critic's *review* of last night's rock concert was devastating to the Punkers." A *review* can also be an examination or study: "Our year-end *review* of the books showed favorable returns on investments."

A *revue* is a musical show that consists of skits, songs, and dances.

revolve, rotate.   *Revolve* means to travel in a circle or an orbit around a central point; *rotate* means to spin or turn on an axis: "The earth *revolves* around the sun and *rotates* on its polar axis; one *revolution* takes a year, and one *rotation* takes twenty-four hours."

Revolve can also mean to ponder: "Her thoughts *revolved* around her boyfriend's plans for the weekend."

Rotate can also imply an indefinite repetition of an order or pattern: "Good farming practice is to *rotate* crops yearly." "The city's hospitals offered a series of *rotating* internships." "These slide projectors *rotate* through the classrooms."

rhyme, rime. The word *rhyme* refers to the regular recurrence of identical or similar sounds, especially at the ends of lines of verse. Until about 1560, the word was spelled *rime*; both forms existed side by side for a time, but *rhyme* is standard today.

Rime is an accumulation of granular ice tufts on objects such as ships' masts or the edges of an aircraft's wings. *Rime* is sometimes referred to as *rime ice* or *hoarfrost*.

SEE ALSO **poetry, verse.**

rigorous, vigorous. *Rigorous* refers to whatever is severe, strict, harsh, or rigid: "Crews subjected the experimental craft to *rigorous* testing." "A *rigorous* ascent of the Sierra Nevada faced pioneers near the end of their westward trek." "Completion of this course requires that you must defend your thesis during a *rigorous* oral examination."

Vigorous means strong, active, and energetic: "*Vigorous* exertions as a youth gave him a robust, solid body." "As a commander, Patton believed in a *vigorous* prosecution of the war." "The agency took *vigorous* steps to combat child abuse."

rite, ritual. *Rite* pertains to the prescribed or customary form for a ceremony, especially of a religious nature: "last *rites*"; "marriage *rites*"; "initiation *rites*"; "the *rites* of courtship."

Ritual can sometimes be substituted for *rite*: Both "initiation *ritual*" and "the *ritual* of courtship" are acceptable. However, "last *rites*" has become such a standard expression for funeral and burial that to substitute "last *ritual*" makes it sound like the final event in a string of ceremonies whether related to death or not.

Ritual can also pertain to a collection of *rites* ("the *ritual* of Christianity") or to that which is ceremonial ("the natives' *ritual* dance in honor of a guest").

SEE ALSO **ceremonial, ceremonious.**

roam, rove. *Roam* and *rove* imply traveling about without plan or purpose: "He spent his summer *roaming* through Europe, having no fixed route or goal." "She enjoyed *roving* through the woods on autumn days."

Rove can imply sometimes vigorous and purposeful travel: "Armed brigands *roved* through the farmland, raiding and looting."

rout, route.   A *rout* is a disorderly retreat: "The infantry was put to *rout* and fled from the battle, leaving behind their weapons and packs."

A *route* is a road, path, or course: "He stopped at every saloon on his favorite *route* home."

ruckus, rumpus.   A *ruckus* is a row or disturbance. A *rumpus* is a noisy commotion.

rural, rustic.   *Rural* describes sparsely settled country-side or agricultural land: "He left the city and returned to the *rural* life of his childhood." "The *rural* architecture of Kansas consists of farmhouses, barns, and one grain elevator after another."

Rustic, which is closely associated with *rural*, describes people or things that are simple, unsophisticated, and perhaps even primitive: "Time seems to stand still for the *rustic* people in the hills of West Virginia." *Rustic* can imply an uncomfortable plainness: "Nothing is worse than spending the night in a *rustic* motel with peeling paint and a sagging mattress."

Russia, Soviet Union, U.S.S.R.   For centuries, *Russia* was the name applied to the empire that occupied eastern Europe and northern and western Asia. In 1922, this area was renamed the Union of Soviet Socialist Republics. *Soviet Union* is a shortened way of saying the same thing, and *Russia* is popularly used to refer to the same area.

S

saber, sword. A *sword* is a hand-held weapon with a long blade; the blade has a sharp point and may be sharpened on one or both edges. A *sword* is used for thrusting or slashing.

A *saber* is a type of *sword*; the *saber* itself exists in two forms. One form is the cavalry *saber*, which is slightly curved and sharpened on one edge. The other form is the fencing *saber*, which has two sharpened edges. In fencing with a *saber*, a touch may be scored with the point or an edge.

SEE ALSO **épée, foil.**

safety, security. *Safety* primarily refers to freedom from danger, injury, or risk: "Your *safety* is not assured on the streets of a city at night." "The *safety* of your money is guaranteed with us." "The canoe carried them in *safety* across the raging river."

Security is sometimes used to mean the same as *safety*, but also has broader senses that pertain to feelings of confidence: "He has true job *security*." "The latest federal budget contains increased funds for national *security*." "The prisoner was transported yesterday to a maximum-*security* prison." "A bountiful harvest provided *security* from famine."

salary, wage. A *salary* is a form of earnings that is usually expressed in monthly or annual terms: "This job pays a *salary* of $35,000 per year."

Wages are earnings based on hourly, daily, weekly, or piecework performance: "This job pays *wages* of $17.50 per hour."

The definitions have little to do with amounts or prestige. Teachers paid *salaries* may earn less than construction workers paid *wages* by the hour.

salon, saloon.   *Saloon* is descended from the French word *salon*, and at one time they meant the same: a social room as in a hotel or on a ship. That use may still survive in some circles, but other uses prevail today.

A *salon* can be a commercial establishment such as a beauty parlor or hair *salon*; a *salon* can also be a rather elegant drawing room for entertaining guests.

The word *saloon* is an old-fashioned and less glamorous way of saying "bar," "tavern," or "cocktail lounge."

Anyone having a hard time remembering the difference between *salon* and *saloon* will note that *booze* and *saloon* both contain two *o*'s.

salubrious, salutary.   *Salubrious* implies that something promotes health and applies chiefly to climatic conditions: "Clean mountain air has a *salubrious* influence on anyone's well-being."

Salutary applies to anything that is beneficial: "The music had a *salutary* effect on his troubled mood." What is *salutary* may not often appear to be so at first glance: "The cannon shot was a *salutary* warning that brought about immediate defensive measures."

SEE ALSO   **healthful, healthy.**

salutatorian, valedictorian.   These words refer to students who give addresses at graduation ceremonies. The *valedictorian* is the highest-ranking student in the graduating class, and the *salutatorian* is the second-highest-ranking.

sanatarium, sanatorium, sanitarium, sanitorium.   *Sanatorium* or *sanitarium* is used in reference to an institution for the treatment of chronic physical or mental illness. *Sanatarium* and *sanitorium* are not correct current usage. However, institutions that have been in existence for a number of years may have any one of the forms as part of their names. The spellings of these are tricky.

sanction.   A newspaper headline read "Oklahoma Officials to Break Silence Today Regarding Sanctions." A

California governmental agency put out a document ti-
tled *Affirmative Action Sanctions Agreement*.

The problem with *sanction(s)* is that it means either to
approve some action or to institute a coercive or restrictive measure against a person or organization. Therefore,
are the Oklahoma officials concerned with approvals or
disapprovals? The same question can be asked about the
affirmative action agreement.

And that raises still another question: Should ambiguity be *sanctioned*?

Answer: Do not use *sanction(s)* unless the surrounding words clearly establish what you mean.

sarcastic, sardonic.   *Sarcastic* implies the intentional hurt-
ing of a person's feelings by taunting, ridiculing, or jeer-
ing: "His *sarcastic* jibes at middle-class values alienated
his audience." "Even if I'm only a minute late, my boss
gives me some *sarcastic* comment about lunch hour ending at one."

Sardonic implies bitterness and scorn along with cynicism or skepticism: "He had a *sardonic* comment to
make about everything, the talk of a man who feels that
life is against him." "The interviewer asked *sardonically*
whether the evangelist practiced what he preached."

SEE ALSO   **cynic, pessimist, skeptic; irony, paradox.**

sate, satiate.   *Sate* and *satiate* may be used interchangeably to refer to complete indulgence, the feeling of being
full or of having had enough: "*sated* with the power of
political success"; "*satiated* after a sumptuous meal."

In current usage, however, either term may imply overindulgence to the point where all pleasure is lost—the act
of making a complete pig out of oneself: "He was so
satiated (sated) with food and drink that he could not rise
from the table." "She was so *satiated (sated)* with fame
that applause and bravos meant nothing to her anymore."

scan, skim.   *Skim* means to look or glance at something
hastily or superficially: "To understand the theme of *Moby-
Dick*, it must be read word for word and not just
skimmed."

Scan has become a true confusable, for it has acquired
two considerably different meanings. In its older senses,

scan meant to look at something repeatedly and point-by-point: "A brain *scan* passes numerous X-ray beams through the brain from various angles and different levels."

In its more modern sense, *scan* means the same as *skim*, a quick survey. Therefore, the proper use of *scan* and the difference between *scan* and *skim* can be important. Suppose that you have an unemployed relative who sits around the house, claiming each day to *scan* the want ads looking for a job. How long you have this freeloader on your hands depends upon what is meant by *scan*. Perhaps *skimming* is all that's going on.

SEE ALSO **examine, inspect, investigate.**

scant, scanty, scarce, sparse. *Scant* suggests a falling short of what is desirable rather than what is essential: "In winter, the daylight hours are *scant*."

Scanty suggests a falling short of what is essential rather than desirable: "Supplies were too *scanty* to prevent starvation during the winter."

Scarce means that something is in short supply or is infrequently seen or found: "Because gasoline was *scarce* during the war, it was rationed." "Good-looking men are *scarce* in my hometown."

Sparse refers to things that are not dense or crowded: "He is not bald, but his hair is indeed *sparse*." "The *sparse* population of Nevada makes for mile after mile of loneliness."

schizophrenia, split personality. *Schizophrenia* does not mean *split personality*, as in a person who has two or more distinct personalities. That disorder is called *multiple personality*. Multiple personality is an abnormality of degree. That is, most normal people show pronounced changes of style and behavior as they move through different situations, yet the underlying integrity of the personality remains intact. In a multiple personality disorder, the different personalities are relatively independent.

Schizophrenia instead refers to the disorder in which a person is "split" from reality. That is, the mind withdraws from everyday social and vocational functioning and becomes disturbed, causing the victim to suffer hallucinations and delusions.

scoff, sneer. *Scoff* means to laugh at or mock; *scoff* implies lack of respect or lack of belief: "People *scoffed* at Newton until his theories were proven." "She *scoffed* at the idea of higher education and went right to work after graduating from high school."

Sneer, as a verb, means to say something that is ill-natured or caustic while putting on a scornful or derisive facial expression; the expression itself is also called a *sneer*: "I was not surprised when his upper lip curled; he always *sneered* at my ideas." "He issued a *sneering* denunciation of the superintendent's program."

scorn, shun, spurn. *Scorn* means to show extreme contempt: "In an industrious society, nonworkers and shirkers are *scorned* as being drones." "One wonders how many good ideas are misunderstood because scientists *scorn* the use of ordinary language."

Shun means to avoid a person or thing: "He *shuns* publicity and prefers to stay in his apartment." "Like a leper, he was *shunned* by his former friends."

Spurn means to reject someone or something while showing *scorn*: "He cultivated certain friends and *spurned* others." "He went against all advice and *spurned* suggestions that he should carry a gun."

Scot, Scotch, Scotchman, Scotsman, Scotswoman, Scottish. A *Scot* is a native or inhabitant of Scotland; *Scotsman* or *Scotswoman* is also used in this same sense. Those three terms are preferred in Scotland over *Scotchman*.

Scotch and *Scottish* are both used as adjectives. Established uses are "*Scotch* whisky"; "*Scotch* broth"; "*Scottish* rite of freemasonry"; "*Scottish* terrier."

scrimp, skimp. *Skimp* is more than likely descended from *scrimp*. The two are used interchangeably to mean be stingy, economize severely, or make something hastily or poorly: "Our school saved money by *scrimping (skimping)* on room for an adequate library." "She paid for her vacation by *scrimping (skimping)* and saving all year."

scrip, script. *Scrip* is a small piece of paper, a certificate representing a fraction of a share of stock, a document representing something due to the bearer, or a substitute for money.

Script refers to either handwriting or the text of a play or movie.

scythe, sickle.   These are tools used for cutting grass, crops, or weeds. A *scythe* has a long handle and can be used while standing erect. A *sickle* has a short handle, and the user must bend over to do any cutting.

seal, sea lion, walrus.   A *seal* is a sleek aquatic mammal with fins and a cylindrical, torpedolike body. *Seals* occur in three main groups. One group consists of eared *seals*; the *sea lion* is in this group, as is the fur *seal*. A second group consists of earless *seals*, which include harbor *seals* and elephant *seals*; an earless *seal* has small ear openings but no ear structure on the outside of its body, The third group consists of *walruses*, which are identifiable by their tusks.

seamy, steamy.   Was the novel *seamy* or *steamy*? It was *seamy* if it was unattractive, unpleasant, or sordid. It was *steamy* if it was erotic.

seasonable, seasonal   *Seasonable* pertains to whatever is suitable for a season: "*seasonable* storms"; "*seasonable* frost."

Seasonal pertains to whatever is caused by a season: "*seasonal* unemployment"; "*seasonal* rates."

secret, secrete.   *Secret* refers to anything concealed or hidden: "Tom and Becky found a *secret* passage into the cave." "She hid her money in a *secret* place in the cellar."

Secrete has two somewhat contrasting meanings. One meaning specifies the act of hiding: "She *secreted* her money in a box in the cellar." The other meaning pertains to the production of a fluid: "Various glands *secrete* the hormones necessary for life."

SEE ALSO **covert, overt.**

sectarian, secular.   *Sectarian* refers to whatever is characteristic of a sect. Although a sect can be any group having a common leadership and doctrine, the words *sect* and *sectarian* are usually used in reference to religious groups: "Many Catholics find it hard to swallow the *sectarian* ideologies of the Jesuits."

Secular pertains to worldly things as distinguished from things relating to religion: "To be a good pastor, one needs to be concerned with both the spiritual and the *secular* needs of the parishioners."

sedate, staid. These two words pertain to very closely related degrees of being serious.

Sedate suggests calmness, a composed and dignified attitude, or the ability to remain uninfluenced by disturbing elements: "She was too *sedate* to participate in the frivolity of the party going on around her."

Staid suggests *sedateness*, self-restraint, or prim and prudent reservation bordering on the colorless or boring: "An influx of younger families, with their noisy children and loud music, proved disconcerting to the *staid* older residents of the village."

SEE ALSO **prim, prissy; prudent, prudish.**

sedition, treason. *Sedition* is conduct or language that incites rebellion, advocates the overthrow of government, or stirs up *treason*.

Treason is the act of attempting to overthrow the government or of betraying the government. *Treason* consists of two elements: adherence to the enemy, and rendering aid and comfort to the enemy.

SEE ALSO **traitorous, treacherous.**

selfish, selfless. A *selfish* person is chiefly concerned with one's own welfare or interests.

A *selfless* person is without concern for self and is devoted to the welfare of others.

sensible, sensitive. Literally speaking, *sensible* and *sensitive* both refer broadly to the ability of a person's senses to perceive something. However, everyday usage has established a difference in the ways these words should be applied to people.

Sensible describes a person who shows good judgment: "The only *sensible* thing to do is wait out the storm before getting back on the road." "She was *sensible* enough to withhold comment until she'd heard both sides of the argument."

Sensitive describes a person with keenly developed senses, or who is acutely responsive intellectually and aesthetically: "She enjoyed his company because he was *sensitive* to her needs." "To appreciate fine wine, a person must be *sensitive* to its bouquet and its more subtle flavorings."

Sensitive can also mean that a person is easily offended and touchy: "He's *sensitive* about his lack of education, even though it hasn't held him back."

sensual, sensuous.   The battle is probably lost on this one, because *sensual* and *sensuous* have become pretty near interchangeable in ordinary usage. However, for anyone interested in preserving the distinctions, they are as follows:

Sensual pertains to the gross gratification of the physical senses, especially those associated with sexual pleasure: "Few sights in the world can surpass the *sensual* appeal of the topless beauties on the French Riviera."

Sensuous pertains to the refined and intellectual gratification of the senses involved in the appreciation of art, music, literature, or nature: "The soft, *sensuous* strains of the cello drifted into the hushed concert hall."

sentiment, sentimentality.   *Sentiment* suggests an opinion that is based on feeling or emotion instead of reason: "His *sentiments* about Lebanon were such that he wanted the country bombed into rubble."

Sentimentality is the condition of being sentimental to an excessive or mawkish degree: "What started out in him as honest *sentiment* became such obvious and distasteful *sentimentality* that he was mocked and laughed at."

SEE ALSO **believe, feel, think; maudlin, mawkish.**

sentinel, sentry.   A *sentinel* is any kind of guard or *sentry*. A *sentry* is specifically a military guard.

serf, slave, vassal.   A *serf* belonged to the lower classes of feudal systems. *Serfs* were bound to the land and subject to the will of the lord who owned the land. To all appearances, *serf*dom was a form of slavery. The essential difference was that the *serf* belonged to the soil, while the *slave* belonged to the lord. Therefore, when the land was sold, the *serf* stayed, while the lord went. Under slavery, the *slave* would have gone with the lord. This is a minor technicality seeing that neither *serf* nor *slave* had any say in who did what anyway.

A *vassal* was part of the pecking order of the Middle Ages, ranking somewhat above a *serf*. *Vassals* were the tenant farmers of the time and could hold and work land on conditions of homage and allegiance to a lord. In modern usage, *vassal* has come to mean any person or thing subject to any controlling influence: "the lesser nations that had become *vassals* of Russia"; "investors who had become *vassals* to stock market trends"; "a fine mind that had become a *vassal* to drink and drugs."

several, various. *Several* implies an indefinite number more than two but fewer than many: "*Several* people came to the meeting, but we'd hoped for a bigger turnout."

Various can be used to mean the same as *several* with respect to mentioning an indefinite number. However, the principal meaning of *various* has to do with people or things that are of different kinds: "birds as *various* as the sparrow and the eagle"; "*various* rate increases for different utility users."

sewage, sewerage. *Sewage* is the waste that flows through *sewerage*. *Sewerage* is the system of pipes, pumps, sewers, and treatment plants used to treat and dispose of *sewage*.

shall, should, will, would. For three centuries, explainers of English grammar have been trying to pound into our thick heads the rules for using *shall* and *will*. These are rules that seem designed for the express purpose of making English more complicated. These rules say: Use *will* for the first person and *shall* for the second and third persons when expressing volition—stating what is mandatory, making promises, or issuing threats or warnings. Do the reverse when expressing what is predictive—foretelling or surmising. In tabular form the rules are usually presented in a simple-looking little table such as this one:

Volitional	**Predictive**
I (we) *will*	I (we) *shall*
You *shall*	You *will*
He (she) (they) (it) *shall*	He (she) (they) (it) *will*

Those distinctions are almost universally ignored in the United States. Who says "You *shall* clean up your room before you're allowed out of this house"? It sounds almost biblical, and we tend to substitute *will* so that we don't sound pompous. Lawyers frequently misuse *shall* and *will* when writing the countless laws and regulations that rule our lives. And in the military, *will* expresses what is mandatory regardless of person or tense.

In the interests of clear communication, there are better ways of expressing volition or stating what is predictive. "I promise to be there tomorrow" is volitional. "I expect to be there tomorrow" is predictive. For describing what is mandatory, *must* is a better word than *shall* or *will*. *Must* presents none of the problems that *shall* or *will* do, and *must* is in the common speech of most people.

In truth, the distinctions between *shall* and *will* are not very important as long as a suitable substitute is chosen from the immense storehouse of our language.

As for *should* and *would*, the rules of traditional grammar say to use them in the same manner as prescribed for *shall* and *will*. Americans, however, have other ideas on the subject and generally use *should* and *would* according to these rules:

Should is used (1) to express conditions—"If anything *should* happen to that dog, I would die"; (2) to express obligation—"You *should* see a dentist at least once a year"; (3) to express what is probable—"If I leave by noon, I *should* be there by supper"; (4) to request in a polite manner or to soften a direct statement—"You *should* finish your work before you go on vacation."

Would is used (1) to express a preference or choice—"I *would* rather eat sooner than later"; (2) to express a wish or desire—"He is one of those who *would* forbid alcohol"; (3) to express a plan or intention—"They said that they *would* come; (4) to express a custom or habit—"They *would* often go to church on Saturday night"; (5) to express a contingency or possibility—"If she were coming, she *would* be here by now"; (6) to express probability—"He *would* have won if he had not stumbled"; (7) to express doubt or uncertainty—"That *would* seem acceptable"; (8) to soften a request—"*Would* you please look into this problem as soon as possible?"

Would is sometimes used in place of *could* ("The tank *would* hold 15 gallons") and in place of *should* ("I knew I *would* enjoy the show").

SEE ALSO **can, could, may, might.**

shear, sheer. *Shear* means to remove fleece or hair by cutting or clipping.

Sheer has a variety of meanings: a sudden change of course ("to *sheer* away from danger"); a thin fabric ("a *sheer* nightgown"); absolute or downright ("the *sheer* persistence of a stubborn person"); and steep or perpendicular ("the *sheer* wall of the cliff").

shovel, spade. A *shovel* is a tool with a broad, deep scoop and a long handle. *Shovels* can be used to lift and move loose material such as dirt or coal. A *shovel* can also be used for digging, but that task is easier with a *spade*. A *spade*'s blade is rounded to make digging easier, and the top of the blade is shaped so that a foot may be pressed against it.

sight, site. *Sight* refers to vision, what is seen, or the ability to see: "a *sight* for sore eyes."

Site refers to location: "a choice *site* for a new office building."

significant. *Significant* is in the same category as *meaningful* in that both say only that some meaning exists. Thus *significant* is a comfortable word for people who wish to refer to some quantity or quality but are hesitant to say how much or to what degree. No precise information is conveyed in expressions such as these: "*significant* levels of pollution"; "a *significant* body of literature on the subject"; *significant* measures to control traffic." On a scale of one to ten, or on any scale for that matter, any interpretation is possible. Even words such as *large* or *major*, as indefinite as they are, would be closer to some ballpark guess than *significant*.

SEE ALSO **meaningful**.

simple, simplistic. *Simple* means having few parts or features, easy to understand, easy to do or use, or bare and unadorned: "The dress was made from a *simple* pattern." "The *simple* sentence has made a fortune for many a writer." "Despite his education and wealth, he is a man of *simple* tastes."

Simplistic means excessively or unrealistically simple: "It is *simplistic* to say that people are either all good or all bad."

skulk, sulk. *Skulk* means to lie in hiding or to move about in a sinister, stealthy manner. *Sulk* means to go into a withdrawn, petulant mood.

Therefore, it is safe to say that the villain in an old-time melodrama both *skulks* and *sulks*. He *skulks* while trying to trap the fair maiden, and he *sulks* when his plans are—"Curses!"—foiled again.

slate, tile. *Slate* is fine-grained rock that splits naturally into thin, smooth-surfaced layers.

Tile is a thin material used for flooring, roofing, countertops, and bathroom walls. *Tile* is manufactured from a variety of materials, including rock, concrete, fired clay, plastic, asphalt, and rubber.

slattern, slut. Either one of these stands for a woman who is sexually promiscuous or who is untidy, dirty, or slovenly.

slew, slough. *Slew* refers to a large number ("a *slew* of gnats") or a skidding sideways movement ("a car that *slewed* around a corner").

Slough (pronounced either the same as *slew* or to rhyme with *how*) refers to a slow-moving, often muddy body of water resembling a creek.

Slough (pronounced to rhyme with *stuff*) means to shed or cast off: "Tissue *sloughing* off caused the ulcer to resume bleeding."

slit, slot. A *slit* is an opening such as a cut, tear, or crack, especially one that is long, straight, and narrow: "The only light in the cave came through a *slit* in the rock."

A *slot* is a narrow groove or opening such as for receiving coins in a vending machine: "For good reason, *slot* machines are known as one-armed bandits."

sliver, splinter. Either one of these refers to a piece, usually long and slender, that is cut or torn off; a few uses have become established: "a *sliver* of cheese on top of a piece of apple pie"; "a quarrel over a *sliver* of land"; "a *splinter* group from the Republican Party."

Otherwise, a *sliver* in the finger is just as painful as a *splinter*, and the meaning is the same.

sociable, social. *Sociable* means friendly, gregarious, agreeable, or characterized by informal companionship: "There is no such animal as an unfailingly *sociable* cat." "It was a *sociable* evening of cards and good conversation."

Social is a broad term that pertains to living or associating together in communities: "Alcoholism had become so widespread in the community that it was a *social* problem and no longer a personal one." "*Social* science is the study of people living together in groups." "Ants are *social* insects, working and thriving together."

solid, stolid. *Solid* generally refers to whatever is firm, filled with matter throughout, and not hollowed out: "statues chiseled out of *solid* rock." Whatever is strong, dependable, substantial, or reliable is also *solid*: "a *solid*, well-built house"; "the *solid* body of a weight lifter"; "a *solid* line of reasoning." *Solid* also pertains to whatever is uninterrupted: "a speech that droned on for a *solid* hour."

Stolid describes a person who has or shows little or no emotion: "Prison had reduced him to a silent, *stolid* creature who took everything as a matter of course."

some day (some time), someday (sometime), somedays (sometimes). As two words, *some day* and *some time* are used when *some* is an adjective modifying the noun *day* or *time* and when the emphasis is to be placed on the *day* or *time*: "Choose *some day* when you're not so busy." "She stayed for quite *some time*." "I want *some time* available for my own purposes."

As one word, *someday* or *sometime* refer to an indefinite or unspecified occasion or instance: "You'll succeed *someday*." "She will be here *sometime* soon." "He is a *sometime* father who is not always present."

Somedays and *sometimes* are near-synonyms for *occasionally*: "*Somedays* I get nothing done at all." "*Sometimes* it snows here."

spaded, spayed. Confusion here is based on inattention to pronunciation. That is, female dogs are *spayed*, not *spaded* unless you go after them with a digging tool. To *spay* means to sterilize a female animal by removing the ovaries. *Spaded* is nonstandard English for the same operation.

specie, species. *Specie* is money in the form of coin or precious metal such as gold or silver.

Species—the same spelling is used in the singular and the plural—means a distinct kind: "a *species* of heroism unknown to his fellow soldiers." *Species* is one of the categories used in the systems of classification of biology and botany.

These systems of classification are called *taxonomies*. The major taxonomic categories in biology, beginning with the broadest and most inclusive and ending with the narrowest, are as follows: kingdom, phylum (division in botany), subphylum, class, order, family, genus, *species*, and sub*species* (variety in botany).

If you were to trace a cocker spaniel through that classification system, the labels would be as shown here:

Kingdom: animal.
Phylum: chordate. Chordates include amphibians, fish, reptiles, birds, and mammals. A chordate has a notochord (a stiff, tubular column that runs down the back of the body) and a nerve tube that runs above the notochord. Some chordates have gill slits.
Subphylum: vertebrate. Vertebrates include fish, birds, and mammals. A vertebrate generally has a bony backbone, a bony skeleton, and a cranium (brain case).
Class: mammal. Mammals include people, cats, dogs,

whales, and cattle. A mammal is a warm-blooded animal that feeds its young on mother's milk.

Order: carnivore. Carnivores include cats and dogs. A carnivore is any animal that eats mainly meat.

Family: canidae. Canidae include animals that are sociable, are awake in the daytime, and attack their prey with jaws rather than claws. This definition excludes cats (felidae) but includes dogs, wolves, foxes, jackals, and hyenas.

Genus: *canis*. Canis includes dogs, wolves, and foxes.

Species: *canis familiaris*. This Latin phrase refers to the domestic dog, the four-legged animal who rules the household.

Subspecies (or breed): cocker spaniel.

specious, spurious. *Specious* applies to anything that looks or sounds good on the surface but is actually not so: "His excuse for being late was *specious*, because he could not have been where he said he was."

Spurious refers to whatever is artificial, invalid, false, counterfeit, or not genuine: "He insisted on collecting original works of art and not *spurious* reproductions."

With either *specious* or *spurious*, the intent to deceive may be deliberate. *Spurious* seems to connote a more evil deed and intent than does *specious*, but dictionaries are not unanimous on this interpretation.

speed, velocity. *Speed* refers to how fast a body is moving without regard to the direction of movement: "The captain ordered an increase in *speed* as we neared the enemy submarine." "Freeways increase the *speed* at which traffic can move through cities."

Velocity, which is sometimes used in place of *speed*, has a restricted technical sense that combines *speed* and direction: "the *velocity* of a bullet between point A and point B."

spire, steeple. A *steeple* is a tower that rises above a building, usually a church. A *spire* is a pointed, upward-tapering object on top of a tower such as a *steeple*.

sprain, strain. A *sprain* is a wrenching or tearing of the ligaments that hold a joint together. A *strain*, or *pulled* *muscle*, is an overstretching of a muscle. None of this makes a lot of difference when you're in pain, except that it is nice from time to time to know the terms that doctors use.

spray, spume.   A *spray* is a cloud or fine mist of liquid: "We were drenched with *spray* from waves breaking over the bow."

Spume is foam or froth: "The sea rolled in, crashing against the rocks, leaving swirling puddles of white *spume* in the shallows."

SEE ALSO **foam, froth.**

sprint, spurt.   *Sprint* means to run at top speed for a short distance; a *sprint* is a short race that is run at top speed.

Spurt refers to a gushing forth in energy or extreme activity: "Blood tends to *spurt* from serious wounds." "He labored in *spurts*, getting his best work done at rare intervals." "The stock market *spurted* upward, and then took a sharp dive."

It may also be said that runners *sprint* or *spurt* toward the finish, just as football players *sprint* or *spurt* toward the end zone.

stable, stall.   A *stable* is a building where horses or cattle are sheltered. Inside the *stable*, a *stall* is a compartment for one animal.

stage left, stage right.   When you stand on the stage and face the audience, *stage left* is on your left, and *stage right* is on your right.

stair(s), step(s).   These words are interchangeable when referring to a flight of *stairs* or *steps* or a single *stair* or *step*.

stalactite, stalagmite.   *Stalactites* point down, and *stalagmites* point up. Both are found in caves and consist of mineral deposits that are transported by dripping water.

stalk, stem.   A *stem* is the main trunk or body of a plant; the *stem* supports branches, leaves, and flowers.

Stem is the preferred term among plant experts; others sometimes use *stalk*, which can refer to any *stem*like part.

stammer, stutter.   *Stammer* refers to involuntary pauses or stops in speech. *Stutter* refers to the rapid repetition of sounds.

stanch, staunch.   These are interchangeable, or becoming so. The more traditional uses that are still honored by many people are given here:
   Stanch means to stop the flow of a liquid: "*stanch* the flow of blood from a wound"; "*stanch* the flow of her tears."
   Staunch means steadfast, firm, and faithful: "always aided by his *staunch* supporters."

stationary, stationery.   *Stationary* means fixed in one place and not moving. *Stationery* means the paper and envelopes used for writing correspondence.

stentorian, stertorous.   *Stentorian* means very loud. *Stertorous* describes snoring, the raspy, labored breathing caused by obstructed nasal passages.

stimulant, stimulus.   A *stimulant* is a drug that provokes increased activity: "Coffee is an acknowledged *stimulant*."
   A *stimulus* is an event that provokes action: "The war proved to be a *stimulus* to industry."

strategy, tactics.   *Strategy* refers to the overall planning and directing of large-scale operations and is concerned with long-range goals: "The *strategy* that led to victory called for invasion and attacks on three fronts." "A clever *marketing* strategy helped the company overwhelm its competition."
   Tactics are maneuvers and actions necessary to achieve short-range objectives, the means of carrying out a *strategy*: "*Tactics* won the battles; *strategy* won the war." "The bullying *tactics* of the defense attorney left witnesses shaken."
   Tactics is also used in the singular: "A clever politician, he was a master of the *tactic* of splitting the opposition."

stultify, stunt. *Stultify* means to make seem foolish or stupid: "Drink made the dullard more *stultified* than ever." *Stultify* also means to render something useless: "It was another internecine faculty war that *stultified* the teaching abilities of the professors."

Stunt means to hinder or stop the growth of: "Acid rain is proven to *stunt* the growth of forests."

stupor, torpor.   A *stupor* is a lethargic condition in which the mind and senses are dulled: "His *stupor* was caused by drugs."

Torpor refers to a condition of suspended animation resembling dormancy or hibernation: "From her heights of intellectual activity she has withdrawn into a deathlike *torpor*."

subconscious, unconscious.   *Unconscious* generally refers to a state of mind characterized by a loss of consciousness, a lack of awareness of internal and external events. In psychoanalysis, the word *unconscious* refers to a domain of the psyche encompassing the repressed functions and primitive impulses that are too anxiety-provoking to be accepted into consciousness.

In general usage, *subconscious* refers to information that exists in the mind just below the level of consciousness, or information that a person is only vaguely aware of: "a person's *subconscious* motives." Instead of *subconscious*, psychoanalysts often use the word *preconscious* to refer to the level of the mind that material passes through on its way toward full consciousness.

subject, topic.   These are frequently interchangeable: "My *subject* (*topic*) today is that diabolical form of self-punishment known as golf." However, a *topic* is sometimes considered to be a division of a *subject*. Thus English teachers require themes to be written on *subjects* and paragraphs to be headed with *topic* sentences.

substantial, substantive.   "An audit of statements revealed no *substantive* problems." That sentence is unclear, because *substantial* and *substantive* are true confusables. Either one can mean ample and considerable in quantity. Or *substantial* can mean ample and considerable in quantity, while *substantive* refers to nothing more than having substance. Therefore, "*substantial* problems" could be large problems, while "*substantive* problems" could be problems of any sort.

supersede, surpass. *Supersede* means to take the place of and implies that something better and more up-to-date has come along: "The automobile has *superseded* the horse." "The telegraph *superseded* the Pony Express." *Supersede* is often misspelled as *supercede*.

Surpass means to excel or to be superior: "She has *surpassed* everyone in generosity." "The beauty of the high mountain valleys far *surpassed* expectations."

sybarite, sycophant. A *sybarite* is a person devoted to self-indulgence and luxury. A *sycophant* is a person who seeks favor by flattering people of wealth and influence.

symptom, syndrome. A *symptom* is any subjective evidence of a patient's condition: "A headache may be a *symptom* of many diseases."

A *syndrome* is a group of *symptoms* that is typical of a condition: "The infant's deformed limbs and outsized skull constituted a *syndrome* of genetic abnormalities."

Each of these terms is used figuratively: "High unemployment is a *symptom* of inflation." "All the signs pointed to a meltdown of the nuclear power plant, another disaster like that in the movie *China Syndrome*."

SEE ALSO **disease, illness.**

T

tamper, tinker. *Tamper* means to meddle or interfere in a harmful manner: "Diplomats *tampered* with the language of the treaty until it was meaningless." "New owners drove customers away by *tampering* with the traditions of the club."

Tinker means to fuss or putter around with something, or to make clumsy attempts to repair: "Like many men, he would *tinker* with something until it no longer worked at all." "She never finished writing anything because she was always *tinkering* with her sentences, trying to make them perfect."

taunt, taut. *Taunt* means to sneer at or ridicule: "Friends *taunted* him about his lack of success with women."

Taut describes something, such as rope or cord, that is so tightly stretched that there is no slack: "Wind filled the sails and made the lines as *taut* as violin strings." "Gaunt and emaciated, her skin was stretched *taut* over her bones." "Constant stress had left her nerves as *taut* as steel wires." And figuratively speaking, "He writes in a *taut*, economical style "

Taut also refers to whatever is in proper order or condition: "A *taut* (disciplined) ship is a happy ship."

SEE ALSO **tense, terse.**

temblor, trembler, tremblor. When referring to an earthquake, *temblor* is the right word to use. *Trembler* refers to anyone or anything that trembles, and *tremblor* is a misspelling.

temerity, timidity. *Temerity* and *timidity* are opposites. *Temerity* means boldness or rashness, especially when brought on by contempt for the dangers or consequences of an action: "Few privates have the *temerity* to talk back to sergeants."

Timidity means being hesitant or easily frightened, or lack of self-confidence: "His *timidity* kept him from asking for a raise, although he certainly deserved one."

SEE ALSO **timid, timorous.**

tenant, tenet.   A bureaucratic document contained this statement: "The tennants of the city's grading ordinance appear to have been met." The sentence is doubly wrong. *Tenants* has only one *n* in its middle, and it's the wrong word to begin with.

The right word would have been *tenets*, meaning principles, doctrines, or beliefs. The word *tenants* refers to people who pay rent to live somewhere or to occupy office space.

tendency, trend.   *Tendency* suggests a predisposition to act in a certain way, especially because of some inherent quality: "My car has a *tendency* to pull to the right." "She has a *tendency* to exaggerate."

Trend suggests a general direction or course that is influenced by external factors: "The long-term *trend* of interest rates is up." "The *trend* of higher education is toward providing more and more practical courses."

tense, terse.   *Tense* describes something that is stretched tight but not necessarily taut: "The muscles around his mouth became *tense* whenever people talked about his lack of motivation." *Tense* also describes a condition of mental strain: "I was so *tense* last night that I didn't sleep a wink." Sometimes the strain can be collective, a feeling of group tension: "The atmosphere in the meeting was *tense* with charges and recriminations." The strain may also be a feeling of suspense: "The novel was written in a *tense*, gripping style that kept the reader turning pages."

Terse describes brief, concise speech or writing that is smooth and polished: "His answers were clipped and *terse*."

SEE ALSO **taunt, taut.**

test, trial.   A *test* is something used to ascertain truth or validity, or to establish whether a person or thing meets a standard, criterion, or norm: "civil service *test*"; "a *test* conducted under rigidly controlled laboratory conditions"; "a *test* on your knowledge of quadratic equations." *Test* can also refer to a trying or troublesome situation: "Today's traffic is a *test* of anybody's patience."

One definition of *trial* is that it is a judicial examination that is conducted according to law, the purpose being to settle an issue between two parties. *Trial* also means the trying of a person or thing to establish worth: "a money-back guarantee after a thirty-day *trial* period"; "an employee hired on a *trial* basis"; "subjected prisoners to the rite of *trial* by ordeal."

testy, touchy. A *testy* person is irritable and peevish: "Like many supervisors, he became *testy* when his instructions weren't followed."

A *touchy* person is oversensitive and too easily offended: "A typical insecure and uneasy artist, he was always *touchy* when his paintings did not receive rave reviews."

than, then. *Than* is a word of comparison: "I like pie better *than* cake." "That's easier said *than* done." "She deceived me worse *than* if she'd told an outright lie." "I'd rather be anywhere else *than* in the dean's office."

Then is a word of time: "*Then* came the dawn." "Math was taught differently *then*." "We had fun *then*, didn't we?"

that (those), this (these). *This* (*these*) refers to the person or thing nearby in space or thought; *that* (*those*) refers to the person or thing further removed: "The book in your hands is *this* book; the book on the shelf across the room is *that* book." "*These* are mine, and *those* are yours." "The paragraph above *this* paragraph is *that* paragraph."

This may be used to refer to what is about to be stated: "As *this* next example shows . . ."

that, which, who. Many users of English have grown accustomed to a set of principles that apply to the use of *that*, *which*, and *who*. These words are used with essential and nonessential sentence elements. The element may be a word, phrase (a group of words), or a clause (a group of words containing a verb).

A couple of definitions—for essential and nonessential sentence elements—are necessary.

An *essential* element is one that *cannot* be removed from the sentence without changing the basic meaning of the sentence. An essential element is also called a *restrictive* element because it restricts, limits, defines, or identifies whatever it refers to. That is, a restrictive element is essential to the basic meaning of the sentence. Therefore, the term *essential* is used here.

By way of contrast, a *nonessential* element *can* be removed from a sentence without changing the basic meaning of the sentence. A nonessential element provides descriptive detail that is useful to the reader. A nonessential element is also called a *nonrestrictive* element.

The difference between an essential and a nonessential element can be seen in the following examples. According to the principles discussed here, *that* is best used with an essential element, and *which* is best used with a nonessential element (we'll get to *who* in a moment):

Essential: Clarksburg is a small town *that is located at the junctions of Routes 10 and 41.* (The clause *that is located at the junctions of Routes 10 and 41* is essential. If you remove those words, readers won't know where Clarksburg is.)

Nonessential: Clarksburg, *which is a small town*, is located at the junction of Routes 10 and 41. (The clause *which is a small town* is nonessential. If you remove it, the sentence still says where Clarksburg is.)

Nothing about the *that-which* code is mandatory, and many good writers ignore it altogether. Nevertheless, the code is a way of helping readers distinguish between essential and nonessential elements. In addition, some people maintain that *that* is informal or colloquial usage and *which* is formal. Nonsense. Either one is used at any level of usage.

Accordingly, *that, which,* and *who* are used in situations such as shown here.

That is used to introduce an essential element that refers to an inanimate object or an animal without a name; commas are *not* used with essential elements: "The services *that* they provide are free." "The program features dogs *that* have been trained to do funny tricks."

Which is used to introduce a nonessential element that refers to an inanimate object or an animal without a name; commas *are* used to set off nonessential elements: "A one-mile run is grueling but not at all like a marathon, *which* goes on for more than twenty-six miles." "Performance testing, *which* is an integral part of modern educational theory, is accomplished at the end of training." "The two pandas, *which* were the first ever to be born in captivity, were trotted out for the press yesterday."

Which may occasionally be used with an essential element to avoid the unwanted repetition of *that*: "He said *that* the training which our organization gives is free."

Now we get to *who*.

Who is used when an essential or a nonessential element refers to a human being or a named animal; commas are *not* used with essential elements but *are* used with nonessential elements: "They flogged the natives *who* did not embrace the new religion." "Johnson, *who* hit three home runs in last night's game, is not playing today." "Best Kitten Award at the show went to Quidalia Pluribus, *who* won handily."

SEE ALSO **he, she, her, him, I, me, them, they, us, we, you; its, it's; myself (and other compound pronouns); who, whom, whoever, whomever; who's whose; you're, your(s).**

their, there, they're. *Their* is the possessive form of the pronoun *they*: "*Their* house is across the street." "She complained to him about *their* large amount of bills." *Theirs* is used without a following noun and often after *of*: "We have a book of *theirs*." "Your cookies taste all right, but *theirs* are better."

Their and *theirs* are primarily used to agree with plural nouns and pronouns. However, there is a long history of mixing the plurals *their* and *theirs* with singular nouns and pronouns: "Anyone in *their* right senses knows he is wrong." "I will do my share if everyone else will do *theirs*." This mixture of singular and plural is frowned upon by devout grammarians, but it exists regardless of the frowning.

There refers to a place: "We're leaving for *there* soon." "*There* I paused, for it was obvious that a point needed explaining."

They're is the contraction of *they are*: "*They're* not going to the party."

therefor, therefore. *Therefor* is a single word that stands in place of *for it* or *for that*: "Let me explain the reasons *therefor*." Little reason exists to use *therefor*, when it is easier and more direct to use *for it* or *for that*.

Moreover, *therefor* is easily confused with *therefore*, a word that means consequently or as a result: "I lost the bet; *therefore*, I've got to pay up." "A equals B, and B equals C; *therefore*, A equals C."

Commas are not placed around *therefore* when it is placed next to the term it modifies: "A *therefore* equals C." When *therefore* appears elsewhere, it is set off with a comma: "*Therefore*, A equals C."

thrash, thresh. These two closely related words mean to beat or flail.

Thresh is the more narrowly defined of the two, used mostly to describe the beating of stems of grain to separate the seed.

Thrash may be used in the same sense as *thresh*, and in other senses: "The Lions *thrashed* the Bears, 31 to 3." "A bird, *thrashing* its wings, flew by." "Fever and delirium caused her to *thrash* about in bed." "The schoolmaster gave the errant boy a good *thrashing*." *Thrash* also means to repeatedly discuss: "They *thrashed* over the plan till late at night, hammering out the fine points."

'til, 'till, till, until. *Till* and *until* are interchangeable: "They stayed *till* (*until*) morning." The wrong usages are *'til* and *'till*.

timid, timorous. A *timid* person shrinks from difficult situations, lacks self-confidence, and is overcautious and shy: "He swindled thousands of dollars from meek, humble, and *timid* people." "He was so *timid* that she had to ask for their first date."

The word *timorous* suggests a stronger showing of fear than does *timid*: "She was so horrified by guns, so *timorous* around them, that she could not even touch one." "Constant criticism from his boss left him dejected and *timorous*."

SEE ALSO **temerity, timidity.**

tinge, tint. As nouns, both refer to a slight shade or trace of a color; as verbs, both refer to the act of applying the color.

Tinge implies color diffused throughout: "white hair *tinged* with blue"; "copper *tinged* with streaks of yellow."

Tint refers to a gradation of color tending toward whiteness and delicacy: "paintings softened with pastel *tints*."

tireless, untiring. Both mean incapable of tiring: "All his life he was a *tireless* (*untiring*) worker."

tocsin, toxin. A *tocsin* is an alarm bell. A *toxin* is a poisonous substance.

tolerance, toleration. *Tolerance* has three principal meanings: (1) freedom from bias and prejudice, the ability to allow and accept views and beliefs other than one's own ("The basis for religious *tolerance* is the belief that a degree of truth can exist in other faiths"); (2) the ability to endure pain, hardship, or insult ("A diseased heart lowered her *tolerance* for stress"); (3) the amount of variation allowed on a mechanical specification ("The shaft was to be milled to a *tolerance* of .0004 inches").

Toleration is sometimes used in place of *tolerance* in the latter's first two meanings but not in the third. Even then, *tolerance* is the more common word.

SEE ALSO **bias, prejudice.**

torso, trunk. Either *torso* or *trunk* is used to refer to the human or animal body excluding head and limbs; *trunk* is the word used in the old standby *Gray's Anatomy*. *Torso* is also used when referring to the *trunk* of a statue of a nude human, especially one lacking the head and limbs.

tortoise, turtle. A *turtle* is a reptile with a shell. Some *turtles* live only on land, while others spend most of their lives in the sea. A *tortoise* is a *turtle* that lives only on land.

tortuous, torturous. *Tortuous* means twisting or winding, and marked by repeated bends and turns: "A *tortuous* road with one switchback after another led up the mountainside." "Rocky negotiations contributed to a *tortuous* settlement of the strike."

Torturous means causing torture: "He regarded a necktie as a *torturous* instrument of the devil."

toupee, wig. A *toupee* is a small *wig* meant to cover a bald spot. A *wig* is a headpiece of artificial hair. Persons concerned about baldness can take comfort from these words on a bumper sticker: "God made a few people with perfect heads. The rest have hair."

track, tract. Confusion over these words could be caused by careless pronunciation or a failure to hear the final *t* in *tract*. Among other things, a *track* is what a train runs on, a course on which races are run, or a path beaten into the wilderness by people, animals, or vehicles. A *tract* is a pamphlet, usually on a religious or political subject. A *tract* is also a piece of land, such as a "housing *tract*."

traitorous, treacherous. One is *traitorous* to a nation but *treacherous* to a trust: "He was *treacherous* in that he would betray his fellow spies to save his own neck." Inanimate objects may be *treacherous* when the word is used to imply danger or peril: "The rapids in the lower stretches of the river were *treacherous*."

SEE ALSO **sedition, treason.**

tramp, tromp. To walk with heavy, noisy steps is to *tramp* or to *tromp*. Dictionaries favor *tramp*.

tramp, vamp. Concerning "loose" women, a *tramp* is a prostitute or one who is sexually promiscuous; a *vamp* is a flirt or seductress who uses her charms to exploit men.

transcendent, transcendental. *Transcendent* describes something that is surpassing, excelling, or extraordinary: "His poetry was compelling and *transcendent*." *Trans-*

cendent is also used when referring to whatever is beyond comprehension: "Her ideas were too obscure, too *transcendent*, to be grasped by readers."

Transcendental can be used in place of *transcendent* or to describe whatever is mystical, abstract, or metaphysical: "He believed in a *transcendental* world of extreme idealism and concepts based on spiritual intuition."

Additional specific, extensive definitions of these two terms are used in philosophy.

transient, transitory.   *Transient* describes whatever lasts or stays a short time: "The levee areas are hangouts for *transients* and the homeless." "The boardinghouse catered to *transient* guests."

Transitory describes something that is bound to change: "Fame in sports is *transitory*." "Life itself is *transitory*."

transverse, traverse.   *Transverse* is an adjective or noun that means crosswise: "*transverse* beams that support the roof." *Traverse* is a verb meaning to travel across: "*traverse* ice fields on their climb up Everest."

triumphal, triumphant.   *Triumphal* applies to things done or made in honor of a triumph: "a *triumphal* feast"; "*triumphal* emblems"; "a *triumphal* procession."

Triumphant is a substitute for *conquering* or *victorious*: "*triumphant* armies."

troop, troupe.   A *troop* is a group of people that are organized as a unit or that work together: "cavalry *troop*"; "Boy Scout *troop*"; "a *troop* of tourists"; "*troops* of servants."

Troupe means a group of performers: "the circus *troupe*."

Tropic of Cancer, Tropic of Capricorn.   The *Tropic of Cancer* is an imaginary line in the northern hemisphere that runs parallel to the equator at 23.5 degrees north latitude; this line is the northerly limit of the sun's travels. The *Tropic of Capricorn* is a similar line in the southern hemisphere.

SEE ALSO **Antarctic Circle, Arctic Circle.**

trustee, trusty. Both of these words refer to one in whom trust is placed. A *trustee* is an appointed overseer of an institution: "Nursing home *trustees* last night voted to build a new wing." A *trusty* is a convict granted special privileges: "As a *trusty*, he was allowed to leave the prison and run errands for the guards."

trustful, trusting, trustworthy. A *trustful* (occasionally *trusting*) person is one who is full of trust, ready to believe or confide in another: "She is so naive and so *trustful* that she can be duped by anyone."

A *trustworthy* individual is one who is worthy of trust, one who can be trusted: "He is a good officer, loyal and *trustworthy*."

tumult, turmoil. A *tumult* is a din or commotion caused by a crowd: "The mob was in *tumult* over the death of the prime minister." "He had to talk loudly to be heard above the *tumult* in the stadium." *Tumult* may also pertain to an individual's emotions or state of mind: "The catastrophe had left her bewildered, her soul in a *tumult*," although *turmoil* could also be used in this sense.

Turmoil is confusion and agitation from any cause: "He savored the excitement and *turmoil* of battle." "Divorce had thrown her life into a *turmoil*."

turbid, turgid. *Turbid* refers to whatever is literally or figuratively stirred up so that it becomes obscured or confused: "Waves surging into the bank washed sand into the water and made it *turbid*." "Dust storms turned the air *turbid*." "The *turbid* state of his imagination left him unable to write for weeks."

Turgid means swollen or distended, figuratively or literally: "Starvation had left their bellies bloated and *turgid*." "His *turgid*, inflated prose guaranteed him an audience of one—himself."

twerp, twit. A *twerp* is a small, insignificant person. A *twit* is a fool.

typhoid fever, typhus. *Typhoid fever* is an infectious disease spread under unsanitary conditions. The disease may be communicated from person to person or through contaminated food or drink. Symptoms include headache, vomiting, diarrhea (usually bloody), high temperature, weakness, and often delirium. The disease may be life-threatening. *Typhoid fever* is rare in Western countries but does exist in underdeveloped areas.

Typhus refers to an infection spread by insects such as ticks and lice. Symptoms include chills, fever, a worsening headache, malaise, aching muscles, and blotches on the skin. Stupor, coma, and death may result. *Epidemic typhus* is spread by human body lice ("cooties" or "pants rabbits") during conditions of overcrowding and uncleanliness found in wartime and in prison camps.

U

usable (useable), useful. *Usable*, which is the preferred spelling over *useable*, means that something can be used. *Useful* means that something is helpful or beneficial or can be used to advantage. Therefore, a *usable* tool is not as good a tool as one that is *useful*.

usage, use. *Usage* refers to customary practice or established *use*. In a book on language, *usage* refers to the way words and phrases are *used*. How anyone *uses* a word can be stacked up against the whole pattern of *usage* for that word. The pattern is determined by the group that *uses* that word. Over the long term, decades or centuries, the group establishes good or acceptable *usage*, along with bad or unacceptable.

As an example, many people say *ain't*, and *ain't* occasionally shows up in edited writing in situations not involving dialogue. Some dictionaries define *ain't*, thereby recognizing its existence, and possibly someday the word will gain widespread acceptance.

For now, however, the users of English as a group have not accepted *ain't*. No logical reason exists for this stand. *Ain't* is a contraction of *am not* or *are not* just as *won't* is a contraction of *will not*. For either one, you have to use your imagination to see how the spelling of the long form carries over to the spelling of the contraction.

Nevertheless, we have accepted *won't* but not *ain't*. At present, *ain't* is indeed used, but it's not (*ain't*?) good *usage*. And although this explanation may help define *usage*, all that it really does for sure is point out the inconsistency of the approach that millions of people take toward language.

V

vacant, vacuous. Both of these words mean lacking content or containing nothing.

Vacant pertains mainly to things: "a *vacant* house"; "a *vacant* seat on the train"; "*vacant* hours with nothing to do."

Vacuous pertains mainly to the absence or near absence of meaning or intelligence: "a *vacuous* expression on his face" (although *vacant* is also used in this sense); "a *vacuous* mind"; "the *vacuous* conversation of idlers at a cocktail party."

vagabond, vagrant. These terms have in common their reference to a person with no fixed home who travels from place to place.

Vagabond at one time implied rascality, shiftlessness, and disreputability: "My husband was such a *vagabond* that he was never home to provide for his family or tend to his property." Today the word may imply nothing more than a carefree, roaming existence: "After four disciplined years of military service, he became a *vagabond* for a year, following his nose across America."

A *vagrant* ekes out a living by begging and is often regarded as a public nuisance subject to arrest: "As a result of the depression, many working men became *vagrants*, waiting in lines of the unemployed and living in hobo jungles."

valiant, valorous. Not confusing. Both mean showing valor, courage, or bravery. *Valiant* is perhaps the more frequently seen of the two: "He made a *valiant* effort to save the drowning boy." "His many medals attested to his *valiant* feats as a soldier." "She was never a perfectionist but always a *valiant* idealist." "The *valiant*, steadfast people of Poland have managed to elect their own government after many years of Communist rule."

The unabridged *Webster III* says that *valorous* sometimes has an archaic or romantic ring, and gives this example from the *Infantry Journal*: "The regiment itself is a proud one, with a *valorous* record."

vampire, werewolf.   In folklore, a *vampire* is a corpse that rises from the grave at night to suck the blood of living people. The most famous *vampire* was Dracula, made famous by Bram Stoker's 1897 horror novel of the same name. By extension, *vampire* has come to refer to any kind of bloodsucker or extortioner: "the *vampires* who charge usurious interest rates."

A *werewolf*, which is also a figment of folklore, is a person transformed into a wolf that usually goes around trying to eat people.

varlet, varmint.   A *varlet* is either a servant, a usage that is largely out of date, or a rascally, unprincipled person.

A *varmint* is a person or animal considered troublesome and contemptible. In a technical sense as applied to animals, a *varmint* is classed as vermin and is unprotected by game laws.

vehement, violent.   *Vehement* pertains to a greatness of force, emphasis, or passion: "He issued a lengthy and *vehement* denial of the charges leveled against him," "She is a *vehement* extremist, totally and loudly opposed to the wishes of her party."

Violent pertains to a greatness of force as used to injure, damage, or destroy: "A *violent* storm tore boats from their moorings." "The coroner's inquest showed that he had died a *violent* death."

venal, venial.   *Venal* applies to whatever is available for a price, the price usually being bribery and corruption: "The clamor for an investigation showed that people were fed up with the *venal* nature of their legislators."

Venial applies to whatever is forgivable, pardonable, or excusable: "Oh, would that all my sins were *venial* and not mortal!"

vice, vise. A *vice* is an evil, wicked, or harmful habit or action: "His only *vice* was smoking."

A *vise* is a heavy clamp usually consisting of two jaws that are opened and closed by a lever or screw action.

vicious, viscous. *Vicious* describes something or someone evil and depraved: "A *vicious* person, she thrived on hatred." "Propaganda was used as a *vicious* political tool." "It was a *vicious* story meant to discredit his former wife."

Viscous describes liquids that are oily or syrupy: "The heavier oils are more *viscous* than the lighter ones."

vigor, vim, vitality. This trio is popularly given as "*vim, vigor,* and *vitality.*" Is there any difference, or are we only dealing with redundancy?

Vim means robust or enthusiastic energy and *vigor.*

Vigor means good health along with active physical or mental strength or force.

Vitality is basically the force that is characteristic of life. That definition is essentially a neutral one that says nothing about good or bad health or *vim* or *vigor.* However, people have used *vitality* in different ways over the years; consequently, dictionaries now show *vitality* as implying outstanding physical or mental energy or *vigor.*

As usual, a true synonym is rare indeed. Shades of meaning exist among these three words, and they have their individual and collective places.

SEE ALSO **élan, verve; enthusiasm, zeal; zeal, zest.**

W

wait for, wait on. *Wait for* means to tarry: "I'll *wait for* you until noon." *Wait on* means to serve, as in providing food to people in a restaurant: "Someone will be here to *wait on* you in just a moment." Substituting *wait on* for *wait for* is informal usage and occurs mainly in rural and Southern dialects.

waive, wave. *Waive* means to give up a right or privilege: "*waive* the right of trial by jury"; "*waived* extradition"; "*waived* a portion of the payment due."

Wave denotes motion: "flags that *wave* in the breeze"; "time to *wave* goodbye."

was, were (subjunctive). H. W. Fowler, in his *Dictionary of Modern English Usage*, said that the subjunctive mood was "moribund." Several sentences later he made the same point by saying "the subjunctive is dying." That was in 1926, and today the death of the subjunctive has yet to occur.

Discerning writers still use the subjunctive *were* to refer to conditions that are clearly hypothetical and contrary to fact: "If I *were* you, I'd be careful." "I wish that the job *were* completed." "It is only a rumor, but suppose it *were* fact." In such cases, *was* might sound better to some people, and indeed *was* is frequently used in spoken sentences in which the subjunctive is being expressed. Nevertheless, the deathwatch on the subjunctive *were* is not yet ended, and the subjunctive is a way of emphasizing that something is not possible.

Was is used when something is possible: "He looked out the window to see if the way *was* clear." "The judge asked if the charge *was* true." "She asked whether I *was* happy to be single again."

waterproof, water-repellent, water-resistant. *Waterproof* means that water cannot enter. *Water-repellent* and *water-resistant* mean that the item repels water for a time but is not thoroughly *waterproof*.

welch, welsh. When a person reneges on paying a debt or doesn't keep a promise, either *welch* or *welsh* applies. In this usage, *welsh* is not capitalized.

were, we're, where. *Were* is the past tense of the verb *are*: "We *were* there yesterday."

We're is the contraction of *we are*: "*We're* (*we are*) going to be there tomorrow."

Where denotes a place: "He didn't say *where* he was going."

what ever, whatever; when ever, whenever; where ever, wherever; who ever, whoever. When making statements, the one-word form is standard: "We will take along *whatever* items we need."

When asking questions, either the one-word form or the two-word form may be used: "*What ever* did you do that for?" "*Whenever* rain is forecast, should I take my umbrella?"

Breaking any of these into two words places added emphasis on *ever*; the writer has to decide whether that emphasis is warranted.

SEE ALSO **who, whom, whoever, whomever.**

whim, whimsy. A *whim* is a sudden capricious idea or event: "The *whim* struck him to be a parachutist." "The servant had to learn to put up with the *whims* of his master." "Life in the wild means tolerating the *whims* of nature."

Whimsy refers to a fanciful or humorous object or creation, especially in writing or art: "He practiced no control over his prose, and he allowed even the most serious subject to quickly degenerate into *whimsy*."

whirl, whorl. *Whirl* specifies action—rapid, circular motion: "Couples *whirled* around the dance floor." "The eddies of the river *whirled* at our feet." "The final act of the gunfighter consisted of walking away twenty feet, *whirling* about to face his opponent, and blazing away." Figuratively speaking, "I was so confused that my thoughts were in a *whirl*."

Whorl refers to appearance—coiled, spiral, or circular: "A *whorl* of smoke rose slowly from the chimney." "A *whorl* fingerprint is one in which the central ridges describe at least one complete circle." "Her hair was all curls, ringlets, and *whorls*."

SEE ALSO **circular, spiral.**

who, whom, whoever, whomever. The following few lines, with apologies to Henry Wadsworth Longfellow, are dedicated to people who insist on saying "*Whom* did you wish to see?"

> There was a perfect man
> Who always used perfect grammar,
> Even when he was talking.
> When he had nothing to say,
> He was very, very good;
> But when he spoke,
> He was very, very boring.

In spoken English, *who* frequently replaces *whom*, the reason being that *whom* sounds stilted, overly formal, and just too fastidious. It's the sort of usage that is like extending the pinkie while (whilst?) sipping tea. Moreover, *whom* in speech tends to be showy and offensive, implying to the listener, "I know good grammar—but do you?"

If this fascination with precision is carried far enough, the traditional high school cheer becomes "Two, four, six, eight. / *Whom* do we appreciate?" It may be good grammar, but it's rotten form.

That's speech, and what works in speech doesn't necessarily follow over to written English. In written English, the rules for *who* and *whom* are generally followed.

The main exception is the asking of a question. In writing, *who* is frequently used to ask a question whether or not *whom* is the appropriate word. Again, *whom* often seems affected.

Anyway, security can sometimes be gained by knowing the rules, so here they are:

- Use *who* (*whoever*) as the subject of a sentence or clause or to refer to or rename the subject.
- Use *whom* (*whomever*) otherwise.

The correct use of *who* is shown in examples 1 and 2:

1. *He* (subject) is *the man* (subject) *who* (subject) came to dinner.
2. *The chief engineer* (subject), *who* (subject) has been with us for six years, left yesterday.

In some instances, it is necessary to break the sentence into clauses and locate the subject of each clause. When doing this, keep in mind that a clause not only has a subject but also has a verb or a verb phrase. Example 3 shows the correct use of *who* in a sentence with two clauses:

3. They do not know *who* is coming to the meeting.

In example 3, the first clause is *they do not know*; the word *they* is the subject, and *do not know* is the verb phrase. The second clause is *who is coming to dinner; who* is the subject, and *is coming* is the verb phrase.

Sometimes the subject doesn't appear at the start of the sentence or clause, and instead pops up at the end of a sentence where the object usually is. The problem with this is that *whom* is used to refer to the object, but the object can be hard to identify if sentence order is other than normal.

When this happens, the writer is required to search for what is known as the true subject. The true subject can be found by remembering that no matter where it appears the subject is the starting or controlling force of anything that happens in the sentence or clause.

Example 4 shows the correct use of *whom* in a clause with other than normal order:

4. I don't know *whom* you mean.

Example 4 has two clauses: *I don't know* and *whom you mean*. The order of the second clause is other than normal; that is, the subject, *you*, does not appear in the first position. When the clause is rewritten into subject-first order, it reads *you mean whom*. *Whom* refers to the object, which is as it should be. Said another way, if the subject is not being renamed or referred to, use *whom*, not *who*.

The same principle applies when asking questions:

5. *Who* is coming to the party?

In example 5, the subject is *who; who* is doing something.

6. *Whom* should I see?

In example 6, the subject is *I; I should see whom* is the subject-first order, and *whom* does not rename the subject, *I*. However, in speech and in edited writing, *who* is often used in place of *whom* in questions like the one in example 6.

Incidentally, some of us have been taught that *whom* (or *whomever*) always appears after a preposition. That advice isn't always infallible, as can be seen in example 7, which shows an *incorrect* use of *whomever*:

7. They lease the plant to *whomever* wants it.

Again, this is a sentence with two clauses: *They lease the plant* and *whomever wants it*. *Whoever* is the correct way to write the subject of the second clause.

In short, to deal with *who* or *whom* the steps are:

• Find the true subject.
• Use *who* (*whoever*) to refer to or rename the subject.
• Use *whom* otherwise.

These same principles also apply to *whosoever* and *whomsoever*, which are rarely seen these days.

SEE ALSO **he, she, her, him, I, me, them, they, us, we, you; its, it's; myself (and other compound pronouns); who, which, that; you're, your(s).**

who's, whose. *Who's* is the contraction of *who is* or *who has:* "*Who's* (*who is*) coming to the lecture?" "*Who's* (*who has*) been to the lecture?"

Whose is the possessive form of *who* and *which; whose* is used with persons and things: "*Whose* car should we take?" "He's like any other animal *whose* coat gets thick in the winter." "It's a symphony *whose* melodies linger on."

SEE ALSO **that, which, who.**

winch, windlass. Of these two, *winch* seems to be the predominant word these days, although either word labels the same kind of machine that is used for hoisting or pulling. The machine consists of a drum or cylinder on which a cable or rope is wound. A crank or motor turns the drum, thereby winding in the cable.

woebegone, woeful. *Woebegone* refers to an appearance that is mournful, sorrowful, or wretched: "The *woebegone* expressions of the villagers mirrored their desperate plight." "Never have I seen a dog look so tired and so *woebegone*."

Woeful—literally full of woe—refers to what is sad and mournful: "Like Romeo and Juliet, their love affair was bittersweet and *woeful*." "Hers was the most *woeful* story I had ever heard." "The play was staged with a *woeful* lack of attention to pacing."

wont, won't. *Wont* means habit: "It was his *wont* to rise before dawn."

Won't is the contraction of *will not*: "You can bet your life I *won't* (*will not*) get up before the sun."

worse, worst. With reference to *bad* and *ill*, *worse* is a comparative and *worst* is a superlative. *Worse* refers to inferior quality, and *worst* refers to the most inferior quality: "It was the *worse* day I'd had in a long time, but not the *worst* day of my life."

SEE ALSO **best, better, good.**

wraith, wreath. A *wraith* is a ghost of a dead person or an apparition of a living person seen just before the person's death. Figuratively speaking, a *wraith* is anything that lacks substance: "The pale *wraiths* of long-dead freedoms were still felt in the conquered nation."

A *wreath* is a twisted band of flowers or leaves.

wreak, wreck. To *wreak* is to inflict vengeance; to *wreck* is to damage or destroy. You don't "*wreck* havoc"; you "*wreak* havoc."

X

X-axis, Y-axis. On a graph, the *X-axis* runs horizontally across the page, while the *Y-axis* runs vertically.

X chromosome, Y chromosome. The *X* and *Y chromosomes* determine the sex of a person, as well as carrying some genetic information that is not related to sex. Sex *chromosomes* are inherited. In a normal female, the *X chromosome* occurs in pairs. In a normal male, the combination is one *X chromosome* and one *Y chromosome*.

The *X chromosome* also carries with it genetic factors that determine conditions such as hemophilia and color blindness. The *Y chromosome* is limited to determining maleness.

SEE ALSO **androgen, estrogen.**

yang, yin. According to traditional Chinese philosophy, *yang* is the active, masculine principle, while *yin* is the passive, female principle.

year-around, year-round. For something that goes on throughout the year, the preferred form is *year-round*: "*year-round* resort"; "commutes via bicycle *year-round*."
    SEE ALSO **around, round.**

young, youngish, youthful. *Young* refers to the early period of life or development: "The menu has *young* lamb listed." The wine is too *young* to be served yet." "The company experienced all the growing pains of a *young* organization."
    Youngish means rather *young* or somewhat *young*: "For a *youngish* man, he possesses the wisdom of the ages." "She is *youngish*, but not an adolescent."
    Youthful refers to what is characteristic of youth: "He is an active, *youthful* senior citizen." "She has a figure that goes well with *youthful* clothing." "The skin loses its *youthful* appearance as we grow older." "She is the very image of *youthful* innocence and girlish happiness."

you're, your(s). *You're* is a contraction of *you are*: "*You're* (*you are*) going to be home on time, aren't you?"
    Your (or *yours*) is the possessive form of *you*. "This is *your* wallet." "Clean up *your* room before you go out." "The house is on *your* left." "You are about to receive *your* first promotion since coming to work here."
    Yours is an independent possessive; that is, it shows

possession without being placed next to a following noun: "This wallet is *yours*." "We'll take my car because *yours* is so ugly."

A question frequently arises as to how this sentence should be worded: "I appreciate *you* (*your?*) taking the time to answer this letter." *Your* is sometimes used in that construction, and that usage is a popular one. However, a usage based on the concept of good grammar is this one:

The word *taking* is a gerund, a verb that functions as a noun. In effect, the gerund turns the rest of the sentence into a noun phrase. To make grammatical sense, a noun phrase can be possessed by something or someone. In this case, the someone is expressed in the word *your*. *You* does not show possession, but *your* does.

In a similar vein is the sentence "I like *your* smile." *Your* shows possession of the noun *smile*. It wouldn't be right to say "I like *you* smile."

SEE ALSO   **he, she, her, him, I, me, them, they, us, we, you; its, it's; myself (and other compound pronouns); that, which, who; who, whom, whoever, whomever.**

Z

zany, zombie. A *zany* is a clown or a buffoon. The word is used as a noun ("He's a real *zany*") or as an adjective ("He's a *zany* person").

Zombie refers to (1) a snake deity in voodoo cults; (2) a drink made with fruit juices, rum, and apricot brandy; (3) in West Indian superstition, an animated corpse that is placed in a trancelike state—the walking dead; or (4) any person who acts like the walking dead: "After thirty-six hours behind the wheel, I was a *zombie*."

zeal, zest. *Zeal* is intense enthusiasm or devotion in working for a cause or in pursuit of a goal: "He is a passionate reformer with unlimited *zeal* for improving public schools."

Zest is added flavor, a stimulating quality, or gusto and rich enjoyment: "A wedge of lime adds *zest* to this drink." "Young children in the house bring joy and *zest*." "He has a great *zest* for life."

SEE ALSO **ardor, passion; élan, verve; vigor, vim, vitality**

zero. *Zero* may mean nothing. *Zero* is also a number between the negative and positive sets of numbers; in that respect, *zero* does mean something. On a graph, *zero* is the usual starting point. We speak of *zero* hour not as the beginning of all time but as the starting time of a military operation such as an invasion. When talking about temperature, we use *zero* degrees Celsius, *zero* degrees Fahrenheit, and absolute *zero*. Absolute *zero* is not the numeral *0* but minus 273.15 degrees Celsius or minus 459.67 degrees Fahrenheit.

All of that is by way of saying that nothing is easy about deciding what a word means.

Nothing?

Or is that *zero*?

Bibliography

Principal General References

Copperud, Roy H. *American Usage and Style: The Consensus*. New York: Van Nostrand Reinhold Company, 1980.

Flexner, Stuart Berg, Editor-in-Chief. *Random House Dictionary of the English Language*. 2d ed., unabridged. New York: Random House, 1987.

Gove, Philip Babcock, Editor-in-Chief. *Webster's Third New International Dictionary of the English Language Unabridged*. Springfield, Massachusetts: G. & C. Merriam Co., 1976. Cited in text as *Webster III*.

Morris, William, Ed. *American Heritage Dictionary of the English Language*. Boston, Mass.: Houghton Mifflin, 1976.

Morris, William, and Morris, Mary. *Harper Dictionary of Contemporary Usage*. 2d ed. New York: Harper & Row, 1985.

Neufeldt, Victoria, Editor-in-Chief. *Webster's New World Dictionary of American English*. 3d College Edition. New York: Simon & Schuster, 1988.

Simpson, J. A., and Weiner, E. S. C., Eds. *Oxford English Dictionary*. 2d ed. 20 vols. Oxford, England: Oxford University Press, 1989.

Webster's Ninth New Collegiate Dictionary. Springfield, Massachusetts: Merriam-Webster, 1983. Cited in text as *Webster's Ninth*.

Principal Specialized References

AFTE Standardization Committee. *Glossary of the Association of Firearms and Toolmark Examiners*. 2d ed. Chicago: Available Business Forms, 1985.

American Psychiatric Association. *Diagnostic and Statistical Manual of Mental Disorders*. 3d ed., rev. Washington, D.C.: American Psychiatric Association, 1987.

Anderson, Kenneth, and Harmon, Lois. *Prentice-Hall Dictionary of Nutrition and Health*. Englewood Cliffs, N.J.: Prentice-Hall, 1985.

Berkow, Robert, Editor-in-Chief. *Merck Manual of Diagnosis and Therapy*. 15th ed. Rahway, N.J.: Merck & Co., 1987.

Black's Law Dictionary. 5th ed. St. Paul, Minnesota: West Publishing Company, 1979.

Cowan, Henry J., and Smith, Peter R. *Dictionary of Architectural and Building Technology*. New York: Elsevier Applied Science Publishers, 1986.

Coyle, L. Patrick. *World Encyclopedia of Food*. New York: Facts on File, 1982.

Dorland's Illustrated Medical Dictionary. 26th ed. Philadelphia: W. B. Saunders Co., 1981.

Edmunds, Robert A. *Prentice-Hall Standard Glossary of Computer Terminology*. Englewood Cliffs, N.J.: Prentice-Hall, 1985.

Gibson, Carol, ed. *Facts on File Dictionary of Mathematics*. 2d ed. New York: Facts on File, 1981.

Glenn, J. A., and Littler, G. H. *Dictionary of Mathematics*. San Francisco: Harper & Row, 1984.

Gunston, Bill. *Jane's Aerospace Dictionary*. New York: Jane's, 1980.

Harris, Cyril M., Ed. *Dictionary of Architecture and Construction*. New York: McGraw-Hill, 1975.

Hunnels, John R. *Facts on File Dictionary of Religions*. New York: Facts on File, 1984.

Isaacs, Alan, and Martin, Elizabeth, Eds. *Dictionary of Music*. New York: Facts on File, 1983.

Kemp, Peter, Ed. *Oxford Companion to Ships and the Sea*. New York: Oxford University Press, 1976.

Kennedy, Michael. *Oxford Dictionary of Music*. New York: Oxford University Press, 1985.

Kennedy, Richard. *International Dictionary of Religion.* New York: Crossroad Publishing Co., 1984.

Lapedes, Daniel N., Editor-in-Chief. *McGraw-Hill Dictionary of Physics and Mathematics.* New York: McGraw-Hill, 1978.

Maggio, Rosalie. *Nonsexist Word Finder: A Dictionary of Gender-Free Usage.* Phoenix, Arizona: Oryx Press, 1987.

Miller, Casey, and Swift, Kate. *Handbook of Nonsexist Writing.* 2d ed. New York: Harper & Row, 1988.

Parker, Sybil P., Editor-in-Chief. *McGraw-Hill Dictionary of Earth Sciences.* New York: McGraw-Hill, 1984.

———. *McGraw-Hill Dictionary of Science and Engineering.* New York: McGraw-Hill, 1984.

———. *McGraw-Hill Dictionary of Scientific and Technical Terms.* 3d ed. New York: McGraw-Hill, 1984.

Reber, Arthur S. *Penguin Dictionary of Psychology.* New York: Viking Penguin, 1985.

Rhea, Joseph C.; Ott, J. Steven; and Shafritz, Jay M. *Facts on File Dictionary of Health Care Management.* New York: Facts on File, 1988.

Rice, Michael Downey. *Prentice-Hall Dictionary of Business, Finance, and Law.* Englewood Cliffs, N.J.: Prentice-Hall, 1983.

Rosenberg, Jerry M. *Dictionary of Business and Management.* 2d ed. New York: John Wiley & Sons, 1983.

———. *Dictionary of Computers, Data Processing, and Telecommunications.* New York: John Wiley & Sons, 1984.

Sax, N. Irving, and Lewis, Richard J., Revs. *Hawleys Condensed Chemical Dictionary.* 11th ed. New York: Van Nostrand Reinhold, 1987.

Sippl, Charles J., and Sippl, Roger J. *Computer Dictionary and Handbook.* Indianapolis, Ind.: H. W. Sams, 1980.

Spencer, Donald D. *Illustrated Computer Dictionary.* Rev. ed. Columbus, Ohio: C. E. Merrill Publishing Co., 1983.

Stedman's Medical Dictionary. 24th ed. Baltimore, Maryland: Williams & Wilkins, 1982.

Steindler, R. A. *Steindler's New Firearms Dictionary.* Harrisburg, Pennsylvania: Stackpole Books, 1985.

Taber's Cyclopedic Medical Dictionary. 15th ed. Philadelphia: F. A. Davis Co., 1985.

Timmreck, Thomas, ed. *Dictionary of Health Services Management.* Owings Mills, Maryland: National Health Publishing, 1982.

Urdang, Laurence. *Dictionary of Confusable Words.* New York: Facts on File, 1988.

Walton, John; Beeson, Paul B.; and Scott, Ronald Bodley, Eds. *Oxford Companion to Medicine.* New York: Oxford University Press, 1986.

Wolmar, Benjamin, Comp. and Ed. *Dictionary of Behavioral Science.* New York: Van Nostrand Reinhold, 1973.

Words and Phrases. St. Paul, Minnesota: West Publishing Co., 1964. Updated annually.

Index